Coach George Allen

ALSO BY LEE ELDER

That Bloody Hill: Hilliard's Legion at Chickamauga (McFarland, 2018)

Coach George Allen
A Football Life

Lee Elder

McFarland & Company, Inc., Publishers
Jefferson, North Carolina

This book has undergone peer review.

Library of Congress Cataloguing-in-Publication Data

Names: Elder, Lee, 1956– author.
Title: Coach George Allen : a football life / Lee Elder.
Description: Jefferson, North Carolina : McFarland & Company, Inc., Publishers, 2023 | Includes bibliographical references and index.
Identifiers: LCCN 2022043409 | ISBN 9781476675008 (paperback : acid free paper) ∞
  ISBN 9781476645988 (ebook)
Subjects: LCSH: Allen, George, 1918-1990. | Football coaches—United States—Biography. | BISAC: SPORTS & RECREATION / Coaching / Football
Classification: LCC GV939.A54 E54 2022 | DDC 796.332092 [B]—dc23/eng/20221004
LC record available at https://lccn.loc.gov/2022043409

British Library cataloguing data are available

ISBN (print) 978-1-4766-7500-8
ISBN (ebook) 978-1-4766-4598-8

© 2023 Leon E. Elder III. All rights reserved

No part of this book may be reproduced or transmitted in any form or by any means, electronic or mechanical, including photocopying or recording, or by any information storage and retrieval system, without permission in writing from the publisher.

Front cover: Washington head coach George Allen in 1971 (Richard Nixon Presidential Library and Museum)

Printed in the United States of America

McFarland & Company, Inc., Publishers
 Box 611, Jefferson, North Carolina 28640
  www.mcfarlandpub.com

To the memory of my father, Leon Elder,
who took me to many games at the Coliseum
in Los Angeles. Dad and I witnessed many of the
Los Angeles Rams games described in the following
pages. We lost Dad before work on this book started,
but he was with me as I wrote every page.
I also dedicate this book to my mother, Dorothy,
and sister, Diane, who never minded when
Dad and I headed off to see a ballgame.

Table of Contents

Acknowledgments   ix
Preface   1

Early Years

1. An Electrifying Moment   3
2. In the Beginning   6
3. Allen at Morningside   9
4. The Green Arrow at Whittier   15
5. An Introduction, a Car Wash and a Return   29
6. Divorce Chicago Style   47

The NFL Years

7. The Turnaround: The 1966 Rams   53
8. Back to the Playoffs: The 1967 Rams   64
9. Out of the Playoffs and Into the Fire: The 1968 Rams   77
10. Out of the Fire and Into the Playoffs: The 1969 Rams   92
11. Lame Duck: The 1970 Rams   98
12. Ascension: The 1971 Redskins   107
13. Checking the Angle of the Sun: The 1972 Redskins   124
14. Chasing the Cowboys: The 1973 Redskins   141
15. "Follow me to the Super Bowl!": The 1974 Redskins   146
16. Chasing Dallas: The 1975 Redskins   157
17. Coping with Quarterbacks: The 1976 Redskins   160

18. A Contract Offer: The 1977 Redskins	165
19. Dumped, Hired, Fired Again	171

The 1980s: Allen's Odyssey

20. Stranger in a Strange Land—Briefly	177
21. Blitzing and Wrangling with the USFL	182
22. Long Beach State	193
Epilogue	211
Appendix 1: Trades	219
Appendix 2: Draft Selections	226
Appendix 3: The Offensive Truth	229
Appendix 4: Coaching Comparison	236
Chapter Notes	239
Bibliography	251
Index	253

Acknowledgments

My thanks go to the team at McFarland for agreeing to publish this book. Mark Durr, my friend and fellow member of the Professional Football Researchers Association, refined my original idea into a better, more interesting and readable project. The book you hold in your hands now is the result.

I have a lot of people to thank for their assistance with the research required for the production of this book and it all starts with long conversations I've had through the years with my treasured friend Max Fields. Max planted the idea of writing a book about George Allen in my mind three decades before I took on the challenge and he has been a big help in getting it completed. It was Max who connected me with fellow Whittier player John McNichols, to whom I also offer my thanks.

Dick Vermeil, the famous coach, television commentator and now vintner, was gracious with his time during our interview. His perspective on George Allen's career is unique and his thoughts were very much appreciated.

This book owes a debt of gratitude to Ron McDole and his family. The Dancing Bear was a joy to interview and his family was quite friendly during the process. Thanks, too, go to Warren Rogan, the host of the *Sports' Forgotten Heroes* podcast, for helping me reach out to the McDole family.

Dave Rebstock, the Sports Information Director at Morningside College, gave me a great deal of insight into that part of George Allen's career.

Roger Kirk, Assistant Athletic Director/Athletic Communications at California State University, Long Beach, helped get me in communication with that school's part of the George Allen story. Chuck Hayes served as an administrative assistant to Allen at Long Beach and Shawn Wilburn played on that team. Both gave insight into Allen's time on that campus. Shane Schroeder also helped with his recollections of working with George Allen.

Acknowledgments

Much of the research for this book was done in the Ralph Wilson Room at the Professional Football Hall of Fame in Canton, Ohio. Jon Kendal, the archivist at the Hall, always finds a way to allow me time in the Research Center when I am working on a project. My work on George Allen, Weeb Ewbank and Joe Stydahar has all been completed with the assistance of Kendal and his co-workers and I am grateful.

My wife, Amy, has been very supportive through my work on this book. Between the time my work started and was completed, Amy was diagnosed with cancer, underwent surgery and then completed post-operative treatment. She recovered in grand style. Amy supported my work on this project through all of that and never once asked me to stop working on it in order to help her with something. My wife is unique and I love her very much.

Preface

This book began, as many do, with my attempt to answer a fairly straightforward question, in this case having to do with a remarkable run of coaching success. What was it, I wondered, about George Allen? Not only did he win at every stop of his career, but often did so right away and against the odds. Whether it was college teams struggling even to keep their programs afloat, NFL teams bedeviled by years of losing, or a start-up franchise in the wilds of the short-lived USFL—when Allen took over, wins followed.[1] I set out to discover the reasons for it.

This is a story of leadership. Allen told his Whittier College players that when the opposition got close to the Whittier goal line, the defense had the advantage. Eventually, those Whittier players believed. He told his crusty, veteran-laden Washington Redskins team, the Over the Hill Gang, that it needed a team song. Eventually, the Redskins sang. And he somehow managed to coach the same roster of players for two different United States Football League franchises. That roster was a winner for both clubs.

How did he do that? I have interviewed coaches who coached for Allen and players who played for him, trying to understand what Allen did to make his teams winners. The reader will see that the George Allen files at the Professional Football Hall of Fame in Canton, Ohio, allow a glimpse into Allen's mind, his relentless need to find a weakness in his opponents and his constant push for players to better themselves. Allen wrote several books, many magazine articles and academic papers. Those publications also give glimpses into Allen's mind and the philosophy that may have gone contrary to the generally accepted framework for team building, but was immediately successful.

George Allen was the first modern NFL coach. He worked seemingly non-stop, even when he coached college teams. As will be seen, he thought nothing of telephoning employees of his own team to discuss some administrative matter in the wee hours of the morning or of calling owners of other ballclubs to discuss a trade late at night.

Allen's dedication to the kicking game is well-known. The incident which led him to hire his first special teams coach for the 1969 season is examined here. The two most memorable plays of Allen's coaching career came on a punt and an opponent's field goal attempt. Those plays will be examined.

Allen preferred established veteran players at the professional level, partially because he gave them great latitude to make adjustments on the fly within the framework of the play calls. Veterans knew how to make those instant adjustments, Allen believed, and young players did not. But Allen gave that same freedom to his college players, men who had much less experience. Allen's quarterbacks and defensive signal callers called their own plays on the field.

And yet, for all of his success, Allen never won a championship. He was fired twice between 1968 and 1979. He was released another time. That brings us to another key question: Why did NFL team owners keep getting rid of Allen? How did Allen lose a court case to gain release from his assistant coaching contract with the Chicago Bears and then immediately gain his freedom? Why was Allen fired four times by the Rams? Allen was never actually fired by the Redskins. He had a contract offer from the Redskins that would have made him the best-paid coach in professional football. He never signed it and the Redskins finally moved on to another coach. Why did that happen? Those questions are explored here.

During the research for this book, I tried to contact George Allen's children. To my everlasting regret, those attempts failed to attract a response. Several men who played for Allen also either politely declined to be interviewed or did not respond to emails or voicemail messages. Attempts to contact the offices of the Los Angeles Rams and National Football League over the course of four years also went unanswered. In some cases, statements from individuals who were not interviewed were found in contemporary print media. Filmed interviews were also discovered and some of those interviews, found online, have also been quoted and cited.

Some former players and assistant coaches agreed to be interviewed. Their insights have been invaluable in the attempt to unravel the Allen story.

Finally, there is the team name of the franchise Allen coached in the nation's capital, the Washington Redskins. During the time this book was researched and written, the franchise temporarily changed its name to the Washington Football Team (now the Commanders). The team is frequently referred to as the Redskins in this book because that was the name of the team when Allen coached it. I mean no disrespect to Native Americans or their supporters.

EARLY YEARS

1

An Electrifying Moment

The Green Bay Packers led the Los Angeles Rams 20–17 as Packers punter Donny Anderson dropped back to punt with less than a minute to go in the game. The Los Angeles Memorial Olympic Coliseum was packed with more than 76,000 fans for the second-to-last game of the 1967 season, a game the Rams had to win to keep their flickering playoff hopes alive.

The Packers had already secured their Central Division championship and knew they would be hosting the first-round game in two weeks. Still, head coach Vince Lombardi said during the week before the game that his Packers played to win regardless of the situation. The Rams could testify to the Packers' philosophy. The game had been tied twice and the teams had exchanged the lead four times.

On the Rams sideline was second-year head coach George Allen, the author of a remarkable two-year turnaround that saw the Rams transform from an also-ran cellar dwelling team to a playoff contender. The Rams were Allen's first head coaching assignment in professional football, but his history included two head coaching stops in college ball and assistant assignments with the Rams and Chicago Bears. Allen's philosophy had been influenced by future Hall of Fame mentors Sid Gillman and George Halas.

Allen was a big believer in stressing special teams play. As Los Angeles lined up its punt defense team against Anderson and the other Packers, three future members of the Pro Football Hall of Fame dug in for a last gasp effort to block the punt. Oddly, none of the men now enshrined in the Canton, Ohio, showplace for football history had any direct influence on what happened next.

Tony Guillory, a back-up defensive lineman, lined up directly in front of the Packers center. Guillory burst through the Packers line and blocked Anderson's punt as it came off the Packer punter's foot. Claude Crabb, also a defensive back-up for the Rams, had lined up furthest to the defensive right. The ball bounced crazily before Crabb bent down to pick it up, then turned around and raced toward the end zone with a large group of white-shirted Rams as escorts. Possibly because his escort service consisted entirely of defensive players, no Rams player got in front of Crabb to block for him. Anderson swept around the group to get in front of Crabb and made contact with him at the Green Bay 16-yard line. Crabb was finally stopped from behind by Doug Hart at the Packer four-yard line.[1]

The Rams scored two plays later but that blocked punt looms decades later as one of the most important, to say nothing of most electric, plays in the history of professional football in Los Angeles. The only play ranking higher was the 73-yard scoring pass from Norm Van Brocklin to Tom Fears that provided the winning points for the Rams in the 1951 championship game against the Cleveland Browns. Guillory and Crabb saved the 1967 season and cemented the Rams' status as contenders. The unexpectedly easy victory over the Baltimore Colts a week later was the icing on the cake for Los Angeles. The blocked punt against Green Bay was the key moment.

To understand what the play meant, one must understand the Rams' situation prior to Allen's arrival. In 1965, for the first time since their move from Cleveland before the 1946 season, attendance at Rams games ranked below the NFL average. Television earnings were far less than the league enjoys now, and dwindling crowds meant less money earned by the club. Under Gillman, the Rams won the Western Conference in 1955 and lost to Cleveland in the title game. The Rams had not played postseason game since. In the seven seasons prior to Allen becoming the head coach in Los Angeles, the Rams won just 25 games under three head coaches. Allen's Rams won 19 in his first two seasons and a symphony of turnstiles could be heard at the Coliseum.

The Rams had finished second in the Western Conference in 1958 with a record of 8–4, but then collapsed to 2–10 in 1959 and Gillman was replaced by Rams hero Bob Waterfield. Waterfield was a quarterback on the Rams championship teams in 1945 and 1951 but he failed to produce the same results as a coach and was replaced by Harland Svare during the 1962 season. Svare failed to make the Rams a winner and later failed as head coach of the San Diego Chargers. The high scoring and successful Rams teams that drew large crowds to the Coliseum in the early 1950s were a vague memory when Allen arrived after the 1965 season. Under Allen the team was winning again in 1966 and, two weeks after the blocked punt against the Packers, they were a playoff team again in 1967.

Allen would later orchestrate a renaissance with the Washington Redskins and then enjoy success during two seasons in the United States Football League. If you take into account Allen's head coaching stints at

1. An Electrifying Moment

three colleges and assistant coaching jobs with two NFL teams, he was a winner everywhere he coached. He was frequently innovative on offense, defense and special teams. But the same coach who turned two National Football League losers into winners and never suffered through a losing professional season would eventually be fired four times by the Rams and let go by the Redskins. Allen was known as a player's coach and generally got along with the local media. But his relationships with team owners were stormy.

Above all else, George Allen was a master motivator. Young college players and crusty NFL veterans alike became enthusiastic followers of Allen's. When Rams owner Dan Reeves fired Allen following the 1968 season, most of the Rams' stars threatened to retire or in some other way not play the following season. Decades later, their time with Allen continues to resonate with men he coached at each stop along his career path. Many of Allen's players eventually became coaches when their playing years ended. One of his former players with both the Rams and Redskins, linebacker Jack Pardee, replaced Allen when the Redskins fired the elder coach.

Allen is frequently remembered as a coach who valued experience over youth and was willing to trade draft choices for veteran players. Yet, when he managed the draft as an assistant for the Chicago Bears, Allen selected future Hall of Famers running back Gale Sayers and linebacker Dick Butkus.

An innovator, motivator and winner with an eye for talent, Allen served in one way or another in three different professional leagues and coached three different schools. He won everywhere he went. Allen would eventually serve as the Chairman of the President's Council of Physical Fitness and Sports, write several books and help raise four successful children. On the flip side of all that, he was also dismissed four times between December of 1968 and August of 1978.

If Tony Guillory's blocked punt was the final step in the Rams development from losers to winners in 1967, it was also a crowning moment for Allen. His team and his players, playing his brand of football, delivered in a clutch situation and produced a key victory at the game's highest level. Allen helped create a rebirth of interest in the Rams and the team was once again filling the Coliseum.

As this book is written, George Allen holds the third most successful winning percentage in NFL history. He had a history of producing winners from the ashes of failure and then getting fired. How did he win? Why was he fired? This book will explore those questions.

2

In the Beginning

George Herbert Allen was born to Earl Raymond Allen and Loretta May Allen on April 29, 1918, in Detroit, Michigan. Earl's occupation was listed on the 1920 United States Census as a chauffeur for a private family. Loretta was a homemaker, as was common at the time. Earl and Loretta had two children, the second being a daughter named Virginia. Virginia was three years younger than George and had not been born at the time of the 1920 Census. Earl and Loretta were both born in New York State, as were all of their parents. George, Earl and Loretta lived on Lake Shore Road in Grosse Pointe Shores, Michigan, in 1920, possibly in the rear of Earl's employer's home.[1] By 1930, Virginia had been born and the Allens had moved to 23511 Allon Boulevard in St. Clair Shores, Michigan. Earl was still working as a chauffeur.[2]

Even though George was born 11 years prior to the stock market crash in October of 1929 and a dozen years before the resulting Great Depression really took hold of America's economy, the Allens were not well-to-do. They struggled to make ends meet, like most American families. George would later write about working as a boy at a nursery owned by a Mr. Couch and about planting crops in planters or flowerpots in the basement of their home in order to help the family get by. As an adult, George would be too busy to make much time for playing golf but as a 12-year-old boy, he got up very early in the morning so he could arrive at a nearby golf course by 5 a.m. and get his name on the top of the list of caddies. In this way, George could caddy twice a day instead of only once and make more money for the family. The drive that turned George Allen into a workaholic as a football coach manifested itself in his early years when his family needed it.

George Allen attended Lake Shore High School in St. Clair Shores, Michigan. He played football and basketball and he set a school high jump record as a member of the track and field team. Allen reportedly had perfect attendance in high school. By 1940, things were different for the Allen

2. In the Beginning

family. George Allen was attending Michigan State Normal College in Ypsilanti, living in the John Munson Residence Hall.[3] Earl, Loretta and Virginia had moved to a home at 23 Nelson Avenue in Rensselaer, New York, by then. It was Loretta who spoke to the Census representative there in 1940. The Census lists no job or even industry for Earl, but the Allens owned the home they lived in.[4] There were times during George Allen's college life that he had to leave school in order to help support his parents by working. Earl's health was not consistently good. The net result for George was that it took him more time than usual to earn his bachelor's degree. Next came the Japanese attack on Pearl Harbor and America's entry into the Second World War. George Allen was placed in the United States Navy V12 program for leadership training at Alma College and then at Marquette University.

The V12 program had a two-fold purpose: to develop leaders to supplement those enrolled in the U.S. Naval Academy at Annapolis, Maryland, and to help the nation's universities by keeping students on campus. As a part of the V12 program, Allen ended up at the University of Michigan. Allen was not the only American to come out of the program and become famous. In fact, Allen was far from being the best-known in his future life. Other V12 students included U.S. senator Howard Baker, Heisman Trophy winner Angelo Bertelli, astronaut Scott Carpenter, actors Jackie Cooper and Jack Lemmon, *Tonight Show* host Johnny Carson and commissioner of baseball Bowie Kuhn. One other member of the program would later cross paths with Allen in two very different roles: football player and team executive Elroy "Crazylegs" Hirsch.

When Allen arrived at the University of Michigan, the head football coach was Fritz Crisler. Crisler stopped coaching after the 1947 season and

George Allen's draft card. Note his birth year was 1918 (ancestry.com).

became the school's Athletic Director. He was replaced by Bennie Oosterbaan in 1948. Allen coached under both Crisler and Oosterbaan and eventually coached a team for players who weighed 150 pounds or less while he was with the Wolverines.

Between his zeal to help his family through tough financial times and doing his part for the war effort, Allen's matriculation through both his bachelor's degree and his master's degree was delayed. He believed the two issues cost him four years of studies and he would soon claim to be four years younger than he really was. It was ironic that George Allen, the coach who valued experience over all other things and became famous for that belief, wanted prospective employers to believe he was younger than he really was. Even his future wife did not know his real age until they had been married for more than a decade.

3

Allen at Morningside

Sioux City, Iowa, sits along the western edge of the state in the northern quarter. The city is across the Nebraska River from the state of Nebraska. Sioux City is the home of Morningside College, where George Allen got his first head coaching experience. If it is true that many football fans don't know Allen ever coached the Chiefs, it is also true that Allen himself never forgot. In three seasons, Allen's Morningside teams went 17–11–2 but, more importantly for him, he met his future wife, Henriette Lumbroso, on campus.

Henriette, whom George Allen came to call Etty, was raised in Tunisia. During the Second World War, her family met an American military officer and Etty went to Sioux City to visit that officer and his wife in 1948, according to Jennifer Allen's book, *Fifth Quarter: The Scrimmage of a Football Coach's Daughter*. In *Fifth Quarter*, Jennifer Allen relates the story of her parents meeting during a play rehearsal. The story goes that the pair held a spotlight on the stage for the length of the rehearsal.

> In the months to come, their dates involved milk shakes, picnics, milk shakes, golf and milk shakes. Mom said she had never met anyone so straight. My father would diagram football plays on picnic napkins, writing "George laterals to Etty," and diagram Xs and Os and arrows on tablecloths and menus, and Mom thought, "How sweet, he's really trying to tell me something about his feelings." After she realized that he wasn't telling her anything, that he was simply doodling football plays during their dates, Mom left Sioux City for Tunis, telling him, "It was nice while it lasted."[1]

It wasn't over, of course. Again, from *Fifth Quarter*: "Dad sent Mom a telegram in 1950 that my mother framed on their bedroom wall: AS THE 1951 FOOTBALL SEASON APPROACHES I WOULD LIKE TO HAVE YOU AS MY TEAMMATE. It was my father's wedding proposal."[2]

Allen flew to Tunis, Tunisia to get Etty's answer to his proposal after writing her that he was coming. The Korean Conflict had started and the world was uncertain what might happen next. In *Fifth Quarter*, Jennifer

Allen noted that her father frequently wrote about himself in the third person and quotes from a letter from George to Etty, "'What if war breaks out and George gets stranded in Africa?' my father wrote. 'Is there football in Africa for George?'"[3]

By the time the 1951 season started, Allen was coaching at Whittier College in California but his long-distance romance with Etty started at Morningside. They were married for the rest of George Allen's life, producing four children. Etty Allen's father, Felix, had been a wine importer in Tunis. Felix Lumbroso was Jewish and was imprisoned by the Nazis when they occupied Tunis. The experience of living in German-occupied territory scared Etty and she initially did not tell Allen that she was Jewish. Allen was a Roman Catholic and so Etty and George did not initially tell George's family about Etty's religion out of concerns that there might be objections to George marrying outside his faith. The Allens eventually raised their four children in George's faith and did not tell them about Etty's heritage until later in Etty's life. She told the *New York Times* in 2006 that she had hid her faith from her children out of concern that they might someday feel the same fear she experienced as a girl. Etty Allen reportedly also worried that the revelation of her Jewish upbringing might somehow be an obstacle in George's career path, asking, "How many Jewish coaches are there?"[4]

Merrian-Webster.com defines loneliness as "being without company" and "cutoff from others." It could just as easily say, "See 'wife of a football coach.'" Coaches constantly plan ahead and scout opponents. College coaches have the extra burden of recruiting high school and junior college players, and in the years immediately after World War II, it was common for coaches to teach. The months during the season are the busiest of all, as Etty Allen found out. It can be argued that George Allen was the first modern NFL coach. His work habits became famous during his years as an assistant with the Chicago Bears and they became almost legendary during his stints as the head coach of the Los Angeles Rams and Washington Redskins. But those coaching work habits really started at Morningside.

During her husband's long absences and even when he was at home, Etty Allen was an organized, determined and fiercely loyal wife and mother. She must have done things right. Daughter Jennifer, the youngest of the Allen kids, became a writer and has worked for the NFL Network. The three Allen sons have also had notable careers: George F. Allen became the governor of Virginia and then a senator, Bruce worked with his father in different roles for many years and then became a team executive on his own, and Gregory became a sports psychologist.

George H. Allen got the Morningside job through dogged determination and after a bout with airsickness. By his account in *Strategies*, Allen

3. Allen at Morningside

sent job applications to 850 colleges, looking for a coaching position. He got two responses, from Trinity College in Connecticut and from Morningside. The Trinity job didn't work out, so Allen flew from Chicago to Sioux City to apply for a job as an assistant coach. The trip left him with a severe case of airsickness. Allen said years later he did not leave his hotel room for a day before going to the school for the interview. He dutifully answered the questions posed to him and then turned the tables.

In *Strategies*, he wrote, "Then I reached into my pocket, took out a sheet of paper with notes on it, and said, 'Do you mind if I ask a few questions?' I had ten or twelve, and I didn't realize that my asking questions would impress them."

Allen was surprised to be offered the head coaching position. "I was caught off guard to be offered the head coaching job," he wrote in *Strategies for Winning: A Top Coach's Game Plan for Victory in Football and in Life.* "I pointed out that they had a head coach, Les Davis, and I had not come there to apply for his job. I was told that Davis was going to retire and that the head coaching job was mine on the condition that I was willing to coach track as well." Then someone said, "One thing you haven't asked about is money and you've been here for two days."

Allen wrote that he told the interview panel, "Well, I'm more interested in beating South Dakota University." South Dakota was Morningside's most important rival, a school the Chiefs had not beaten in 16 years. Allen was offered $3,900 for the year, which he accepted. He asked for an assistant coach and was not granted that expense. Instead, he found a member of the faculty who was willing to be an assistant football coach.[5] Clayton Droullard joined the Morningside faculty as a mathematics instructor about the same time Allen

George Allen, the new football coach at Morningside College, in 1948 (courtesy Morningside University Archives).

was hired. Allen learned from the university president that Droullard had played college football at the University of Dubuque. Droullard told *The Sioux City Journal*'s Terry Hersom, "George is a very persuasive fellow and, of course, he talked me into serving as his assistant."[6]

Droullard told Hersom that Allen's recruiting bases included Detroit, New York, and Chicago. Droullard, who was born in Sioux City, would later succeed Allen as the head coach at Morningside before completing his doctorate in mathematics and moving to the University of Wisconsin at Whitewater.

Allen was not due to begin coaching the Morningside team until August, but he was on campus as early as May 17. He was honored at a dinner on campus that night. The dinner was held in the Women's Residence Hall and 60 high school athletes from the surrounding area were invited in order to meet the new coach.[7]

Allen's first game as the head coach of a program went well. The Chiefs beat Midland Lutheran 33-0. But Morningside lost its next three, scoring only 14 total points while surrendering 65. The Chiefs won two of their final five games and the scores were closer in the losses. With three weeks to go in the season, Morningside lost to rival South Dakota 14-7. They finished with a 3-6 record in 1948. Morningside scored just 12.7 points per game that year and gave up 17.5.

Morningside College football coaches (from left) George Johnson, Al Buckingham, Allen, and Bill Pritula (courtesy Morningside University Archives).

3. Allen at Morningside

Allen was a lifelong writer, as will be discussed in the next chapter. He wrote of the 1948 campaign, "During the past season, Morningside won two conference games, which was two more than in 1947; defeated two teams which Morningside had not beaten in 11 years; and, except for an early game fumble, might have trounced the highly-rated Coyotes from South Dakota."[8]

The 1949 team went 7-3-1 and did not surrender a point until the third game of the season, a 27-20 loss to South Dakota State. Next, the Chiefs rattled off three straight wins and then tied South Dakota 6-6 before losing to Northern Iowa, 30-10. Morningside averaged 19.8 points per game that year and gave up just 13.7. Perhaps most importantly for history, Morningside's 34-7 victory over Concordia in the sixth game of the 1949 season put Allen's head coaching record above .500 at 8 wins and 7 losses. His record briefly slipped below the breakeven point during his first years at Whittier College, but once he got back into plus territory again, George Allen spent the rest of his life with a winning record. His final record, not including professional league preseason games, was 192-99-13.

The best player Allen had at Morningside was probably Connie Callahan, who was a senior in 1949. Callahan was named First Team, Little All

Allen (center) with his 1948 team captains, Connie Callahan (left) and Leon "Shorty" Shortenhaus (courtesy Morningside University Archives).

America in 1949 and did just about everything. He led the team in rushing with 1,284 yards, completed 55 of 103 passes for 722 yards and scored 16 touchdowns. As a punter, he averaged 43.7 yards. Callahan's career total of 1,574 yards stood as the school rushing record until 1970 when Dave Bigler surpassed him.[9]

The 1950 season started oddly with a Morningside win, a loss and then a tie. The Chiefs won five of their last six and finished at 6–2–1. Most importantly, Morningside beat South Dakota 10–0 in the sixth week of the season, the only shutout of the season for Allen's Chiefs. Morningside averaged 19.5 points that year and gave up 11.2.

Joseph S. Vadini played on Allen's 1948 Morningside squad and then coached at the high school level for 27 years, most of that as a head coach. Shortly before Allen died, he wrote a letter under the heading "Recollection of George Allen."

Vadini wrote that Allen's enthusiasm for the game was contagious. "Coach Allen was well organized and left nothing to chance. There was no time lost in practices. This helped the team to be well prepared for the games to [sic] that we could do our best. He also had a few practice 'gimmicks' that were new to me, such as, when we practiced shifting from the 'T' to single wing, we did it to music. He introduced a canvas strip with hole designations and line spacing so that we could practice more efficiently. There were other drills that he initiated that were innovative. Football music was played in the locker room as a source of inspiration and relaxation."[10]

Allen's offense, which included both the T and the single-wing formations, went with him when Allen became the Whittier College coach and will be discussed in that chapter.

Allen's impact went beyond coaching his players. Radio broadcaster Gene Sherman wrote that he met Allen for the first time when Sherman started his career in 1949. In a November 5, 1990, letter, Sherman wrote, "To Whom it might concern."

"Coach Allen who was also a young coach at that time was very much concerned that this rookie announcer would be well prepared to cover his games," Sherman wrote. "One example would be that Coach Allen took the time to explain the complicated Michigan single wing offense that he coached at Morningside."[11] Talk about attention to detail! Not many football coaches have ever taken the time to be sure the local play-by-play announcer understands the offense the coach plans to use. Sherman said Allen remained helpful after leaving Morningside. Allen invited the announcer to attend the Chicago Bears Media Day twice while Allen was an assistant and went so far as to assist Sherman in setting up player interviews for Sherman's television show.

4

The Green Arrow at Whittier

Unlike his other coaching assignments, Allen did not take over a loser when he started at Whittier College before the 1951 season. The Poets had gone 10–1 in 1950, won the Southern California Intercollegiate Athletic Conference championship and played in a bowl game.

Whittier is a suburb of Los Angeles. Whittier College's best-known alumnus would become Vice President of the United States while Allen coached at Whittier. Richard M. Nixon, who played basketball and football at Whittier, would serve two terms as the back-up for President Dwight Eisenhower. A decade later, Nixon became President and was a fan of Allen's Redskins teams before resigning in the wake of the Watergate fiasco.

The Whittier football team is best known as the program where one Hall of Fame coach succeeded another in the 1950s. When Allen left Whittier to join the Rams coaching staff as an assistant coach in 1957, Don Coryell took over the Poets program. Coryell brought with him an offense that changed football and famously generated Heisman Trophy–winning tailbacks at the University of Southern California, the I Formation. Coryell had developed the I when coaching at Wenatchee Valley College, a junior college in the state of Washington. Coryell called the new formation the I-T Formation when he arrived at Whittier.

Whittier's program was not the only school in the Conference to generate well-known personalities. Jack Kemp, later a quarterback for the Chargers and Bills before serving in the United States House of Representatives, played at Occidental College during that era, as did future NFL coach Jim Mora. And a player of a different sort, singer-songwriter and guitar player Kris Kristofferson, played football at Pomona.

According to Allen's *Strategies*, one of his first moves as a head coach at Whittier was a big mistake. He said: "I once thought I was

Former Whittier Poets player Richard M. Nixon, then president of the United States, and George Allen (to Nixon's left) in a team photo with the Washington Redskins. Assistant Coach Marv Levy is at right, in a Redskins cap (Alamy).

communicating to others very well in a brief span of two weeks on a new job as head coach at Whitter College. I wanted an easy game (spelled w-i-n) before we swung into the regular season's schedule. I asked our assistant athletic director, Bob Clift, to schedule an extra game to be played at home, a chance to show off the team and my new system to the home fans and alumni. We booked a team called Sub-Pac, supposedly a service team based on a submarine out at sea. I was so naïve that I thought these guys must surface every day to work out, and they would have sea legs. There was no way they could work on their kicking game at sea—ball handling, kicking, absolutely not. To make a long story short, Sub-Pac defeated us 51–0 and I lost three players for the season, including my captain, Ed Vanderhaven. We had only seven lettermen to start the season."[1]

His time in the Navy's V-12 program did not prepare Allen for the quality of play military service teams had in those days and he had not been in Southern California long enough to learn that some service teams were better than others. It was a gaffe that slowed Allen and the Poets for a year, but Allen said the lesson he learned was even more important than the one about scheduling military service teams. He wrote in *Strategies* that the biggest lesson was one about communicating well. The 1951 Poets did not recover from that opening loss and finished the season 2–7, although they split their SCIAC games, finishing with a 2–2 mark in conference play.

The program recovered in a big way in 1952, going 9–1 overall and 4–0 in conference play. All told, Allen's Poets went 32–22–5. They split the six games with Whittier's chief football rival in those days, Occidental, in the annual Shoes Game (although Allen's Poets outscored the Tigers 54–40 in the six meetings). According to legend, the trophy is a pair of shoes worn by Whittier's Little All American, Myron Claxton. Claxton's shoes were swiped by enterprising Occidental players before the 1939 renewal. Whittier won that game and Claxton found his shoes on the Occidental sideline after the contest had ended. After the Second World War ended, Claxton's shoes were bronzed and the teams played for the trophy each year until Occidental dropped football in 2017.

John McNichols went to Whittier as a junior college transfer from East Los Angeles College, where he had played for Clyde Johnson. McNichols played at Whittier in 1955 and 1956, a fullback in Allen's offense.

"At 83," McNichols told the author in 2017, "[Allen] is still an influence on my life."[2]

McNichols spent the remainder of his life around the game. He was briefly in a tryout camp with the Colts ("I competed with a guy named Lenny Moore, whom you might have heard of," McNichols told the author), then played minor league ball. McNichols coached at the high school level for decades. He remains involved as an administrator for the National Football Foundation.

Allen's offense at both Whittier and Morningside merged the offense of the 1930s and 1940s, the single wing, with the more modern T-Formation. The Poets would line up in the T, then shift to the single wing and run a play. The idea was to give opponents two offensive looks to prepare for and to try to induce offside penalties with the shift. McNichols said the pre-snap shifting paid dividends.

"He ran a lot more single wing than he did out of the T formation. We'd line up in the T and then shift to the single wing. I was always a fullback," McNichols said.

Max Fields, a tailback and another transfer from East Los Angeles, said, "That funny shift.... When you'd shift, you'd shift to the right or the left. I didn't like the offense too much, but that's the way it was. The key to that offense was the center had to snap it accurately. We had some good snappers. One of our centers was a guy named Jim Carlisle."[3]

Fields played at Whittier in 1956 and 1957. He was among the Poets who played under both Allen and Coryell.

"It was a three-step move from the T to the single wing," McNichols said. "We made a living on five-yard penalties. George was sneaky. If there was a way to get an easy five yards, George would do it." He added, "George was good at figuring out a way of getting the other team off balance.... Concentrating on the cerebral part of the game."

If the shifting between the single wing and the T formations seems odd today, what really matters is that it worked. McNichols said, "My senior year, I had one play for negative yardage. We didn't make mistakes." That play was against Cal Tech, he said.

Fields recalled that the first time he heard Allen speak was at a banquet before a high school football game between Fields' school, Mark Keppel High School, and its rival, Alhambra High School, when Fields was a senior. A few years later, after playing for two years at East Los Angeles, Fields was recruited by both Whittier and San Diego State. He eventually picked Whittier. "I was almost set to go to San Diego State when George called my coach at East LA. Our coach [Johnson] called me in and said that Coach Allen wanted to talk to me. Coach Johnson returned the call and I went over to Whittier. I was sold when Allen said, 'I want you to play for me.' He got me enrolled that day. Classes had been going for about a week."

"I really didn't know too much about [Allen]," Fields added. "When I was in junior college I went over and watched out of curiosity." Once he got to Whittier, Fields came to be happy with his decision. "I really liked him. I got along with him. Even after he left, I got notes from him." Fields said Allen's coaching staff at Whittier was much smaller than the number of coaches most programs have today. Fields said "they" didn't have an army out there" and that Allen spent time coaching both offense and defense.[4]

Like McNichols, Fields spent much of the remainder of his life around the game. He was among the last players cut by the 49ers in 1958 when he tried to make the team as a rookie running back with the likes of Pro Football Hall of Famers Joe Perry and Hugh McElhenny already on the roster. Fields coached junior college and high school ball for decades and was a radio broadcaster in Southern California's Imperial Valley for many years.

The author asked Dick Vermeil, who was an assistant coach for Allen with the Los Angeles Rams in 1969, why Vermeil thought Allen was successful as a college coach when he was so veteran-oriented as a professional coach.

"It's all relative," Vermeil said. "He found people who could play and fit into his scheme. I would say he probably did a little more teaching of each position at that level."[5]

"He surrounded himself with guys who could coach, too," McNichols said.

In 1953, Allen published the book, *How to Scout Football*.[6] The small book is not surprising for the in-depth treatment of its subject. Attention to detail was the first trait of Allen's that everyone interviewed for this book described to the author. Interestingly, the back cover of the 2009 edition correctly notes the year of Allen's birth as 1918 while the Library of Congress notation in the original text has Allen born in 1922. The book was dedicated to his parents, "for their many sacrifices." Predictably, Allen wrote in a series of conclusions that "it is essential to have detailed information on both offense and defense in order to have a complete scouting report." Then, he wrote, "it is the general opinion that offensive reports are more reliable and should be given more attention because offenses do not vary much from game to game, whereas most teams change their defenses frequently. Offensive scouting determines the type of defenses that will be employed." He also wrote, "It, as a rule, is easy to get the offense of a team when this team has a fairly easy game. Defensive points are brought out more clearly when a team has a hard game." Allen recommended no more than two scouts per game and that they sit together except that one of the pair should spend a quarter behind one of the end zones when possible. Only one of the scouts should use field glasses. Allen recommended scouting opponents three or more times when possible.

For all his determination to scout the opposition as fully as possible, the thirty-five-year-old Allen also cautioned against what he called "overscouting." He wrote, "It is possible to overscout [sic] and thus lose a football game. The danger of overscouting in the sense of drilling your own team too rigidly so that any slight change by the oppositions [sic] may confuse them, results in one's squad losing flexibility to adjust quickly to meet unfamiliar situations that might occur." The book is packed with suggestions for the best scouting forms for the purpose for taking notes, but Allen also wrote, "Ninety percent of the scouting forms used are too detailed and contain superfluous information." A page later, Allen wrote that coaches should revise their scouting report forms frequently.[7]

The recommendation to revise the forms is interesting, if for no other reason than it shows how life can be cyclical. Chapter 16 begins with the words, "Throughout our coaching career we have always stressed the importance of our centers. Perhaps the emphasis may be due to the fact that we have always been a single wing football machine." In the decades after the single wing offense disappeared, the shotgun formation and all of its variations became commonly used at every level of the game. The center is as important as ever for a football team's offense.[8]

No football book authored by George Allen would be complete without pointers about the kicking game. He wrote, "Every coach is vitally concerned about the kicking game. Sometimes we fail to get the necessary details. By simply answering these key questions a scout will have graded the opposing kickers." For punters, Allen wanted to know the player's name and number, the distance behind the line he stood to receive the center's snap, the distance of the punt from the line of scrimmage, whether the punt was high or low, whether a punter's kicks spiraled and whether the punt tended to go toward one side of the field or the other. He wanted to know how quickly the punter got the ball away. Allen also wanted to know the wind conditions at the time of each punt. For kickoffs, Allen wanted to know the kicker and his number, the distance the ball traveled, whether it was high or a line drive and what direction the ball went. In each case, for both for the punter and the kicker, Allen wanted a judgement from the scout about the ability of the punter/kicker.[9]

Sometime during his stay at Whittier, Allen wrote an article about football on the Pacific Coast as compared to the Big 10 Conference. He contacted a magazine about the piece and was rewarded with a cautionary reply that he was welcome to write the article, but the editors did not expect to use it. He titled it "The Big 10 Is Not That Good!," and cited regular season games between Big 10 schools and schools from what Allen termed "The Western Conference." Allen mentioned Howard Jones' tremendous USC teams and the outcome of Rose Bowl games. Allen wrote that the weather in the Midwest made Big 10 players harder and that the good weather on the coast could be a distraction for college players during the off season.[10]

Allen's hard work ethic, the same one that had Etty Allen calling the police to search for her husband in Iowa, came with him to Whittier. In those days, assistant coaches at Whittier also taught classes. Fields said he remembered hearing a story from assistant coaches, who said they'd be in Allen's coaching office until 10 p.m. or later and an assistant would realize that he had to teach a class the next morning. Allen's enthusiasm, which later invigorated even the saltiest veteran pros in the National Football League, eventually caught on with the players and coaches he led at Whittier.

McNichols said, "When coach started talking, you thought he was full of bull. The more he talked, the more sense he made. Pretty soon you believed. He had a barbeque at the park by the college and we were all there. We thought we were all just getting a free hamburger but he was team building. His kids were there and so was his wife, but he was teambuilding."

McNichols specifically recalled Allen's theory about playing defense near the goal line. Somehow, Allen wanted his players to believe the defensive team with its back to the goalposts and just a few yards from surrendering a score actually had an advantage. "George preached things that didn't make any sense," McNichols said with a grin in his voice. "If the other team got inside the 10-yard line, George would say, 'Now we've got them where we want them.' His theory was that there are only so many things a team can do inside the 10. We'd already taken away all these other things. Now there isn't much they can do. It must have worked; we had a lot of goal line stands."

Allen's Whittier teams used the 5–2 and 4–4 defensive fronts. Fields said, "We were not too big and we ran a lot of 5–2. We ran a lot of stunts out of the 5–2 or the 4–4."

Allen would never be known as a yelling coach and he didn't shout much at the Poets. After all, who yells at poets? But Allen got his points across. His book, *Strategies*, reads like a primer for using hard work and enthusiasm to build the practice habits of students or football players.

In a letter he wrote to the players on the 1955 Whittier team, Allen wrote, in part:

> The game of football is built out of a number of individual fundamental acts coordinated into team play and maneuvers. The fundamental acts are the foundation. The team play is the superstructure and as in the case of any structure, the superstructure can be no better in the long run than the foundation. A poor foundation means a poor building. Poor fundamentals mean a poor football team. A great football team can be developed only when all fundamentals are mastered and carried out with a high degree of perfection.... The strength and character of the personnel determines the strength and success of the team.... [Aggressiveness] ... is the most important single quality for a football player. At least 80% of the success of the football team is determined by the fight and spirit that they put into their play. The biggest and fastest material, superbly coached, would fail miserably without this indispensable characteristic.

Allen added that concentration, determination, obedience, reliability, confidence and cooperation "will broaden your personality. Apply them to your football, apply them to your college work and apply them to your life after leaving the classroom. They will help make your associations and employment pleasant and successful."[11]

That 1955 Whittier team was remarkable, so much so that Allen dedicated his book, *George Allen's Guide to Special Teams* (which was published in 1990), to that 1955 squad. Allen wrote, "In 1955, my Whittier College football team blocked eight kicks (we led the nation for small colleges). The team was outweighed in every game we played, sometimes as much as 24 pounds per man, as we still won eight games and lost only two that season. We upset San Diego State and Chico State, which was undefeated at the time. I always held that 1955 team in particular esteem, and I have always considered my special teams as superior and unique.... This book is dedicated to that 1955 Whittier College team."[12]

George Allen was a master motivator. He motivated players everywhere he coached. While he labeled himself as a self-starter, he also understood that others were not the same way. Allen generated followers at the college level and, as will be seen, he motivated heavily experienced grown men to sing fight songs in NFL locker rooms. His generation had experienced the Great Depression and won the Second World War. Some people with that background achieved great things, but others from the same era did not. So how did Allen pass his energy level and his commitment on to others?

There are clues in a paper Allen titled *Motivation in Athletics*, written while he was at Whittier.[13]

"To understand motives is both to observe and interpret what goes on for an individual as he plays, competes, co-operates, or withdraws from contact with others," Allen wrote. Later on, he continued, "To make use of motives for the purpose of coaching requires not only that the motives serve the purposes of learning, but also that the motives themselves be shaped and modified in desirable directions. ... If there is any conclusion from recent research of which the coach may be sure, it is that there is no known formula or infallable [sic] set of procedures to motivate pupils at all times." Allen alluded to Edward Thorndike's "Law of Effect" that covers behavioral conditioning.[14] Thorndike basically said that responses that produce a satisfying effect in a particular situation become more likely to occur again in that situation. Further, according to Thorndike, responses that produce a negative effect becomes less likely to happen again. Coleman R. Griffith, considered by some to be the father of sports psychology, said (according to Allen) that if the "Law of Effect" is valid, then memories would almost always be happy ones. Allen contradicted Griffith. The coach wrote, "In reality some of the sharpest remembered images are the unhappy occurrences. The wild pitch that cost the ballgame or the missed free throw in the waning seconds of play—these are remembered along with successful achievements. One is just as likely to remember the night spent on a park bench as the night spent in a luxurious hotel."

Allen then applied the law to sports learning, where he wrote there were some effects. "The beginning hurdler who takes a painful fall may become inhibited in his technique and reluctant toward further practice. The coach who drives his player beyond their span of readiness, attention and constructive energies may find that the disagreeable effects will discourage some players from further participation. ... Obviously, factors other than effect must be present. In conclusion, it may be said that the law of effect is very important in situations where the motivation or competitive prestige isn't strong. In other situations, the law of effect may be over shadowed by motivation and social prestige."

Motivation in Athletics covered evaluation practices, punishment in learning, a child's need for approval and the use of success and failure as regulators of learning. "Every child needs to find some way to give expression to anger, hostility and destructiveness which arise out of the thwartings which he forces. Frustration is inevitable in growing up," Allen wrote.

According to his players, George Allen put into practice what he seemed to preach in the paper. "He did not really chew you real bad," Fields said of Allen. "For what he wanted to do, he was well prepared. He got that across to us."

In the same paper discussed above, Allen wrote, "Immediate goals usually are more strongly motivating than remote goals, but good methods of working toward goals may help insure the existence of desirable long-term goals. The habit of clarifying goals may help the youth." A paragraph later, Allen wrote, "Finally, motivation is important not only as an energizer and director of learning but as a habit system in itself."

Allen's lifelong calling cards were established by the time McNichols and Fields arrived at Whittier. His work ethic, enthusiasm for his job and even a somewhat academic approach to leadership marked Allen's coaching process. Through his career, Allen never stopped looking for ways to understand himself and the men he coached. In January of 1977, his career fully entrenched as a winner at the highest level of his profession, Allen was still searching. He answered a survey titled the *Communicating Styles Survey* offered by Graytek Associates Incorporated of Rockville, Maryland. According to an April 4, 1977, letter to Allen from Graytek, Allen was interviewed. The results were to be published the following summer. The same group had done a similar article on Dallas Cowboys coach Tom Landry.[15]

The 1977 letter from Graytek said, in part, "Your primary style [of communicating] is that of THINKER and SENSOR." The emphasis is in the original. The letter included the tabulated scores of test results. Under favorable conditions, the Graytek test said Allen's highest score was for THINKER, with SENSOR showing to be his secondary style. Under stress, Allen's style of communicating was that of a FEELER, with SENSOR the secondary style again. The THINKER style, Graytek wrote Allen, is characterized by heavy emphasis on logic, ideas and systematic inquiry. SENSOR style communicators, the letter said, thrive "on getting things done here and now, without unnecessary and time-consuming deliberations." The FEELER style typically heavily emphasizes human interaction. "Individuals operating in this style seek and enjoy the stimulation of contact with others and typically try to understand and analyze their own emotions and those of others." The FEELER, the report said, "is likely to be perceived as being dynamic and stimulating."

Fields suffered an injury while playing for Allen and had to sit out a game and part of another. He recalled, "I had a shoulder separation.

I missed the next game and played slightly in the next game after that. We were walking down for practice and he just said, 'By the way, Fields, you're starting Saturday,' and I said, 'Okay.' He made a special pad for my shoulder. He rigged that up and I used it all season." There was no call to the office and no dramatic pep talk. Allen simply told his tailback that he would be starting the next game. It was all the motivation Fields needed. Nothing is perfect, of course. Fields recalled a screen pass from Whittier quarterback Gary Campbell during a close game. Campbell threw the ball too high for Field's right arm, the injured one, to catch due to the restrictions of the new protective pad. "I could not get my arm up," Fields recalled. "If I had done so, there were blockers in front and a sprint [was open] down the sideline for a score." This game was against the Air Force Academy and the game ended in a 14–14 tie.[16]

After winning the conference championship in 1952, the Poets went 6-3-1 (2-2 in the SCIAC) the next season, then 3-6-1 (1-3), 8-2 (3-1) and 4-3-3 (2-1-1). Allen's record at the school was 32-22-5.

Most college football coaches look to their senior players for leadership. Allen, who later became the coach of the NFL's Over the Hill Gang in Washington, could be expected to be more senior oriented than most college coaches. But McNichols said that was not necessarily the case. One of the keys to Allen's success at Whittier, McNichols said, was "how he selected his personnel that was going to play. I don't think George cared about next year until next year. ... One of the things I had to face was [that a senior] was the starting fullback because he was a senior. I got in the game pretty soon but [the senior] was the starter."

Another of the habits Allen became known for manifested itself at Whittier: Spending money. He bought a special projector to help the players and assistant coaches prepare for games. On a list of Visual Aids and Ideas for 1954, Allen wrote that there were "few colleges, large or small that possess a machine like ours." Another goal was to get every game, both home and on the road filmed "as long as the money lasts." He wanted to use a closed-circuit television system he'd seen advertised in a magazine for use on the sidelines during games, a teletype for self-scouting, mirrors on the field (presumably at practice) and a Polaroid camera. He also wanted to scout every opponent "even if we have to go to Alaska." Most of Allen's ideas were left unused while he coached the Poets but the fact that Allen generated such far-reaching dreams for improving his teams pointed toward a coach who was dedicated to winning and did not want to allow anything to get in the way of producing victories.[17]

One of the most important figures for the program at Whittier was a local businessman named Rufus Trueblood. The rules for collegiate players were different in the 1950s than they are today, and some college

4. The Green Arrow at Whittier

players had off-season jobs. Trueblood was among the Whittier supporters who assisted players by helping them to get jobs. Even with a scholarship, those jobs made the difference between attending college and dropping out for some guys.[18]

Allen became a prolific writer. He wrote articles for sporting and athletic magazines constantly. During his last year at Morningside, he wrote "Defending the Running Pass" for *The Athletic Journal*, a detailed breakdown for stopping a specific pass play by single wing offenses. The article was submitted prior to Allen's arrival at Whittier. "It is our belief that the running pass off the single wing formation is the most effective maneuver in football today. We have been confronted with the problem of defensing the single wing running pass for some time. When we came to Morningside College in 1948, seven of the nine teams on our schedule were using the single wing. ... As a result, we have worked many months on research in attempting to solve our problem of defensing the running pass."

The article went in depth. For example, he wrote:

> The territorial responsibility of the strong-side halfback, the left halfback extends from a point about six yards downfield from the line of scrimmage to the goal line, and laterally, from a point in line with the offensive end to the sideline. From the aspect of a possible running threat his vision is keyed on [offensive backs 4 and 5 in Allen's system]. One or both of these men must block on the line of scrimmage for a running play to be a threat into his territory. Thus, he has an immediate tip-off as to whether a run or pass is developing.[19]

Like others of its kind, this article included diagrams of ways to defend against the running pass. Included with the article and diagrams was a bit from the editors of the magazine: "George Allen learned his football under Crisler and Oosterbann. Hence, it is not surprising that he is a strong advocate of single wing football. Playing in the tough North Central Conference, Allen's Morningside teams have won three-quarters of their games, which Allen attributes largely to the quick kick. Mr. Allen resigned at Morningside recently to accept a similar position at Whittier College."

Allen was a voracious reader. He collected similar magazine material written by others. His collection included articles about conditioning and drills, new practice aids (such as the latest developments in blocking sleds and tackling dummies), offensive theories and ways to defense them.

Allen exchanged letters with other coaches constantly, a common practice at the time. There were no computers, email or texting in the 1950s and some the answers to Allen's letters survive. In some cases, Allen wrote asking questions about fine points of the game and in other cases he asked about practice planning.

He exchanged letters with Duffy Daugherty, then an assistant coach at Michigan State, about pass protection. He wrote to and then heard back from Charles W. Caldwell, Jr., of Princeton, about the veer buck play. Eddie Teague, an assistant at the University of North Carolina, replied to a letter from Allen about the Gap 8 defense and Allen asked E.R. Godfrey about the finer points of placekicking. Al Johnson, the head coach at New Mexico Western College, traded letters with Allen several times. In 1956 Johnson sent Allen game films of his team's game against New Mexico Highlands, a future Whittier opponent. It was a major no-no for Johnson to share the films with Allen because New Mexico Highlands and New Mexico Western were in the same conference and most conferences had unwritten rules against exchanging information about conference teams with non-conference schools.

"Do not let anyone know that I am giving you some information on Highlands as they are in our conference," Johnson wrote. "The only reason that I am is because of their coaching staff." Johnson had a beef of some sort with the Highlands staff. Whittier tied New Mexico Highlands, 21–21, that season.

In the 1950s, the he-bull of college football was Bud Wilkinson, head coach at the University of Oklahoma. Wilkinson's Sooner teams won three national championships and 14 conference titles between 1947 and 1963. Best known for his team's 47-game winning streak between 1953 and 1957, the Sooners also had a 31-game win streak between 1948 and 1950. Oklahoma won Wilkinson's first 79 conference games over a span of a dozen seasons. In 1956, Wilkinson invited Allen to observe Oklahoma's spring practice sessions. Allen had a scheduling conflict. In an April 17, 1956, note, Wilkinson invited Allen to attend the start of Oklahoma's fall practice. Allen scrawled in blue pencil across the top of Wilkinson's invitation. "I'll be there."[20]

From Duffy Daugherty to Bud Wilkinson, and many others in between, Allen was getting his name recognized in coaching circles. His magazine submissions and coaching clinics introduced his name to some who had not met or exchanged letters with the young coach at Whittier. The effort resulted in at least one job offer. Frank D. Clayton, at Wisconsin State College, Whitewater, wrote to Allen on July 3, 1956. Wisconsin-Whitewater had a sudden need for a football coach.

Dear George,

The head football coach here the past 15 years has decided to become the athletic director only. This just came about yesterday. The president asked me to be one of 3 on a screening committee to select a new coach.

The job pays $6000 plus $1000 if you teach 6 weeks of summer school. I do think you could get more, however.

We are located 50 miles from Milwaukee (40 from Madison) [and] 100 from

4. The Green Arrow at Whittier

Chicago. If you are at all interested, send your credentials to me and I will follow through. I know you are set at Whittier, but you might be interested in this area and a state school.

I'll try to get a more personal [and] informed letter out to you later.

Regards,
Clayt

P.S.—We will take 3–4 weeks to decide.

Allen turned down the job and Clayton wrote again on July 27, 1956. In part, Clayton wrote,

I could have gotten you the job here at $6500 plus $1083 for 6 weeks of summer school. However your reasoning to staying seems logical.

The best to you,
Clayt

George Allen's coaching career is among the most notable in the history of the game. After coaching college winners at Morningside and Whittier, he started a long and headline-grabbing coaching career at the professional level. He coached winners in two professional leagues and served briefly in management for a team in a third league. But Wisconsin-Whitewater's next coach, Forrest Perkins, did that school well. From 1956 to 1984, Perkins' teams went 189–87–8. The school split its two postseason appearances for a total of 190 wins, 88 losses and eight ties. Perkins' winning percentage over 29 seasons was 66.43 percent.

Allen's reasoning for turning down Clayton's job offer might have had something to do with Allen's family, which was growing,[21] but a more likely reason for staying in Southern California was Allen's cultivating connections with the major college programs in the area through an annual coaching clinic he held during his years at Whittier. Jess Hill, then coach at the University of Southern California, was among those who attended the event and there were others. The event raised funds for the football program at Whittier and it served to help Allen make connections he might not have made otherwise. Allen addressed the clinic and he probably impressed his audience.

The college coaches, however, were not the only connections Allen made during his tenure at Whittier. The Los Angeles Rams held their preseason camp at the University of Redlands in the 1950s and Allen spent time with the pros during the early portion of some of their training camps during those years. Redlands was a conference rival for the Poets. Whittier's summer workouts did not get under way until August, allowing Allen time to volunteer with the Rams. Sid Gillman became the Rams head coach in 1955 and the team responded by winning the

NFL's Western Conference. They lost the NFL championship game to the Cleveland Browns at the end of that season. Gillman would later become better-known as the developer of the modern passing game while he coached the San Diego Chargers in the early years of the American Football League but while he was with the Rams, he had Hall of Fame quarterback Norm Van Brocklin passing to Hall of Fame receivers Tom Fears and Elroy "Crazylegs" Hirsch. Allen was around those men during the summers at Redlands and he had become familiar to them.

5

An Introduction, a Car Wash and a Return

When the Rams hired Allen to coach the offensive ends for the 1957 season, it put him in position to work with one of the most creative coaches in the history of the game, Sid Gillman. It put Allen in position to work full-time with future Pro Football Hall of Fame inductees, quarterback Norm Van Brocklin and wide receiver Elroy "Crazylegs" Hirsch. It was also Allen's first year as an assistant coach at any level since he left Michigan to coach at Morningside.

The Rams had been up and down in the 1950s. They played in the championship games in 1950 and 1951,[1] losing the first and winning in 1951. Joe Stydahar, the head coach who led the team to the 1950 and 1951 title game appearances, was fired one game into the 1952 season. Hamp Pool replaced Stydahar and watched over the club as it finished increasingly worse for three seasons before Gillman was hired. Gillman led the club to the Western Conference title in 1955, resulting in a championship game loss to the Browns. The Rams' record was 8–3–1 in 1955 and fell to 4–8 in 1956.

The team had internal problems in 1957. The star quarterback and head coach had differing opinions about who should be calling the offensive plays.[2] There was a power struggle among the owners. The team's stars were aging. Van Brocklin was 31 that year and Hirsch was 34. Flanker Bob Boyd was 29, fullback Tank Younger was 29 and guards John Hock and Duane Putnam were 30 and 29, respectively. Most of the defensive starters were younger.

Allen coached ends Hirsch and Leon Clarke and flanker Boyd. "We had a veteran group of ends," Hirsch said. "Most young coaches are full of fire and want to put in new ideas right away. But George just let us do what we had been doing most of the time. If he did have something he wanted to get in, he brought it up as a suggestion. He'd say, 'Have you ever tried it this way?' He'd never say, 'This is the way we're going to do it.'"[3]

The Rams led the NFL in scoring that season, averaging 25.6 points per game. But the defense surrendered 23.2 points a game, tenth worst in the 12-team league and the Rams completed the year with a 6-6 record, finishing fourth in the Western Conference.[4] Cleveland's Jim Brown broke his own single-game record by gaining 237 yards against the Rams on November 24.[5]

In today's world of televised games, with networks bidding against each other to put pro football on the air more and more nights every week to the point where the market is over-saturated, it is hard to understand what the Los Angeles franchise meant to the NFL in 1957. In that era, teams had to depend upon the ticket-buying public for funding and, as the only major sports franchise in all of Southern California, the Rams drew very well, especially when they were winning. The November 10, 1957, game between the 2-4 Rams and the 5-1 San Francisco 49ers drew 102,368 to the cavernous Coliseum. The bigger statistic was the NFL's total attendance for that day: 312,131. In other words, 32.7 percent of the people who attended an NFL game that week were in Los Angeles for the game with the 49ers. For the entire season, counting both home and away games in the preseason and regular season, the Rams drew a pro football-best 1,051,106.[6] The Rams beat the 49ers on that November day, 37-24, as Van Brocklin completed 14 of 23 attempts for 224 yards and two scores. The Rams rushed for 193 yards on 47 carries that day and Lamar Lundy, a future member of the most famous defensive line in pro football history (the Fearsome Foursome), caught a pass for an 18-yard gain. Lundy played both offense and defense his first two years as a pro and finished his career with 35 receptions, gaining 584 yards and scoring six times.

Allen was fired after the season but he wasn't alone among ousted Rams assistants. Gillman kept line coach Joe Madro and backfield coach Jack Faulkner but eliminated Allen and defensive line coach Lowell Storm. Bill Swiacki replaced Allen as offensive ends coach and former Rams hero Bob Waterfield was brought in to coach the quarterbacks.

The time with Gillman and the Rams introduced Allen to the fine, old art of spying in the National Football League. Gillman's biographer, Josh Katzowitz, described Gillman's devotion to collecting information on his opponents.[7] Allen, who went to great lengths to scout his opponents at Whittier, was a willing student and when Allen reported to his next professional football job, he went to work for a spy master. In fact, that was the reason Allen got his next chance in the NFL. The Chicago Bears needed information about the Rams' potent passing attack.

5. An Introduction, a Car Wash and a Return

But George Allen's job with the Bears was in the future and, at the end of the 1957 football season, Allen wasn't just out of football; he was out of work entirely. What was next?

In *Fifth Quarter*, Jennifer Allen picked up the story. She wrote, "Dad bought a car wash and named it, 'Rams Car Wash—Best Car Wash in the World.' But the car wash was failing and he had a wife and my three toddler brothers in a crummy house in Encino to support."[8]

Some of Allen's balance sheets from Rams Car Wash, Inc. survive in the Allen files at the Pro Football Hall of Fame and Jennifer Allen appears to be accurate in her description of the business' fortunes. A balance sheet for the period between September 17, 1958, and October 31, 1958, showed a loss of $2118.61. A balance sheet for January 31, 1959, shows the figures for the total assets and total liabilities and capital to be the same amount. A second sheet for the period between September 17, 1958, and January 31, 1959, shows a net loss of $3,521.12, although the business turned a small profit ($378.49) in the month of January 1959 alone.[9]

Jennifer Allen continued: "One night, on his walk home from the car wash, Dad stopped at a Catholic church. The doors were locked. Through a window, he could see candles burning inside. Dad knelt on the steps of the church and prayed that, God willing, God would find him a coaching job. A few days later, George Halas called ... would my father be interested in a job? Dad shut down the car wash, packed a bag, and hitched a ride to Phoenix, where Halas was attending an owners' meeting. Leaving the car wash, my father left behind him the same kind of blue-collar, assembly-line work his father had performed at the Ford auto plant. My father always feared working at a faceless job with his Christian name sewn on his chest pocket, all his education in vain, his potential wasted."[10]

George Allen's first introduction to the Chicago Bears had been during the training camp prior to the 1958 season when Allen arrived, attempting to sell weighted footballs to the club for Voit, the sporting goods manufacturer. The heavy footballs could be used as a training aid, the pitch went. The Bears were not buying but Allen befriended assistant coach Chuck Mather. After he returned home to California, Allen wrote a letter to Mather, saying how lucky Mather was to be coaching in pro football. The visit and Allen's letter were part of an odd chain of events. More than a month later, on September 5, 1958, Frank Korch, who handled the publicity for the Bears and was also the team's personnel director, had a heart attack and died in Dallas, Texas, where the Bears and Lions had played a preseason game. Then the Bears opened the 1958 season with a victory over Green Bay and a loss to the Colts, 51–38, in a game where Johnny Unitas threw four touchdown passes. Unitas completed just 10 of 23 passes against the Bears for 198 yards and the Bears intercepted a pass. But Chicago's defense also surrendered 147 rushing yards.[11]

The Bears' next four games were at home against San Francisco and Los Angeles followed by a West Coast swing through the Bay Area and then tinsel town. According to Jeff Davis' book, *Papa Bear,* Mather convinced Chicago owner/coach George Halas to bring Allen to the Windy City to help prepare the Bears for the Rams' high-powered offense. Halas agreed and the Bears won three of four, losing only to the Rams in Los Angeles.

Davis quoted Mather: "We brought George in and he helped us win when we got an interception off an audible. Halas didn't want anyone to know we had Allen here, so he said, 'Get him the hell out of here.' So I had to tell George I was sorry—that's all there was."[12]

In *Papa Bear,* Davis wrote that the Bears saw in Allen "the arrival of the coach who, years later, not only should have replaced Halas but also might have won multiple Super Bowls had he done so."[13]

As we have seen, Allen got his NFL indoctrination as a volunteer camp coach in the early 1950s when offensive maestro Hamp Pool was the Rams' head coach. Allen spent a year as a full-time Rams assistant and learned some of the tricks of the trade under Gillman's tutelage. He had been the head coach of two college programs and knew the value of a well-defined organizational doctrine. His decision to work for the Rams, leaving behind a dependable job at Whittier, was costly in the short term. But by this time George Allen knew his craft well and must have believed in himself enough to understand that, sooner or later, a job would open up somewhere in the football universe and he would get hired. He did, shortly after moving the family from Whittier to the San Fernando Valley city of Encino. Mather had worked on Halas to hire Allen as the Bears' personnel director. Finally, Allen was summoned to Chicago and hired. Etty and the kids remained in their home in Encino. Davis quoted Etty Allen: "I stayed in the house in Encino for nine months while George lived at the Y ... in Chicago. He would send me the paycheck. I don't know how he survived."[14]

Eventually Etty and the children came to Illinois and the family lived at 636 Ambleside Way in Deerfield. George Allen rode the train to and from work each day, earning a salary of $4,800 a year.[15] He famously rode the slower train, one with more stops, home so that he could accomplish more work while commuting.

In George Allen, George Halas had a willing, even eager student. It is not over-stating the case to say Halas invented the professional game. From the business side to the play on the field, Halas had seen everything and refined the things he did not invent. He had played against Jim Thorpe, promoted Red Grange as a superstar and coached against

5. An Introduction, a Car Wash and a Return

Jim Brown. Every coaching strategy, trick and plan was available for use because Halas knew them all. Allen knew that and spent two years as the personnel director listening to and watching as the two-legged NFL encyclopedia worked.

Jennifer Allen wrote, "Halas hired my father, and Dad learned much from the great man, including his need to control, his desire to win at all costs, and his famous paranoia."[16]

While Allen worked with Sid Gillman, there had been accusations from around the NFL that Gillman's Rams spied on other teams and pulled other shenanigans of the sort. Halas was not above that sort of action. After all, he'd originally paid Allen to teach the Bears' defensive players the Rams' audible system. The only two head coaches George Allen ever worked for at the professional level were masters of what politically correct punsters today might term extracurricular scouting. Allen learned well. Still, he did no coaching for the first two years of his time with the Bears.

Halas soon learned that Allen was an uncommonly good judge of talent. In 1959, the Bears' first draft choice was Don Clark, a back from Ohio State, who was a bust. But their next selection was Richie Petitbon, who played through the 1972 season and was later with Allen in both Los Angeles and Washington. Five of the first six selectees and seven of the first ten drafted by the Bears that year played somewhere in the NFL for at least one season.[17] The resurgent Bears finished second in the NFL Western Conference with a record of 8–4. The Baltimore Colts won the West and won their second straight NFL title that year.

In 1960, the Bears selected SMU quarterback Don Meredith, but Meredith never played for Chicago. He went to the Dallas Cowboys as part of the expansion draft. Dallas had not taken part in the draft. Allen could not predict what would happen to the men he recommended for the Bears' draft, and it could be argued that Meredith was the most successful passer George Allen ever drafted.

The Bears struggled in 1960, as a new power rose in the West: Vince Lombardi's Green Bay Packers. Chicago beat the Packers in Green Bay on opening day, 17–14, but later lost badly to the same team in Chicago, 41–13. The Bears lost twice to Baltimore. Green Bay eventually lost the 1960 championship game to the Philadelphia Eagles, 17–13.

Allen's first pick in the 1961 draft can probably be credited with reconstituting the Bears' reputation for gritty toughness. That draftee nearly invented the tight end position and was eventually inducted into the Pro Football Hall of Fame. His name was Mike Ditka and he played his college football at Pittsburgh. He played six seasons for the Bears, four for the Cowboys (catching passes from Meredith during part of that time) and two more for the Eagles. He later became the Bears' head coach and led them to a Super Bowl victory.

Ditka was also drafted by the Houston Oilers of the AFL. The competition for college players was heading toward the all-out spendathon it became a year later and Ditka almost certainly could have made more money playing for the Oilers. Ditka said later that he felt he would have played linebacker if another team from either league drafted him. Halas told Ditka that Ditka would play tight end with the Bears. Whether the Bears owner/coach projected Ditka as a tight end on his own or did so due to the recommendation of the personnel director is still unclear, but the decision changed professional football. The tight end position as it came to be in modern day football was born when Ditka began playing for the Bears.

Davis quotes Ditka's story about signing his contract in *Papa Bear*. In January of 1961 Ditka flew home from playing in the Hula Bowl in Hawaii. Ditka's flight stopped in Chicago and Allen flew with him to Pittsburgh. "He came right to our house and we did the contract," Ditka recalled. He said his deal paid Allen $12,000 with a $6,000 bonus.[18]

In the second round, Allen picked running back Bill Brown, who played a year for the Bears and 13 more with Minnesota. The third-round pick was defensive lineman Claude Gibson, who played five seasons with the AFL's Chargers and Raiders. Massive defensive lineman Ernie "The Big Cat" Ladd, who played eight seasons in the AFL with the Chargers, Oilers and Chiefs, was picked in the fourth round. Keith Lincoln, a running back who went on to star for the AFL's Chargers and Bills for eight seasons, was picked in the fifth round. Running back George Fleming, who ran back kicks for the Raiders for a season, was the sixth rounder and Mike Pyle, who played center for the Bears for nine seasons, was grabbed in the seventh round. Looking back at those seven selections, each of them played at least a season of professional football, most had long careers and the first of the bunch ended up in the Hall of Fame.[19] Of all the players the Bears drafted and did not sign that season, Ladd is the most intriguing. A defense that matched the six-foot-nine-inch Ladd on the same defensive line as the six-foot-eight-inch Doug Atkins under the coaching of George Allen might have changed the history of the game.

It was during his time with the Bears that Allen confessed to his wife that he was four years older than he had originally told her. Before he had completed his schooling, Allen had needed to help his family financially and he stopped working on his master's degree at Michigan so he would work. Earl Allen had suffered a work-related injury and neither the medical profession nor the workers' compensation laws were as helpful in the late 1950s as they have become in more recent times. Allen did not want

5. An Introduction, a Car Wash and a Return

the world to see him as a 27-year-old without much working experience when he finally did complete his master's degree and so he changed his age to 23.[20]

The Bears used two starting quarterbacks in 1960, veterans Ed Brown and Zeke Bratkowski. Brown, who was drafted by the Bears in 1954, had started most of the games since that time and the Bears were 36–23–2 in those games (through the 1960 season).[21] In 1960, Brown started 11 games and Bratkowski started one. The Bears won Bratkowski's start and were 4–6–1 with Brown starting. Neither man was efficient, as both threw more interceptions than they did scoring passes, and as a team the Bears completed just over half of their passes.

The Bears acquired another quarterback, Billy Wade, along with receiver Del Shofner and linebacker Jon Guzik, from the Rams in return for two players and a draft pick. Wade was the NFL's passing yardage leader in 1958. He also led the league by throwing 22 pass interceptions (against 18 scoring passes). Neither Shofner nor Guzik ever played for the Bears. Shofner ended up with the Giants and was selected to the first team, All Pro list from 1961 through 1964 and still later was named to the Professional Football Researchers Association's Hall of Very Good. Guzik played for the Oilers in 1961, his final year in pro ball.[22]

It was Wade who threw to Ditka for weeks as former Bears quarterback Sid Luckman coached the rookie tight end the art of playing receiver.[23]

The 1961 Bears improved to finish third in the Western Conference at 8–6. Wade had a fine season, completing 139 of 250 pass attempts for 22 touchdowns, against 13 interceptions and 2,258 yards. Those figures seem pedestrian compared to the numbers passers such as Tom Brady and Kurt Warner would post decades later, but Wade's numbers were impressive for the time. He was second in the league in scoring passes and only three quarterbacks with 250 or more attempts had fewer interceptions that year. Future Hall of Famers John Unitas, Bart Starr and Sonny Jurgensen all threw more interceptions that year, for example. The Bears finished fifth in scoring in 1961 at 23.3 points per game.

The Bears' problem in 1961 was the defense. Chicago surrendered 21.6 points per game, ninth best out of the 12 teams in the NFL. Clark Shaughnessy was the defensive coach and had been for several years. Shaughnessy had been a part of the Bears organization, in different capacities, for a long time. As a head coach, he led the Rams to the 1949 title game, losing to the Eagles. He was also the head coach of several collegiate programs. While some have described Shaughnessy as the father of the T-Formation, it is more accurate to describe him as an early proponent of the scheme. His defensive schemes, however, were not effective by the early 1960s and Halas made a change: Halas promoted George Allen. For 1962, George Allen coached the defense for the Chicago Bears. Shaughnessy remained on the coaching staff as the season started but he quit and went home to California during the season. Allen's defense, which was a refined version of something an injured player named Jim Dooley cooked up for Halas, was fairly straightforward and the players grasped the intent easily.[24]

In *Papa Bear,* Davis quotes defensive end and future Hall of Famer Doug Atkins: "When George Allen got [control], we went to basic defenses, and he turned us loose. The coverages were simple."[25]

The 1962 Bears defense finished fifth in the now 14-team league in points allowed, surrendering 20.5 points per game. Chicago registered three shutouts that year, two coming in the last four games. George Allen had arrived as an NFL coach. Atkins said, "I thought George Allen was the reason we won the '63 championship. ... Allen came along and rewrote the rules of how to play defense, like breaking down opponents four and five ways. ... We knew exactly what we were gonna do in '63. We'd line up and just tee off and play football."[26]

"We all knew he was the man," Ed O'Bradovich said. "He had the youth. He had the knowledge. And he treated us like men, not like some retarded escapees from an institution who gotta be guarded and watched. He threw all that stuff out the window."[27]

The 1963 Bears finished the regular season with an 11–1–2 record. The Bears' defense allowed opponents to score just 10.3 points per game over the 14-game season. Only two teams scored as many as 20 points against Chicago that season. Rosey Taylor led the Bears with nine interceptions, one of which he returned for a touchdown. Petitbon had eight picks. Dave Whitsell and Bennie McCray had six each. In the 14 games, the Bears allowed 17 offensive touchdowns. One of the interceptions Wade threw was returned for a score and shouldn't be credited to an opposing offense. Wade completed almost 54 percent of his passes for 2,301 yards that year. He threw 15 touchdown passes and had 12 passes intercepted. Joe Marconi led the Bears with 446 rushing yards, averaging 3.8 yards per carry. Ronnie Bull rushed for 404 yards, averaging 3.5 yards.

Green Bay was the two-time defending NFL champion when the 1963 season started but Chicago's 11–1–2 record narrowly beat Green Bay's 11–2–1 mark and earned the Bears the Western Conference championship. Both of Green Bay's losses in 1963 came at the hands of the Bears. The Bears beat the Packers 10–3 at Green Bay in the season opener. Chicago held Green Bay's proud running game to only 77 yards in the opener and intercepted Bart Starr four times. The second meeting came in the 10th week of the season and the Bears handed the Packers a 26–7 beating in Chicago. Bart Starr, Green Bay's future Hall of Fame quarterback, was injured and did not play. The Bears intercepted Starr's replacements, Zeke Bratkowski and John Roach, five times and limited the Packers' running game to just 71 yards.

Chicago's only loss in 1963 was a 20–14 defeat at the hands of the San Francisco 49ers in San Francisco. Through the years ahead, the 49ers would become a special problem for Allen-coached teams. Late in the season, Chicago tied the Steelers and Vikings in consecutive weeks. It was an odd circumstance that the scores of the two games were both 17–17. The Bears avenged their loss in the 13th week of the season with a 27–7 victory over the 49ers in Chicago.[28]

The playoffs in those days consisted entirely of the championship game between the champions of the Western and Eastern conferences. The Eastern champs in 1963 were the New York Giants. The Giants advanced to the title game with a record of 11–3, leading the NFL in scoring with an impressive average of 32 points a game. Quarterback Y.A. Tittle threw a league-best 36 scoring passes and just 14 interceptions, hitting on 60.2 percent of his passes, which also led the NFL, for 3,145 yards. Del Shofner led the Giants with 62 receptions for 1,181 yards and nine touchdowns, and future Hall of Famer Frank Gifford caught 42 passes for 657 yards and seven scores. The New York defense was not stressed to stop the opposition since the offense put plenty of points on the scoreboard. But the Giants finished the season fifth in points allowed, surrendering 20 points per game. New York defensive back Dick Lynch grabbed nine interceptions and returned three for touchdowns, while another defensive back, Jimmy Patton, intercepted six passes.[29]

The author has read a number of descriptions of the weather conditions for the day of the championship game. The game was played December 29, 1963, at Chicago's Wrigley Field and, regardless of which report one accepts, it was flat out cold. No report viewed by the author put the temperature above 10 degrees. Pro-football-reference.com has a grim reading of four degrees with a wind chill reading of 11 miserable degrees below zero.[30]

The Giants scored first when Tittle hit Gifford for a 14-yard touchdown pass but, still in the first quarter, Chicago's Larry Morris intercepted Tittle and returned the ball 61 yards before he was stopped on the Giants five-yard line. Wade plunged in from two yards out to tie the game. A field goal gave the Giants a 10–7 halftime lead. Chicago's Ed O'Bradovich intercepted another Tittle pass in the third period and set the Bears up at the New York four-yard line. Wade plowed in again, this time from a yard out, to put the Bears ahead and the scoring was over.

In *Papa Bear*, Davis wrote that Allen and Dooley prepared the

Chicago defenders for the New York screen passes. Davis quoted Morris as describing his big play like this: "I didn't know the screen was coming until Tittle sent a guy in motion. His key was to look right and give the left tackle and end time to slip over to the left." Morris jumped the route and was moving forward when he caught the ball.[31]

Dooley said, "If you get a team that screens and you take that away from them, they're in trouble. George Allen took away the screen."[32]

Tittle completed 11 of 29 passes to Giants receivers for 147 yards and the scoring pass but the Bears intercepted him five times and recovered a New York fumble. The six turnovers were too much for the Giants to overcome.

Wade completed 10 of 28 for 138 yards and he was not intercepted. The Bears did turn the ball over twice on fumbles, but Allen's defense did not allow the Giants to convert those mistakes into enough points to win. In the Chicago locker room after the game, linebacker Bill George awarded the game ball to Allen. The ball could have been given to Halas, the 67-year-old head coach and owner or to Morris or O'Bradovich, the two defenders who had key interceptions. Instead, the players handed the ball to George Allen. Richie Petitbon was a fourth-year safety for the Bears in 1963. He said, "The defense, we kind of dominated that game. We just got in the locker room, grabbed the game ball and said, 'We're going to give it to George.'"[33]

Jennifer Allen wrote that her earliest childhood memory is of that night, when she was three years old, when her father came home "with a game ball in his hands. I remember climbing out of bed and running down the stairs to greet my father. I remember my father tossing the ball up in the air, and my brothers, below him, reaching, stretching to catch the prize possession of the Chicago Bears 1963 championship game. I also remember my mother crying."[34]

George Allen would later become recognized as a master of turning losing NFL franchises into winners in amazingly short periods of time. He coached winners in the United States Football League and, in his final year as a coach, he grinded the team at California State University, Long Beach into another winner. Allen would be posthumously be inducted into the Pro Football Hall of Fame with one of the best coaching records of all time.

But George Allen would never again win a league championship.

The seeds of Allen's departure from Chicago may have been planted in that victorious Bears locker room. Davis quoted Ed O'Bradovich this way, "George Allen called us 'men.' Men. And call you by your first name and always give you respect. Instead of cussing at you constantly and doing everything to bring you down, his philosophy was just the opposite.

5. An Introduction, a Car Wash and a Return   39

And what greater time for Halas to step out, when we won the world championship, on December 29, 1963.... What greater time for him to step down and go out and to this day still be remembered for doing that? ... We had George Allen. I remember Paul Hornung telling me, 'With the talent you had, you should have won three or four of them.' When Allen left, that was the demise."

It is intriguing to consider what the future might have brought the Bears, had they been able to keep Allen in the fold. Halas had stepped away from coaching several times during his long career that was vital to the survival of the NFL. In George Allen, Halas had a disciple who believed in the Halas way and had demonstrated his ability to recognize talent, mold players into a strong unit and win. What might have the Bears' future held with Allen's energetic coaching under Halas' steady hand as the owner? We'll never know but the bald facts are ugly: From the time Allen was hired away by the Los Angeles Rams before the 1966 season until the Bears produced a winning record in 1977, Chicago Bears fans endured eight losing seasons, two seasons when the team broke even with records of 7–7 and one winning season. Halas had retired from coaching by then, but he had not generated a front office and coaching staff that could produce consistent winners.

The 1964 Bears' season started with a tragedy. Star running back Willie Galimore and starting split end Bo Farrington were killed in an automobile accident on July 27 on their way to training camp in Rensselaer, Indiana. Galimore was 29, Farrington was 28. Galimore played seven seasons for the Bears and gained 2,985 yards, averaging 4.5 yards per carry and scored 26 rushing touchdowns. He gained another 1,201 yards, scored 10 more touchdowns as a receiver and had another 1,100 yards as a kickoff returner. He returned one kickoff for a touchdown. For his career, Galimore gave the Bears 5,286 total yards and 37 touchdowns. Farrington played four seasons for the Chicago, catching 55 passes for 881 yards, averaging 16 yards per reception. He caught seven touchdown passes, the longest a 98-yarder in 1961.[35]

Losing that kind of production to injury would have been a difficult adjustment for a coaching staff, but to have two veteran players killed during preseason camp left Halas, Allen and the other coaches with a tough task ahead. Jon Arnett, whom the Bears acquired from the Rams, replaced Galimore in the lineup and gained 400 yards rushing. Arnett also caught passes for 223 yards. Rich Kreitling started at split end, caught 20 passes and scored two touchdowns. But Chicago averaged just 18.6 points per game, 10th best in the 14-team NFL. Allen's defense was worse, finishing 13th in points allowed, surrendering 27.1 points a game.[36] Chicago won five games and lost nine in 1964, finishing sixth in the Western

Conference. The Baltimore Colts won the West and were beaten by Cleveland, 27–0, in the title game.

Davis' book hints that the Bears players began the season nursing a grudge against Halas. Green Bay coach and general manager Vince Lombardi had famously gifted the wives of his players mink stoles after the Packers won the 1961 title game. Lombardi gave the players televisions after the Packers secured the title in 1962. Halas did not gift his championship players with anything, other than their championship rings, for the 1963 title.[37] The incident probably impacted George Allen's career. As coach of the Rams and again in Washington with the Redskins, Allen helped his players secure better contracts than the team administrators wanted to pay. Allen gave away weekly awards to players for good plays—a television for a blocked punt or a case of beer for a fumble recovery. The author heard arguments that no prize system existed on NFL teams, but in Allen's book, *Strategies,* there is a photograph of Allen handing a portable color television set to Redskins player Joe Lavender as a prize for being named the defensive player of the week. The gifts may have seemed like outlandish expenditures in the early 1960s, before professional football franchises began to earn very large sums of money, but Allen believed the gifts were small change compared to the team camaraderie they helped build. Halas had nursed the Bears and the entire NFL through The Great Depression and the Second World War. Like many American business owners who lived through that era, Halas ran his business in a parsimonious manner. Anyone who lived through Halas' lifespan could understand the legend's determination to watch his team's bottom line very closely. But that philosophy might have cost the team the cohesiveness that it played with in 1963.

Allen wrote in *Strategies* that, as a head coach, he used small bits of cash to keep his players alert at team meetings. He asked them to spell certain words or the names of players from the next opposing team. "I gave them $10 bills if they could spell difficult names. One time, Manny Sistrunk won $20 for spelling Cincinnati[38] and Mississippi. ... Does this approach sound schoolboyish, undignified, adolescent? Maybe so. *But it worked.*"[39]

On February 12, 1965, Halas held a meeting with his assistant coaches to discuss how to keep the Bears from going out of style. Allen spent three days working on a letter to Halas addressing the topic. An abridged version of the letter appears in *Strategies.*

In the letter, Allen addressed topics all over the map.

- Team morale was at a low ebb. Allen cited the shocking deaths of Galimore and Farrington, injuries to other players and the

resulting losing season for the drop in morale and then addressed the issue of the lack of gifts or bonuses for winning the 1963 title. Allen wrote that some players felt that they would not be treated worse for producing a losing team. Allen suggested an incentive plan.
- Allen recommended better facilities for office space, specifically an improvement in restroom facilities.
- The NFL had grown so quickly in recent seasons, Allen wrote, that a better-defined organizational outline of the coaching staff and front office was needed. Allen suggested that unit coaches have their responsibilities defined more specifically and suggested the implementation of a Head Offensive Coach and Head Defensive Coach, both of whom would report to the Head Coach. This is basically the same as today's offensive and defensive coordinators.
- Allen believed the Bears should join the handful of other NFL teams that had retirement plans for coaches.
- He recommended reorganizing training camp to give players a day off every other week.
- Allen wrote, "we stand to lose a great deal if we do not either expand our scouting forces tremendously or form a scouting combine with several other clubs."
- A Player Grievance Committee—composed of Allen; George Halas, Jr.; and assistant Luke Johnsos[40]—was needed so the players would feel that had a place to go when they had problems.
- Allen suggested a revolutionary idea where the Bears would contract with semi-pro teams or college teams and provide those programs with new plays or offensive schemes, both offensive and defensive. The Bears would help with what Allen termed "professional use of game films." After the plays or schemes were further refined at lower levels, the Bears could adopt the ideas and spring them on NFL opponents. All of the Bears' coaches, Allen said, had ideas that might be explored in this way. Allen also suggested that the Bears stock a farm club with drafted talent that did not make the NFL squad but appeared to have the talent to do so.
- Allen suggested something he later made his coaching calling card: a stronger emphasis on special teams. He suggested the kicking and kick coverage teams have their own team captains.
- He suggested expanding the Taxi Squad effort, giving this group of 15 players its own coach.
- Allen wanted a special tryout camp for free agents. Allen eventually did this in Los Angeles, Washington, and in the USFL.

- On a personal level, Allen wrote that in eight seasons Halas had not once sat with Allen to discuss his future with the club. Allen was grateful, he wrote, but "I believe I have delivered on every assignment you have given me. In addition, I am continually taking on extra projects to try and improve our football program without you asking me."
- Allen wrote that he was frustrated with what he called Halas' "lack of accuracy" with keeping appointments and delays in receiving decisions. Allen also complained that it seemed the Bears had penalties for staffers who did things pertaining to football that were encouraged by other NFL teams.[41]

It was an extraordinary letter. According to Allen, Halas acknowledged receiving the letter but never sat down with Allen to discuss it. Many of Allen's ideas were far-reaching, some were futuristic and most would be expensive to implement, while Halas was in his fifth decade of doing things his way. Halas' way had been successful, as witnessed by the championship won one season earlier, so Allen's letter may have been far too suggestive.

Still, George Halas had asked for ideas and George Allen gave him some. Reading the letter with the knowledge of 20/20 hindsight vision, the letter reads almost like a job application. Allen wrote that he reviewed his notes from his years in Chicago before writing his boss the letter. "Here is how carefully I have observed every facet of our operation since I have worked here," he seemed to say. "Here are some ideas that will help us avoid becoming stagnant. I am able to see the big picture and ready to take the next a step up. Can I be confident that, one day, I will be the head coach of the Chicago Bears?"

The answer to the final question was apparently no because George Allen became the head coach of the Los Angeles Rams less than a year later.

The failure of the 1964 season set the stage for the 1965 draft. As well as Arnett played in place of Galimore, Chicago needed a halfback who could be more of a game breaker. Wade, the quarterback who scored Chicago's touchdowns in the 1963 title game, turned 35 years of age that year and the Bears were aging at middle linebacker. They had needs. The Bears also had the third, fourth and sixth overall selections in the college draft that year. The Bears had drafted well in recent years with Allen calling the shots, but they needed to be successful again.

If you accept the selection of two future Hall of Fame inductees with their first two picks as successful, then Allen was successful. Typically thinking defense first, Allen selected Illinois linebacker Dick Butkus with the third pick overall and then nabbed Gale Sayers, a halfback from Kansas, with the fourth pick. Two picks after Sayers, Allen selected Steve DeLong, a defensive end from Tennessee. DeLong had an eight-year career in professional football, but all of it was with the San Diego Chargers in the American Football League.

The AFL-NFL brawl over college players was in full rage by 1965. Rookie salaries were jumping into new tax brackets. The veteran players, especially those who started in the NFL before the advent of the AFL, wanted contract increases to keep their earnings equitable with the untested college kids. The results of the competition between the leagues eventually formed the NFL into the league it was during the decades of its greatest growth, the 1970s and 1980s. There was no championship game between the leagues in 1965; bragging rights were more or less earned by signing the best college players.

Butkus eventually became the prototypical middle linebacker. The only other linebacker selected in the first round by NFL teams that year was Duke's Mike Curtis, who was taken by Baltimore with the final pick of the round. The University of Pittsburgh's Marty Schottenheimer, who went on to become a very successful coach in the NFL, was also selected by the Colts in 1965.

Allen ranked Butkus third on his list of all-time linebackers, behind Chuck Bednarik and the man Butkus supplanted as the Bear in the middle, Bill George. Allen wrote in *Pro Football's Greatest Players: Rating the Stars of Past and Present*, "Butkus came in and took over in George's last year with the team. And he was darn near as good as George. Of them all, only Bednarik hit as hard as Butkus. Butkus played with the ferocity of an angered animal. He was mean. ... Not that he wasn't smart. I think he was more of an instinctive player.... We were short staffed when I helped coach the Bears and I had a lot of jobs to do. I couldn't get the scouting reports ready before Thursdays. Butkus was always wondering why he couldn't get them on Wednesdays. He would study them on the plane flights while the others played cards."[42]

Somehow, with Sayers available, two white running backs were selected before him, leaving Sayers for the Bears. The New York Giants selected Auburn running back Tucker Frederickson (the 1965 Heisman Trophy winner) with the overall first choice in the NFL draft and the San Francisco 49ers picked Ken Willard of North Carolina second. Both Frederickson and Willard had productive NFL careers. Allen snapped up Butkus and Sayers and gave the Chicago franchise its faces for most of the next decade.

Sayers, Allen wrote in *Pro Football's 100*, might have been the greatest running back of all time, had he not suffered the knee injury that eventually shortened his career. "I was personnel director of the Bears as well as defensive coach in 1965 when I recommended we draft Sayers, who had been a successful runner at Kansas but was not a big name All-American. He didn't have much help there and the films showed me he had moves few backs have had. ... We needed a running back to replace Willie Galimore, who was on the verge of greatness when he was tragically killed in an automobile accident. ... Sayers was the most exciting running back I ever saw, the best long-gain guy I ever saw. ... He was one of the best I ever saw at returning kickoffs and punts. He caught and ran with passes brilliantly and even passed well. He was also an effective blocker."[43]

Allen and the Bears drafted other impact players. They included fourth-rounder Jim Nance, a running back from Syracuse, who chose the AFL instead and had a successful career with the Patriots and Jets; Dick Gordon, a seventh-round pick and wide receiver out of Michigan State who had an 11-year career with the Bears, Rams, Packers and Chargers; Brian Schweda of Kansas, a defensive lineman who played three seasons with the Bears and New Orleans Saints; Frank Cornish, a defensive lineman who eventually played six seasons with the Bears, Bengals, Dolphins and Bills; and Dave Pivec, a tight end from Notre Dame, who never played for the Bears but played for Allen in Los Angeles before ending his career with the Broncos.[44]

After the draft ended, the Bears and all the other teams from both leagues began the process of snapping up undrafted players who showed promise. Among the players Allen convinced to come to the Bears training camp was a running back from Wake Forest. His name was Brian Piccolo. Piccolo was not on the Bears roster for the 1965 season. He spent that year on what was called the Taxi Squad. He was a Bear, but he was not on the active roster. Piccolo made the roster for 1966. Piccolo, who was white, and Sayers, who is Black, became friends and their friendship was the basis for the film *Brian's Song*, which was a made-for-television film starring Billy Dee Williams and James Caan that first aired in 1971 and was then remade in 2001. Piccolo and Sayers became roommates when the team traveled and they were among the first mixed-race roommates in the NFL. Piccolo's career was cut short when he was diagnosed with cancer during the 1969 season. He died in June of 1970 at the age of 26, leaving a wife and three daughters. Piccolo finished his NFL career with 927 rushing yards and four touchdowns. He caught 58 passes for 537 yards and had one touchdown as a receiver.[45]

The Chicago Bears franchise has a history of great players, such as Red Grange, Bronco Nagurski, Sid Luckman and Walter Payton. Towering above them all is George Halas. Those are household names for sports fans and historians. Brian Piccolo's story transcended sports. The Bears later retired Piccolo's number, 41.

Drafting a boatload of talent was one thing. Inking contracts with those players was different and the Bears could have lost Butkus to the rival league. Denver selected Butkus with the first pick in the second round of the AFL draft, the ninth overall selection in the AFL draft and the first linebacker picked.

Allen wrote in *Pro Football's 100* that Butkus and his agent, Arthur Morris, came to talk to Halas about a contract. "Butkus and Morris left furious. Halas could be a little close with a buck. For example, when Morris said Butkus wanted a car for a bonus, Halas hemmed and hawed and said he'd look around for a used car. This was before the pros paid unproven rookies big bucks. But the AFL was driving up prices. And Butkus knew he was good. And I knew he was good. They stormed out of Halas' office with Butkus growling profanities. I intercepted them in the corridor and had the darndest time pacifying them. I promised to make Halas see reason. I had the darndest time with Halas. But Butkus got his car; we got Butkus a new one."[46]

The Bears got off to a slow start in 1965, losing their first three games. Chicago was out-scored 105–66 by the 49ers, Rams and Packers in those games. Billy Wade and Rudy Bukich both played quarterback. But starting with week four's 31–6 pasting of the Rams, the Bears went on a tear and won nine of their last 11 games. The Bears averaged 31.18 points per game and gave up a miserly 15.45 points over that stretch. The Bears finished at 9–5, but it was not enough. The Packers and Colts finished tied at 10–3–1 and Lombardi's Packers won the tie-breaker playoff game to advance to the NFL title game against Cleveland, beating the Browns 23–12.[47]

Chicago split its games with both the Colts and Packers in 1965, so they were at the very least competitive with those teams. A quicker start to the season would have given the Bears a chance to compete for the Western Conference title.

Allen later said that a letter he wrote to the league office changed the way the NFL distributed its postseason awards. He said he wrote that both Sayers and Butkus were so good that it would be "a shame if either lost the Rookie of the Year award, so maybe they should have an award for offense and another for defense. That's when they started the two awards, and both Sayers and Butkus won them."[48]

Allen might well have written a letter of the sort he cited in his book, but there was no Rookie of the Year award for defensive players until 1967 when The Associated Press named a top rookie on both sides of the ball. *Pro Football Weekly* started naming two top first-year players in 1969. Most of the major rookie awards went to Sayers.

The final game for the Bears in 1965 was played on December 19, a 24–17 loss to the Vikings in Chicago. At that time, some of the teams in the National Football League were looking for new head coaches. It was clear that the Chicago Bears were not one of them. While George and Etty Allen both had formed emotional attachments to Halas and the Bears, George wanted to take the next step in his profession. He believed he would be an effective head coach. For that reason, George placed a telephone call to the Los Angeles Rams, asking whether the team would be interested in interviewing him for its vacant head coaching position. The Rams' answer was yes.

6

Divorce Chicago Style

By the last month of 1965, George Allen had come a long way from his days as a failing owner of a car wash. He had risen to extraordinary authority within the Bears organization. He was the architect of one of the best defensive units in the National Football League, had been handed a game ball in the locker room by players on the freshly-minted 1963 NFL championship team, directed the Bears' draft decisions and had become the team's Personnel Director. Allen had observed and worked with Halas, who not only coached and owned the Bears but had also helped found the league 45 years earlier.

If Allen had not enjoyed a meteoric rise, his progress had at least been constant. Allen was now among the most highly-regarded assistants in the league and was a prime candidate for a head coaching position. His three-year assistant coaching contract with Chicago still had time left on it but, within the NFL culture, it was common for teams to allow top assistants to accept head coaching positions with other clubs.

Allen may have felt his time to advance in his profession was slipping away. Ever since his time in the military, Allen had been conscious of his age and had told potential employers and the media that he was four years younger than he actually was. In December of 1965, George Herbert Allen was 47 years of age. Newspaper reports of the day wrote that Allen was 43, but he was born in Detroit on April 29, 1918. It is one of the great ironies of the Allen story that a man best-known for valuing age and experience claimed to be a younger man throughout his professional career.[1]

The Rams had suffered through a terrible season in 1965 and for the first time since their move from Cleveland in 1946, the Rams' attendance was below the NFL average.[2] In that era, game attendance played a bigger role in team finances than it does now because network television contracts of the day did not support teams as well as they have since that time. Head coach Harland Svare was fired after the end of the 1965 season for failing to turn the club's fortunes around. The Rams had an opening and

Allen saw an opportunity to return to the Los Angeles area where he had coached successfully in the past. Indeed, the Rams general manager in 1965 was Elroy Hirsch, the Hall of Fame receiver Allen coached during his brief stint coaching ends under Gillman in 1957.

The opportunity was too much to pass up. Allen called the Rams sometime after Svare was fired in order to ask about the vacant head coaching job. He was granted an interview. Only then did Allen contact Halas about getting permission to meet with Rams owner Dan Reeves about the opening. At that point, things became a little murky. Halas would maintain for the rest of his life that he granted Allen permission to talk to Reeves only because he believed the Rams contacted Allen first and by granting permission for Allen to talk to the Rams, Halas was saving Reeves from violating a league rule against tampering with the employees of fellow ballclubs. Reeves was supposed to ask Halas for permission to talk to Allen, Halas maintained, and Halas would not have granted the Rams the opportunity to interview Allen otherwise.

Allen and the Rams reached an agreement quickly, but Allen was under contract with the Bears for two more years. He could not sign a contract with the Rams while still under one with the Bears.

A legal hearing was quickly arranged to consider an injunction requested by Halas and the Bears to prevent Allen from joining the Rams. In the history of NFL-involved legal proceedings, the *Chicago Bears vs. George Allen* is one of the oddest. Judge Cornelius J. Harrington heard the case in Circuit Court beginning on January 12, 1966. In requesting the injunction, Halas wrote that Allen had "special, exceptional and unique knowledge and skill as a coach which cannot be measured in monetary terms and cannot be adequately compensated." Halas continued that "unless he is restrained he will use this information in coaching the Rams against the Bears."

This was an odd complaint since Halas originally brought Allen to Chicago to help the Bears' defense prepare to play the high scoring offense the Rams expected to produce in 1958. Halas, it seems, did not want the Rams to do the very thing to him that he asked Allen to do for the Bears eight seasons earlier. Of course, Allen was not governed by an NFL contract when the Bears brought him out from Los Angeles to help prepare for the Rams offense.

Only one witness was called to testify during the hearing and that witness was George Allen. Allen said under oath that he had yet to sign a contract with the Rams but that he had reached agreement with the Los Angeles club during a Tuesday, January 4 telephone call. Charles F. Short, Jr., the Bears' counsel, told Allen, "On December 30 you were told by the Bears you would not be given a release."

6. Divorce Chicago Style

Allen replied, "That's news to me."

Short pressed Allen and said, "Prior to reaching an agreement with the Rams on January 4 you were told by the Bears they would not release you from your contract."

Allen said, "That is incorrect."

Allen's version of the story, the one he told in court that day, was that the Rams contacted him on December 28 while Allen was in New Orleans to sign a player and scout the Sugar Bowl. Rams personnel director John Sanders asked Allen if Reeves had Allen's permission to contact Halas about getting Allen released from his contract with the Bears. Allen said he called the Bears office six times in the coming days and eventually drove straight through from New Orleans to Chicago in order to talk to Halas about his Rams opportunity. Allen arrived back in Chicago on January 4, but the Bears' owner would not see him until the next day.

Allen said in court, "I figured if they were going to play a waiting game, to heck with it, and I put in a call to Mr. Reeves and agreed to terms."

Short asked Allen if the Bears had released him from his contract, which Allen admitted they had not. Then Short asked Allen, "Did you ask him [Halas] for a release in writing?"

Allen answered, "I did not. I didn't know I had to."

In *Fifth Quarter: The Scrimmage of a Football Coach's Daughter,* Jennifer Allen wrote, "In court, my father admitted that even though he had made the call to the Rams, he didn't know it had been a violation of his contract. Fact is, Dad said, 'I didn't read my contract.' Dad not reading his contracts would always plague our family."[3]

Allen's attorney, Albert E. Jenner, asked Allen whether Halas ever withdrew his permission for Allen to talk to the Rams and Allen testified, "He did not."

It was Jenner's assertion that the case did not belong in court to begin with, as he said NFL rules stipulated that beefs between two or more owners would come under the jurisdiction of NFL Commissioner Pete Rozelle. The dispute over the services of George Allen had become a difference of opinion between the owners of the Rams and Bears. Later in the proceedings, Judge Harrington asked Allen whether he would be willing to have the matter settled by Rozelle and Allen indicated that he was willing for that to happen. Halas absolutely did not want Rozelle to settle the issue and he went to court specifically to avoid allowing the league office to do so. According to a January 12, 1965, story in *The Evening Sun,* reporter Joe Mooshill wrote that Rozelle had already told Halas that NFL assistants had long been allowed to take advantage of the opportunity to advance their careers.[4] Mooshill's story quoted the commissioner as telling Halas,

"On the basis of this historical precedence, in fact as it is now known, this office finds no cause at this time to interfere with the Los Angeles Rams' signing of George Allen as head coach. It is hoped that the matter can be amicably resolved by the two clubs."

Thus, before the matter ever got to court, Rozelle had already indicated to Halas that he was inclined to side with Allen and the Rams. Halas' rush to court was an end run around the league office he had helped to found. Further, as indicated above, Halas' public reason for going to court to block Allen from leaving the Bears was to keep the Rams from hiring a coach whose value could not "be measured in monetary terms and cannot be adequately compensated." For these irreplaceable services, George Allen was paid $19,000 a year.

Allen's nervous system got worked up before standard, daily team meetings, so the three-week period between his initial contact with the Rams and the moment when he was finally freed from the Bears must have been torturous. Jennifer Allen wrote, "My father adored Halas."[5] Etty Allen told James C. Mullen, Executive Sports Editor of the *Chicago Sun-Times*, "It wasn't an easy thing for George to make this decision. He called me four times Monday. He got sick, he couldn't sleep. Finally, he said he agreed to terms," with the Rams.[6] In the same newspaper story, Etty Allen was quoted as saying, "I love Mr. Halas and I love the Bears. I've told my husband many times that the three men I respect most, excluding him, were my grandfather, my father and Mr. Halas."

In fact, Allen tried to find ways to stay with the Bears, even after he had reached agreement with the Rams and before the matter went before Judge Harrington. Some of Allen's solutions seem a little strange now but others are similar to contract deals offered to high-dollar coaches in today's football world. Over the course of several days and during different meetings with Halas, Allen, according to published reports in the Chicago media at the time, asked for assurances that he would someday be the Bears' head coach. Allen offered to stay with the Bears as an assistant if they matched the salary offered by the Rams and then later offered to stay if the Bears would offer him 10 percent ownership of the club. Finally, Allen proposed the Bears allow him to coach the Rams for a few years and then return to the Bears.

Halas declined each of Allen's proposals. When Allen resigned from the Bears on January 8, 1965, Halas refused to accept the resignation, saying the contract Allen had with the Bears was still in effect. In his resignation letter, Allen wrote, "No man ever owed more to another than I do to you for all you have done for me. No one has ever had a more agonizing experience in arriving at a decision than I have had in bringing myself to this final act of resignation."[7] Etty Allen told a newspaper reporter that her husband's easiest course of action would have been to stay with the Bears.

6. Divorce Chicago Style   51

But, she said, George Allen wanted to test himself as the head coach of an NFL team. What the Allens did not know and nobody else knew was that George Allen's days as an employee of the Chicago Bears were over. The Bears had gone to court to retain his services with no intention of actually keeping Allen on staff.

When Harrington announced his findings, he ruled in favor of the Bears and their contract. Allen was to remain an employee of the Chicago Bears. The three-year contract Allen had signed a year earlier was valid. But as soon as Harrington announced his ruling, Halas stunned everyone in the courtroom and around the league by immediately releasing Allen from his contract. The point to requesting the injunction, Halas said, was to establish the validity of the contract between the Bears and their tremendously valuable assistant coach. Once the Bears made their point, Allen was free to go. Despite the legal effort to keep him, the Bears and their owner did not want George Allen anymore.

It appears the Bears' players wanted him. In the 1960s the NFL Pro Bowl, football's version of baseball's Major League All-Star Game, was played in Los Angeles. *Los Angeles Times* columnist Sid Ziff approached Dick Butkus, still a Bears rookie, at Pro Bowl practice and reported the possibility that Allen would soon be named the Rams coach. Ziff wrote, "'Oh no,' exclaimed Butkus. 'Gee, I hope we don't lose him. He's a real good football man. I work with him all the time. Gee, I mean I like to see a man better himself but I'd just hate to lose him.'" Ziff wrote that Butkus seemed genuinely shook up over the news that Allen might be leaving the Bears. Ziff further quoted Butkus, "He is such a conscientious football man. He eats and sleeps football. Look how we came together this year after our poor start. I mean, this is a coach."[8]

This was now the Los Angeles Rams' coach.

Over the next five seasons, while Allen coached the Rams, the Bears compiled a record of 26 wins, 41 losses and three ties. In the seven years after that, while Allen coached the Washington Redskins, the Bears generated 37 wins and one tie in 98 games. Their total record while Allen coached in the NFL was 63 wins, 101 losses and four ties, a winning percentage of 37.5. Allen's teams had records totaling 116 victories, 47 losses and five ties, a winning percentage of 69. His teams advanced to the playoffs seven times.

George Halas coached the Bears for two more seasons, then gave way to Jim Dooley. Two more men, Abe Gibron and Jack Pardee, would coach the Bears during Allen's tenures with the Rams and Redskins. Ironically, when Allen coached his final complete NFL season, his Redskins went 9–5 and failed to reach the playoffs. The Bears had the same mark, just their second winning season since Allen left for Los Angeles. That year, the Bears made their first playoff appearance since Allen joined the Rams.

THE NFL YEARS

7

The Turnaround
The 1966 Rams

The Rams had not been winners since 1958. Sid Gillman was the head coach, but Gillman was gone after the 1959 season with a record of 28–31–1. Rams hero Bob Waterfield, the starting quarterback on two championship winners for the Rams, was next, but Waterfield compiled a record of failure at 9–24–1 and he resigned after the first eight games of the 1962 season. Harland Svare replaced Waterfield to complete the 1962 season and then lasted three more seasons. Svare's record was far worse than Waterfield's at 14–31–3. Svare's 1965 Rams went 4–10.

As poor as those records were, the Rams' roster was not without talent. Future Pro Football Hall of Famers David "Deacon" Jones and Merlin Olsen anchored the so-called Fearsome Foursome defensive line on the left side. Roosevelt "Rosie" Grier and Lamar Lundy filled the right side. The defensive backfield included cornerback Clarence "Clancy" Williams and safety Eddie Meador. Offensively, the starting line was a good one. The center was Ken Iman, the guards included Joe Scibelli and Don Chuy and the tackles were Joe Carollo and Charlie Cowan. Running back Dick Bass would finish his career as the all-time franchise rushing leader. Bass averaged 4.5 yards a carry in 1965. Split end Jack Snow caught 38 passes for 559 yards in 1965 and tight end Billy Truax also returned.

The quarterback situation continued a fine, old Los Angeles tradition: Indecision and controversy. Bill Munson started the first 10 games in 1965 before an injury ended his season. His results could have been better. Munson completed 144 of 267 attempts for 1,701 yards. He tossed 10 scoring passes but also gave up 14 interceptions. Roman Gabriel played in seven games and started the last four, hitting 83 of 173 attempts for 1,321 yards and 11 touchdowns. Gabriel threw five interceptions, or one every 264 passes. Munson averaged an interception every 121 passes.[1]

Rams fans were accustomed to arguing over the merits of

quarterbacks. In 1951, when the team brought Los Angeles its only NFL championship of the 20th century, Waterfield and Norm Van Brocklin shared time in the huddle. Later in his time with the Rams, Van Brocklin shared passing duties with Rudy Bukich and Billy Wade. Wade and Frank Ryan continued the uncertainty in 1958 and 1959. Even Buddy Humphrey, by then a second-year man out of Baylor, got a start in 1960. Van Brocklin, a Philadelphia Eagle by then, won his second NFL title in 1960. Wade moved on to the Chicago Bears in 1961, leaving Ryan and Zeke Bratkowski to settle matters for the Rams. The Rams drafted Gabriel in 1962 and then Gabriel shared roster space with Bratkowski and Ron Miller. In 1963 (after Ryan was moved to the Cleveland Browns), Gabriel started nine games, Bratkowski started four and Terry Baker, the 1962 Heisman Trophy winner and first overall pick in the NFL draft, started once. Munson joined the fray in 1964, starting eight games for the Rams to Gabriel's six. Ryan and his Browns won the championship in 1964.[2]

George Allen as head coach of the Los Angeles Rams against Green Bay in 1966 (Vernon J. Biever photograph).

After Allen left the Rams and became the Washington Redskins coach, he created his own controversy with tough guy and great leader Billy Kilmer playing ahead of the best pure passer of the era, Sonny Jurgensen. Later in Allen's Washington tenure, he sat Joe Theismann against the wishes of his owner. But one of the first decisions Allen made as coach of the Rams was to elevate Gabriel to the role of starter.

Before he could use Gabriel, Allen had to convince him to stay with the club. The Oakland Raiders had offered Gabriel a four-year contract worth $400,000, which was a lot more than he could have made playing for the Rams. Gabriel left California for his home on the East Coast and was driving across country when he learned Allen was the new Rams coach.

Gabriel told author John Klawitter, "At this time, I'd already left the

7. The Turnaround

Rams in my mind. ... Well, George Allen came to my home, the first time any coach had seen fit to do that. He told me we were going to build a winner, and I was his man, I was going to be his quarterback. He fought with [owner Dan] Reeves to get my contract up to $40,000 a year. It was nowhere near what the Raiders were offering, but George got to me in another way. He said, 'You don't want the fans in Southern California to think you can't play. Show them your stuff first—and then you can go if you want to.' That really got to me. I knew then that it wasn't the money. I had to prove myself, and George was giving me the opportunity to play. That's why I say he's a completely different coach than anyone I had ever met, or ever met after."[3]

Munson stayed with the ballclub through the 1967 season and was traded away before the 1968 season. More on that trade later.

Allen had to recruit another player to return to the Rams for 1966, but this one played defense. Linebacker Jack Pardee had been drafted by the Rams in the second round of the 1957 draft, the 14th player overall in that year's selection process. He was a fullback and linebacker from Texas A&M, where he'd played for head coach Paul "Bear" Bryant. Pardee was among the survivors of Bryant's infamous preseason training camp at Junction, Texas, in 1954. In his first eight seasons with the Rams, Pardee started all but five games and was an All-Pro selection in 1963. But before the 1965 campaign, Pardee had been diagnosed with a malignant melanoma in his left arm. On his 28th birthday, he underwent an 11-hour surgery which included chemotherapy, a complete blood transfusion and a procedure which lowered his body temperature to 86 degrees. Pardee was a tough, smart guy, an Academic All American in college, and Allen wanted Pardee on the defense he was building for the Rams. Pardee did not play football in 1965 but Allen wooed him back for 1966. From the start of the 1966 season through the end of the 1972 campaign, his last as a player, Jack Pardee started 96 of 98 regular season games for Allen and started every postseason game.[4]

The Rams had other players returning from 1965, too, men who formed the foundation for Allen's winning teams in Los Angeles. But those players, good as they were, went 4–10 in 1965. The franchise had been in or near the NFL's Western Division cellar through the first half of the decade. In 1966, they won four of their first five games, lost four straight and closed by winning four of five to go 8–6. What happened?

Dick Vermeil was an assistant for Allen in 1969 before moving on to UCLA, where he was the offensive coordinator for a season. Vermeil returned to the Rams as an assistant from 1971 to 1973 before returning to UCLA, this time as the head coach. His Bruins went 15–5–3, winning the Pac 8 conference title and the Rose Bowl in two years. From there Vermeil went back to the NFL as the head coach of the Eagles, where his teams made one Super Bowl appearance and compiled a record of 54–47. He left the game in 1982, returning as head coach of the Rams in 1997. After a masterful rebuilding job, Vermeil's Rams won the 1999 championship. He retired again after that game and came back a year later to coach the Kansas City Chiefs for six seasons. Dick Vermeil rebuilt the Eagles and Rams into winners and he made the Chiefs a contender. With that experience behind him, and having coached with Allen for a season, Vermeil understood what made Allen a winner.

"His passion for the game was outstanding," Vermeil said. "An overwhelming passion for the game. He was intense in his preparation. He was so driven to teach the game as it ought to be played. I think he was ahead of his time in his breakdown and preparation for an opponent's offense."[5]

Successful coaches have those traits in common: passion and intensity. But even very good coaches might not be able to turn a struggling franchise around in a short period of time as Allen and Vermeil did. What was different about the Rams in 1966 from the year before? Vermeil said Allen's ability to match another club's veteran player with a position of need on his own team made a difference.

"The key was that he [Allen] knew the importance of each position," Vermeil said. "He understood how long it would take to teach each position. He knew [veteran players] could adjust quicker. It really helped me to have worked for George. I remember my first or second year with the Philadelphia Eagles, the San Francisco 49ers let Woody Peoples go, they thought he was too old. He played three more years for us." Vermeil listed several other players that he got extra mileage out of, as examples.

The struggles between the NFL and the still-young American Football League were at high pitch at the time and the 1966 draft was held in November of 1965, before Allen was finally free of his contract with the Bears. The Rams had the second overall pick that year and they selected Tom Mack, an offensive lineman from Michigan, with that choice. Mack played for 13 seasons with the Rams and was later elected to the Pro Football Hall of Fame. He became a starter before the end of his rookie season. The Rams also drafted Heisman Trophy winner Mike Garrett of Southern California, but Garrett never signed with the Rams. Instead, Garrett inked a deal with the AFL's Kansas City Chiefs and played in two of the first four Super Bowls, winning once. Henry Dyer, a running back from Grambling, was the Rams' fourth round pick. Dyer had no carries in 1966 but he did spend four years in the NFL. The fifth-round pick, the last member of the Rams 1966 draft class to make a meaningful contribution, was defensive tackle Diron Talbert of Texas. Talbert's 14-year career spanned four years with the Rams and then a decade with the Redskins.

The Rams had depended upon the draft to get the players the team needed to become winners for years without success. They had drafted good players—Gabriel, Mack, Jones, Olsen, Bass and many others—who played well for Allen in 1966. The difference between Allen's 1966 Rams and the teams Waterfield and Svare coached was that Allen replaced lesser players with proven veterans. Remember Vermeil's note that veterans could adapt to changing teams and schemes quicker than rookies could adapt to playing pro ball.

In his book *Strategies for Winning: A Top Coach's Game Plan for Victory in Football and in Life*, Allen wrote, "Trading was a part of the mental game for me, and I enjoyed it. Trading is to coaches what cutting a deal, closing a contract or making a big sale is to a businessman. This is where you move the chess pieces; it provides a feeling of power, a clash of wits. You have to know what you want and what you are willing to give up, and you have to work hard at it."[6] Knowing what he wanted was not a problem for Allen. He was a keen judge of talent. He preferred veteran players who could step in and make the Rams better immediately and his record shows that he readily went after players he thought his teams needed.

Allen said in *Strategies*, "I don't think you can always be building toward the future. People are constantly looking for a player who is 22 with eight or nine more years ahead of him. In baseball you always hear about the great young pitching staff, where the oldest starter is 24. That has nothing to do with it. How much ability do they have? How much of it are they using? How badly do they want to win? To me, the best years of an athlete's life are after 30, provided he has taken care of himself. I think he appreciates more, he has more leadership, is smarter, more dedicated, and makes more of a contribution to the entire team than he did when he was 24."[7]

Once he joined the Rams and filled his coaching staff, George Allen started earning his reputation as a coach who preferred veterans to rookies and as a shrewd dealmaker. The first trade George Allen completed as a head coach was, fittingly, for Cleveland Browns kicker David Ray. Allen sent Cleveland a draft pick for Ray.

Allen acquired 37-year-old middle linebacker Bill George for his 1966 Rams. George Allen had coached Bill George in Chicago and the coach knew the linebacker's experience and study habits would help the Rams. In his 1982 book, *Pro Football's 100 Greatest Players*, Allen ranked George second among linebackers in history to that point, behind only Chuck Bednarik. Allen wrote, "[George] was the smartest defensive player I ever coached. He called defensive signals for the Bears when they were at their best defensively. He studied films, kept a notebook of his own, did his homework every week, and always prepared to play his best." Once Allen became head coach of the Rams, Allen, "picked him up because he could still contribute to a team with his intelligence even when his body was beat up. ... He played 15 years of superb pro ball and there hasn't been anyone I've admired much more." That is high praise, especially when you consider the man Allen ranked third among all-time middle linebackers was Hall of Famer Dick Butkus.

Allen and the Rams acquired halfback Tom Moore from the Packers. Moore started every game for the Rams in 1966, rushing for 272 yards and a touchdown. Moore caught 60 passes, three for touchdowns. Perhaps more importantly, Moore had played for the Packers from 1960 through 1965, winning three championships in that span under Vince Lombardi. Moore understood the intensity of preparation that winning teams must undergo. As much as Allen figured Moore could contribute on the field, the new Rams coach knew Moore could also be a positive influence in the locker room. A man who owned three championship rings would understand what had to be done and could help guide other players.

Training camp was a new experience for the Rams who played under the previous regime. Gabriel recalled three practices a day for the first few weeks, each workout lasting three and a half hours. The typical NFL team practiced twice a day in training camp during that era and most sessions lasted about two hours.

"He wanted your will," Gabriel told NFL Films during an interview for a retrospective on Allen's career. "He was going to give us an example that if you wanted victory, this is how it had to be done."[8]

Deacon Jones said, "It was a bitch. ... Ain't no other way to describe it because it was. See, we needed to learn how to practice hard. We were losers when he took over. We had the theory that you draft to make a championship. George brought in that you take the veteran, cultivate him and you get to that point a lot quicker."[9]

Training camp during Allen's time with the Rams was significantly different from what it became four decades later. Allen and every other NFL coach invited a hundred players or more to try out for one of the 40 roster spots. There were six preseason games to play and endless hours of film to watch. Judgments had to be made about which players to keep and who to cut. Most coaches have a formula for how many spots to keep for each player group (for example, how many offensive linemen, how many linebackers and so forth) and the assistant coaches have to report their judgments to the head coach.

Jennifer always stayed home with Etty during training camp, but Allen's sons—George, Bruce and Greg—were with the team and their father during the summer. Training camp was almost pure football because there were fewer distractions. It was disciplined and straight forward, a total emersion into the game. It was a busy, demanding time for head coaches and Allen loved it. His single-minded devotion to building a winning team was a perfect match for everything that must happen during training camp.

Gabriel said, "You talk about George Allen, there's only one thing that counts: Winning. Nothing else. Everybody has that little deal where it's God, family and football. George would tell you today: Football, family and God."[10]

Allen constantly wrote himself notes. Following the 1966 season, he wrote notes about preparing negotiations for a trade involving the Rams, 49ers and Atlanta Falcons. The Rams would send running back Moore to the 49ers and eventually get wide receiver Bernie Casey from the Falcons. Casey played for the 49ers at the time but the deal would send Casey to the Falcons on paper before he finished the deal as a Ram.

The note read:

Moore for Casey
1. Team man [meaning Moore]
2. Played every game [Moore started all 14 games for the Rams in 1966]
3. White [Moore][11]
4. Hustle's all time [sic]
5. Can play [fullback] or [halfback]
6. Best receiver we had
7. 60 new league record [Moore caught 60 passes]
8. Popular deal in your area—Vanderbilt [Moore played his college football at Vandy]
9. He will play longer than Casey. [Allen was wrong, Casey played a year longer than Moore]
10. Casey like act over football [sic].
11. Popular—not a loner.

Allen's third point, that Tom Moore was white, does not indicate that George Allen was racially motivated. Keep in mind that Allen was trying to swing a deal that would allow him acquire Bernie Casey, who was Black. The three-team deal Allen wanted to put together did involve a team in the deep south, the Atlanta Falcons, and Allen wanted to sell Atlanta on the trade. Had either Moore or Casey been a native of the planet Mars, Allen might have praised the virtues of Martian athletes in his notes and while pitching the trade to the 49ers and Falcons. In the end, Moore went to Atlanta and played a year with the Falcons before retiring. Allen got Casey for two seasons before Casey retired.

The notes also show Allen considered proposing a trade sending Moore to Atlanta for kick returner Ron Smith or Ron Smith and running back Junior Coffee. Smith eventually joined the Rams in 1968. Then there were more notes about the possibility of trading Moore for Casey straight up, Moore for Casey and a draft pick, Moore for Casey and Falcons center Bob Whitlow and Moore for Casey and Falcons back Perry Lee Dunn. There was also a note that someone, probably Allen, contacted a former member of the 49ers coaching staff about Casey and the note said the former coach was not complimentary towards Casey. There is another page with ideas for a trade which might have sent Moore to the New Orleans Saints.[12]

Howard Schnellenberger was the offensive coordinator for Bear Bryant's Alabama program in the early 1960s. Schnellenberger was a part of Bryant's early championship runs and Allen called Bryant shortly after the courtroom dust cleared in Chicago, making Allen the coach of the Rams. Allen talked to Bryant about Schnellenberger and Bryant recommended that Allen hire Schnellenberger. Allen wanted Schnellenberger to coach the receivers, the same job Allen had when he started with the Rams in 1957. However, Bryant told Allen that Schnellenberger could not possibly go to Los Angeles without a significant raise over what Schnellenberger earned at Alabama, plus the use of a car. Alabama coaches had cars as part of their pay. After the conversation with Allen, Bryant called Schnellenberger into his office and recommended that Schnellenberger accept the chance to coach with the Rams, as it would help further Schnellenberger's career. Then Bryant told Schnellenberger about the salary and need for a car that Bryant had explained to Allen.

Schnellenberger called Allen, who attempted to retain Schnellenberger's services for a lower salary than what Bryant had dictated. Schnellenberger held his ground and eventually Allen agreed to the salary Schnellenberger wanted, plus the car. Not long after he arrived in Los Angeles and started working for the Rams, Schnellenberger had to start looking for a place to live and he needed a car to do that, so he talked to Allen's secretary, who said she had no knowledge about a deal for Schnellenberger to have a car at the Rams' expense. Schnellenberger talked to Allen about the matter and shortly after that, a car was delivered to the Rams facility for Schnellenberger. The 1966 season went along and ended. One day, while the Rams were preparing for the 1967 pro football draft, Schnellenberger got a call from the dealership that had supplied his car. Thinking it was time to get a new car, Schnellenberger greeted the caller warmly, only to discover that Schnellenberger was on the hook for more than $27,000. The car that Allen had so quickly arranged for his ends coach was a rental, hired at a daily rate. The debt was more than Schnellenberger's annual salary with the Rams. Eventually, the front office had to settle the matter and Schnellenberger did not have to pay for the car. But decades later, Schnellenberger was still telling the story.[13]

Once the regular season opened, Allen's Rams started gathering the attention of Los Angeles sports fans. The Rams gained 421 yards and allowed just 237 while beating the Atlanta Falcons 19–14 in Atlanta. The Falcons accused the Rams of conducting a type of spying on the Falcons by talking to Bob Jencks, a former Falcons kicker who had been cut recently. Jencks had played for the Bears when Allen was an assistant in Chicago. Allen said that during the week before the game, the Rams held a closed practice on Thursday in Atlanta. During the practice, a Coca Cola supply truck was allowed into the practice facility and Jencks walked in behind the truck.

"I saw Robert Jencks—after all, he's 6-5 and you could hardly miss him," said Allen. "He asked for a tryout at tight end, having heard that Marlin McKeever was hurt. ... He talked with me a little and then with [Bill] George and mentioned little things about the Falcons, odds and ends. ... It's ridiculous to think that anything he said could help your team." Allen said he had contacted Falcons coach Norb Hecker after Jencks' visit. Then Allen added that two players cut by the Rams in the preseason, defensive linemen Bob Sherlag and Joe Szezecko, played for the Falcons against the Rams.[14]

In their home opener, the Rams beat Halas' Bears 31–17 in front of 58,916 fans, perhaps drawn by the history between Allen and Halas.[15] The Rams lost on the road to the Packers 24–13 and then came home to wallop the 49ers 34–3. Then the Rams beat the Lions 14–7 in Detroit.

Allen prepared a Quarterback Game Guide for each game and wrote an introduction on the first page. The introductions give the reader a glimpse into the intense preparation Allen's teams became known for. Prior to the September 16, 1966, game with the Bears, Allen wrote, in part:

> This week we face the best defensive unit we have encountered. It will be a real test of our offense. We have advanced the ball against every opponent to date so keep up the good work. You must control the ball and keep it away from Sayers & Co. [sic] Don't let the changing defenses bother you. Keep your poise and be a leader.

Before the September 25, 1966, game against the Packers, Allen wrote:

> This game has now become the most vital of the year. To whip the Packers we must play sound fundamental football for a *full* 60 minutes. We must not make mistakes. Last week the offense had little fire. Get yourself ready and be leaders all the way.

Then came the September 30, 1966, game against the 49ers:

Forget last week and look only ahead. This game with the 49ers has now become the pivotal game of the year on our schedule. We are sure to face an inspired team and everyone must be emotionally ready and mentally tough. We have a good offensive football team and we are going to prove it. Nothing more needs to be said.[16]

In their first five games, the Rams averaged 322.6 yards of offense and gave up just 267.4. Those numbers turned around in a 35–7 loss to the Vikings in week six. The Rams mustered just 84 passing yards against the Vikings and only 230 overall, surrendering 313 passing yards and 378 yards overall. The loss to the Vikings started a four-game skid during which the Rams totaled just 33 points in losses to the Vikings, Bears, Colts and 49ers. Allen's defense gave up 90 points in that stretch. But the Rams rallied to win four of their last five games, starting with a 58–14 blowout win over the New York Giants. Los Angeles gained 572 yards against New York, their best output of the season, and gave up 103, the fewest they allowed all year. The Rams followed with revenge wins over the Vikings (in Los Angeles) and Colts (on the road), then beat the Lions (at home) again before losing to the Packers at home. The Packers loss drew 72,416 to the Coliseum.

Football history is replete with stories of teams with a recent history of losing getting off to a hot start, suffering a few losses and then folding up for the remainder of the year. But the Rams did not do that. Instead, they rallied in week 10 to overwhelm the Giants and then out-score their next

Rams quarterback Roman Gabriel with Allen (Vernon J. Biever photograph).

7. The Turnaround

three opponents 67–16. Even the season-ending defeat to the Packers was a close loss, 27–23. The Rams' 8–6 record left them third in the NFL West, a game behind the second-place Colts. The Packers won the West easily with a 12–2 record, beat the Cowboys in the NFL championship game and then won the AFL-NFL World Championship Game, later named the Super Bowl, beating the Chiefs and Mike Garrett 35–10.

Bass had a career season, rushing for a franchise record 1,090 yards and eight touchdowns. He averaged 4.4 yards a carry and caught 31 passes for 274 more yards. Gabriel started all 14 games, completed 54.7 percent of his passes and tossed 10 scoring passes. He also threw 14 interceptions. The Rams scored 20.64 points per game, tenth-best in the league. They gained 4,282 yards, seventh-best. The offensive statistics did not bring back memories of the high-flying days of the record-setting Rams offenses of the early 1950s, but one important stat generated attention: The Rams were winning. It was their first winning season since 1958.

The defense played very well, finishing the season ranked second in scoring defense (allowing 15.14 points per game) and fourth in yardage allowed (269.35 per game). Clancy Williams intercepted eight passes, returning one for a touchdown. Safeties Eddie Meador and Chuck Lamson snagged five interceptions each and Lamson returned one for a score. The NFL did not count quarterback sacks as an official statistic in 1966, but defensive ends Jones and Lundy each intercepted a pass.

Meador ranked ninth among Allen's list of all-time best safeties. In his *100 Greatest* book, Allen wrote that he, Allen, "studied films of the Rams and really admired Eddie. I felt he was one of the players I could build a winner around. Eddie was smart, tough and had good hands. He was a bit of a gambler. He gambled on an interception against Bob Hayes, missed, and got burned for a long score. He didn't gamble against guys like Hayes again. Eddie had such good hands he held for our extra point and field goal tries, and one time he went on his own, took the ball, and ran with it for a first down. But he almost didn't make it. He had to break a tackle to make it. And, afterward, he admitted to me he'd made a mistake. He laughed and said there was no way he wasn't going to make it because he knew I'd have killed him otherwise. Sometimes you had to go with a guy like Meador because he wanted to win so much he'd do anything he could to do it."

The Rams did not earn a spot in the playoffs, but the 1966 campaign was still a breakout season.

8

Back to the Playoffs
The 1967 Rams

The Los Angeles sports scene was tailor-made for the resurgent Rams to burst onto the local, regional and national stage as headliners. In a town that worshipped stars, the Rams were reaching for the spotlight.

The Los Angeles Dodgers were coming off back-to-back National League pennants but there was no three-peat. The Dodgers were playing their first season since the retirement of the great pitcher, Sandy Koufax. Koufax's popularity was an important factor in Los Angeles and Dodgers fans missed him. The ballclub, which still had future Hall of Fame hurler Don Drysdale, missed Koufax as well and finished second-to-last in the National League with a record of 73–89. The Dodgers did not get back to postseason baseball until 1974. The California Angels were playing in Anaheim Stadium in 1967. While the Angels compiled the second-best win-loss record in franchise history up to that time, they still finished fifth in the American League.

Thus, the baseball season ended without the Dodgers making a World Series bid during the first month of the NFL season. The Angels, by that point in their history, had never been serious World Series contenders.

The Los Angeles Lakers were playing their first season in the brand-new Forum in Inglewood, a short distance from Los Angeles International Airport. In a move the Rams would eventually learn from, the Lakers' owner, Jack Kent Cooke, grew tired of waiting for the Los Angeles Sports Arena to be improved by the powers that be and he built his own building. The same group that oversaw the Sports Arena also managed the Los Angeles Memorial Olympic Coliseum and the Rams franchise would leave the Coliseum years later. The Lakers were perennial challengers for the NBA title and their season started during the second half of the football season. John Wooden's UCLA basketball machine would win its second straight national championship and its fourth in five years during the

1967–68 season. The Bruins had their own on-campus arena, Pauley Pavilion, and college basketball was in the midst of domination unlike anything it had seen before nor has seen again.

The Los Angeles Kings were a National Hockey League expansion team in 1967. The Kings played home games in the Long Beach Sports Arena, the Los Angeles Sports Arena and the Forum. The Kings surprised many by finishing second in the NHL's Western Division. They drew an average of 8,084 to their home games.

There was direct competition for the attention of football fans in the area. The USC Trojans won the 1967 national championship with a record of 10–1. Junior tailback O.J. Simpson sparked USC fans to an average attendance of 62,849 for USC's five home games that year in the same stadium where the Rams played. The USC-UCLA city title game drew 90,772, matching Simpson against the 1967 Heisman Trophy winner, UCLA's Gary Beban.

UCLA's season started well but the Bruins finished at 7–2–1. Still, Beban's Heisman-winning performance was great football. So good, in fact, that he was later drafted by the Rams.

For all of the drama that marked Allen's tenure as head coach of the Rams, he did manage to meet with owner Dan Reeves and other members of the front office. As late as June 9, 1967, Allen met with Reeves and General Manager Elroy Hirsch, along with front office members John Sanders and Jack Teele. The meeting began at 2:25 p.m. Reeves suggested at the start of the meeting that the staff meetings be held weekly and asked Allen to pick a day and time and a format was agreed upon. They discussed the responsibilities of the team's traveling secretary and Reeves suggested "greater communication among all concerned parties," according to the minutes of the meeting. Reeves requested that Allen make his initial roster cuts of rookies to get the roster down to 50 men as quickly as possible after a scrimmage with the Cowboys rookies. The group discussed relations with minor league teams in the area and how some players cut by the Rams might be farmed out to minor league operations, an echo of Allen's letter to George Halas. There was a conflict between the reporting date for Rams veterans and a rookie scrimmage with the Cowboys at the Cowboys training facility. Reeves wanted written rookie reports on a daily basis for the first two weeks of training camp and then multiple times each week for the remainder of training camp. Allen suggested his coaches use a tape recorder to get their notes down and it was agreed that Sanders would accumulate the reports. The men spent 15 minutes discussing a tarp to cover the practice field at Blair Field in Long Beach but eventually Allen said, "Forget about the tarp." They discussed various organizational aspects of training camp. Allen indicated that he wanted a weekly trophy for special teams players, something just for the players and Reeves agreed with the idea, but the owner did not like Allen's suggested name for the award: Jock of the Week Award. Reeves suggested that all taxi squad players sit in the stands during games, Hirsch asked Allen for the preferred location for the photo tower at training camp and Hirsch asked the group to consider whether it was a problem for the players' wives to sit together during games. Finally, they agreed that the best time for cutting players during training camp would be shortly after breakfast.[1]

Once training camp started, there was a significant change in the Rams defense. Rosie Grier, the veteran defensive tackle, injured his Achilles tendon and was lost for the entire season. Allen immediately acquired Roger Brown from the Detroit Lions and the Rams defense played as well that season as any team in the league.

As has been noted, Allen's sons attended training camp and Deacon Jones told a story about his time with the Rams and a training camp incident involving one of them. Bruce Allen was retrieving footballs as Jones practiced kicking extra points after practice had ended. Jones considered himself the Rams emergency extra point man. Eventually the young Allen asked to be excused and Jones kicked a few more balls before ending his practice day. Jones passed Coach Allen's office and overheard the coach talking to his sons.

In *Headslap: The Life and Times of Deacon Jones*, by Jones and John Klawitter, Jones recalled the conversation this way: Coach Allen told his son, "Now Bruce, you know you kids have the run of the camp. I want you here. I like you here. But you have to remember. You have a responsibility to do your schoolwork, and your chores at home for your mother."

Bruce Allen said, "But I was helping the kickers."

George Allen replied, "Yes, and that's good. But I expect you to live up to your responsibilities first. You never saw Doug Atkins shirking his responsibility! You don't see Lamar Lundy or Deacon Jones shirking their responsibilities! Those players work hard, and that's how they get to be the best! You take after them, and you're on the right track!"

Jones, who lived through the ugliness of racial bigotry before coming to the Rams, had just heard a white man describing him as a role model. Allen, according to Jones' book, had seen something within Deacon Jones that wanted to be recognized and Allen recognized it.[2]

Jennifer Allen, who was not taken to training camp with her brothers, wrote in her book about the same incident. "Deacon said he had once heard my father reprimand my brothers for avoiding their many duties at Summer training camp. 'You don't see Deacon shirking his responsibilities,' Deacon heard my father say. 'How do you boys expect to grow up to be like Deacon if you keep goofing off?' Deacon said it was the first time he

8. Back to the Playoffs 67

ever heard a white man view him, a black man, as a role model. After that, Deacon looked to my father for guidance on the field."

But off the field, in the hours before games, particularly Rams home games, Deacon Jones superstitiously met with Etty and Jennifer Allen in the Coliseum's tunnel that led to the locker rooms. Etty Allen would ask the massive defensive end who was the terror of the NFL quarterbacks whether he was going to "sock it to 'em, sock it to 'em, sock it to 'em?" Jones would respond, "You ain't seen nothing yet," hug Etty and pat Jennifer on the head. "Years later," Jennifer Allen wrote in her book, "Deacon told me that his affection for my mother was based on his deep respect for my father."

The respect went both ways for Jennifer Allen. She named one of her sons Deacon. She named another son Roman, after the quarterback.[3]

According to Jones, Allen's Rams teams did not have racial problems. There was an incident involving Gabriel, who was of Filipino heritage, and African American running back Willie Ellison. Ellison, according to Jones in *Headslap*, missed some pass-protection blocks during a game against the Bills in Buffalo and Gabriel ran Ellison off the field. Allen brought the subject up at team meetings. Jones said it was determined that while the quarterback should not have sent the running back off the field, Gabriel did not do so out of bigotry. Rather, the missed blocks got the quarterback hit and the quarterback wanted better pass protection.

The season did not start in a good way. The Saints' John Gilliam returned the opening kickoff of the opening game 94 yards for a touchdown. It was the first league game for the New Orleans franchise and a great start for the home team. The Saints later scored on two field goals and the second one tied the game at 13–13 in the third quarter, but the Rams pulled away to win, 27–13. In their home opener, the Rams thumped the Vikings 39–3 and then they went back on the road and beat Dallas 35–13.

The Cowboys game was notable for the fact that Dallas accused the Rams of spying on Cowboy practices. It was not the first nor last time the charge would be made against Allen's teams. Allen's rivalry with the Cowboys grew to be great drama when Allen became the coach of the Washington Redskins.

The October 9, 1967, edition of *Sports Illustrated* covered both the game and the allegation by the Cowboys that the Rams spied on Cowboys practices during the week leading up to the game between the teams. According to the *Sports Illustrated* story, the Cowboys noticed a yellow Chevrolet parked near where the Dallas squad practiced. The Cowboys were temporarily using a local high school field while the normal location had work performed on it. After practice ended, Dallas coach Tom Landry sent a security guard to look at the yellow Chevrolet and find out who was sitting in it. The car was driven away before the Dallas security guard reached it, but the license plate number, which *SI* said was KRZ 308, was recorded.[4]

A call to the Hertz desk at the Dallas airport uncovered the information that the car belonged to Hertz and that it was rented by J.R. Sanders of the Los Angeles Rams at 7813 Beverly Boulevard in Los Angeles. The Dallas organization, which had enough connections that it should have been working for the Central Intelligence Agency during the off-season, then searched around town and discovered that Johnny Sanders (J.R. Sanders), who worked in the Rams scouting department, and Norm Pollom, who also worked for the Rams, were registered at a Dallas hotel. While it would not be unheard of for an organization's personnel to be in town early for a road game, those early travelers would more likely be logistical personnel and not the head of a team's scouting department. The Cowboys lodged a complaint with the league office. Confronted with the Cowboys' accusation when the Rams arrived in Texas, Allen had a counter claim. The Rams coach charged that a man looking like Dallas scout Bucko Killroy was seen climbing a eucalyptus tree that overlooked the Rams' practice facility. The *Sports Illustrated* article noted that Kilroy weighed about 300 pounds and did not seem to be a likely candidate to climb a tree and spend a long period of time watching practice from there. Landry was quoted as saying that spying on the Cowboys was an unethical thing for the Rams to do.

It was a fast start for Los Angeles, similar to their burst out of the gate in 1966. In the first three games, Gabriel completed 37 of 81 passes for 581 yards and two touchdowns. He was intercepted once. The Rams rushed for 507 yards, giving them better than a thousand yards from scrimmage over those three games. The defense allowed just 795 in the same period. More importantly, the Rams scored 101 points while allowing just 29.

The next three games mimicked the mid-season slump of the previous season while also setting the stage for the late-season charge which earned Los Angeles a division title. Game four's contest in Los Angeles against the 49ers saw the Rams fall behind 20–0 in the first half. San Francisco quarterback John Brodie threw scoring passes of 59 and 55 yards to spark the visitors. He finished with 269 passing yards and three scores. The Rams charged back in the second half, starting with an interception by Pardee that the linebacker returned two yards for a touchdown. Gabriel ran for a touchdown and threw for another, to put the Rams ahead 21–20. A later field goal gave the Rams a 24–21 lead, but Brodie hit Sonny Randle for a 28-yard score and the winning points. It was the lowest scoring output for the Rams to that point of the season and the most points they had allowed. The defeat dropped the Rams from the first-place tie with the Colts.

8. Back to the Playoffs

And it was the Colts whom the Rams played the following week in Baltimore.[5]

The Colts were off to a fast start, too, in 1967, with a 38–31 victory over the Falcons, a 38–6 victory over the Eagles, a 41–7 clubbing of the 49ers and a 24–3 victory over the Bears. Unitas was in the midst of one of the best seasons of his Hall of Fame career. In the first three games of the season, he threw six scoring passes and just one interception. In the week four victory over the Bears, he threw one scoring pass and three interceptions. Altogether, Unitas had 80 completions on 137 attempts in the first four games, good for 1,170 yards and seven touchdowns. The Baltimore defense had not allowed a team to score in double figures since the season opener.

In Baltimore, the Rams opened the scoring when Gabriel hit Snow for a 53-yard scoring pass in the first quarter, but Baltimore took the lead before the end of the first half on a Lou Michaels field goal and a short run by halfback Lenny Moore. Gabriel hit Snow on an 80-yard bomb in the third quarter and Unitas countered with a 14-yarder to Alex Hawkins. The Colts took a 24–14 lead when Unitas hit Willie Richardson for a 31-yard score in the fourth quarter, but the Rams scrambled back with a 47-yard field goal by Bruce Gossett and a game-tying, 16-yard scoring pass to flanker Bernie Casey. The game ended in a 24–24 tie.

The Rams did not stop the Baltimore offense. Unitas completed 21 of 34 passes for 288 yards and two scores, although the Rams intercepted Unitas once. The Colts rushed for 98 yards and the Moore score, giving Baltimore 388 yards from scrimmage. But the Colts did not stop the Rams, either. Gabriel hit 19 of 31 for 297 yards, had the three scoring passes and was intercepted once. The Rams rushed for 128 yards, led by Josephson's 62 yards on nine carries. Bass gained 56 yards on 14 attempts. All told, the Rams gashed Baltimore for 425 yards from scrimmage.

The good news was that the Rams had gone to Baltimore and left without losing. The bad news was that the Rams failed to win for the third consecutive week when they tied the Redskins 28–28 in Los Angeles a week later.[6] But the Colts supplied the Rams with good news when they tied Minnesota, 20–20, on the same day that the Rams tied the Redskins. The Rams could still win the Coastal Division by winning the remainder of their games, including the season-ender against the Colts in Los Angeles.

In 1966, after a hot start, the Rams lost four straight in the middle of the season. In 1967, the Rams lost once and tied twice after a hot start and were seemingly poised to fail again in mid-season. But they didn't. Los Angeles rattled off six wins and out-scored opponents 160–54 leading up to the do or die games against the Packers and Colts, both in the Coliseum.

The Rams and Packers squared off on December 9, 1967. The Packers were coached by Vince Lombardi and packed a punch with a roster so full of future members of the Pro Football Hall of Fame that some deserving Packers have failed to be elected to the shrine in Canton, Ohio, because so many other Packers had been elected. The Packers had defeated the Kansas City Chiefs in the first AFL-NFL World Championship Game one season earlier.[7] Green Bay arrived in Los Angeles with a record of 8-3-1, their Central Division championship already assured. Due to the NFL rules of the era, the Packers knew they would host the Western Conference championship game even though both the Colts and Rams would finish the season with better records.

The Packers did not seem to have much to play for, but in his classic book, *Instant Replay*, Packers offensive guard Jerry Kramer wrote he and his teammates had a reason for wanting to beat the Rams. "We want to beat the Rams Saturday for a very selfish reason. ... We think the Rams are a much more dangerous team. ... There are only a few dissenting opinions on the team, and they all come from the defensive unit. They're not anxious to face Johnny Unitas again. I don't blame them. But, given the choice between going up against Unitas and going up against Los Angeles' defensive Fearsome Foursome, the consensus is: Bring on Unitas."[8]

The game drew a crowd of 76,637. The Packers' Don Chandler missed a field goal and Gossett had one blocked, but Carroll Dale caught a pass from Bart Starr near the end of the opening quarter and opened a 7-0 lead. Gabriel hit Snow for a 16-yard score before Chandler converted a field goal attempt and the Rams were down at halftime, 10-7. Gabriel hit Snow for a scoring pass in the third quarter, giving LA a 14-10 advantage, and then Gossett booted a field goal to give the Rams a full touchdown lead. On the play immediately following Gossett's field goal, Green Bay's Travis Williams returned Gossett's kickoff 105 yards for a touchdown and tied the game. Gossett kicked another field goal, giving the Rams a 20-17 lead, but Chuck Mercein's scoring run put Green Bay ahead 24-20 late in the final quarter. The Rams were unable to move the ball on their ensuing possession, but the Packers had to punt a short time later, too, setting the scene for the dramatics featuring Guillory and Crabb with 54 seconds left in the game.

The Rams put nine men on the line to rush Anderson's punt. Those punt rushers included future Pro Football Hall of Fame enshrinees Deacon Jones and Merlin Olsen on the Rams' left side. Guillory lined up directly in front of Packers center Ken Bowman and Crabb was the end Ram on the right side. Crabb was standing up, as opposed to launching from a three-point stance. The Rams put each of their rushers in a gap between blockers. Guillory and Dave Cahill were in the center of the line and then there was a gap between them on Guillory's right and Cahill's left. Diron Talbert, Maxie Baughn and Crabb were arrayed on the Rams'

8. Back to the Playoffs

right. Guillory's goal was to pick a side of the Green Bay center and go around him.

"The center's got his head down for the snap, so you get a good jump on him and I got off right with the ball," Guillory said. "My assignment on the play is really to draw a block from the fullback so one of the outside guys can come in free. This time nobody touched me and I came right up the middle." After the punt was blocked, Guillory said, "I can't see at all without my glasses. I didn't know Claude had the ball and I couldn't read the numbers anyway."[9]

Tommy Joe Crutcher, the Packers' upback charged with protecting the punter, drifted to his left to cut off Crabb's charge. That left Guillory with a clear path to Anderson, the punter.

"For some reason Tommy Joe Crutcher picked me up instead of Tony," Crabb said. "I don't know why. I couldn't see it but when I heard the thud I knew the punt was blocked so I started looking around for the ball. We're trained to do that. The ball was bounding around and there was nobody near so I just picked it up and ran with it. Maybe I could have scored but I wasn't going to take a chance of losing the ball because we still had time to get the touchdown. I wasn't going to fumble."

Anderson said, "It looked to me like they were set a little tighter in the middle than usual. I was already in the process of kicking the ball when I saw this guy [Guillory] coming in at me. There was nothing I could do then. I rushed the kick as much as I could, but it was too late."[10]

Kramer wrote in *Instant Replay*, "On a punt, the center isn't responsible for blocking anyone; he's got his head down in a very awkward position and his main job is to get the ball back to the punter. Chuck Mercein, who was new to the punting team, was supposed to check Guillory. But Guillory jumped around Bowman at center, and Mercein didn't pick him up, and Tommy Joe Crutcher, who was back blocking for the punter, was looking from side to side, expecting someone to come charging in from the outside, and didn't even see Guillory coming up the middle."[11]

Video of the play makes Crabb seem as safe from harm as a Hollywood starlet emerging from a limousine to step on a red carpet. Crabb scooped the ball into his hands and headed for the end zone surrounded by teammates. Guillory nearly decked Crabb as the phalanx escorted the ball toward the goal, but Green Bay's Doug Hart and Anderson managed to get in front of all the Rams and make the tackle.

Allen said, "We've worked on that blocked punt play since last July and spent a little time each week sharpening it up, but we don't use it much because you always run the risk of getting a 15-yard penalty for running into the kicker. This time it was a desperation move. The penalty wouldn't have meant anything, but blocking the kick did. What we do is put everybody in the gaps in their line and come in with more men than they've got blockers. It was no time to give up. As long as there was time on the clock we figured we had a chance. This was the opportunity of a lifetime and we could not pass it up."[12]

In his book *George Allen's Guide to Special Teams*, Allen wrote about the preparation for the possibility of attacking the left-footed punter, Anderson. "As head coach of the Rams," Allen wrote, "I thought that we needed an heroic effort by someone to win this game—time was running out on us. ... We had worked all week with Tom Mack, our starting offensive guard [who was not a punter but was the only left-footed player on the squad], trying to imitate Anderson. The work paid off."[13]

Allen's devotion to the kicking game is his greatest legacy to professional football. During his time with the Rams he devoted more coaching time to that aspect of the game than any NFL or AFL coach. Since that time, every team has hired an assistant coach whose only job is to coach the kicking game, which has come to be known as Special Teams. But even in the era of specialization, which was made easier since Allen's era by the expanded roster limitation, few coaches would follow Allen's example and find a left-footer on the roster and use that player to give punt rushers the experience of charging a lefty during practice. Allen's devotion to details and to the kicking game were directly responsible for the heroics of Guillory and Crabb against the Packers and saved the 1967 season for the Rams.

Washington Post columnist William Gildea wrote of Guillory and Crabb, "they were the most devastating one-two punch since Bonnie and Clyde."[14]

The Rams ran one play before Gabriel hit Casey on a touchdown pass for the game-winning points. The Packers got the ball back in the final seconds, but the Rams defense denied the miracle comeback and the game ended.

Had the Rams beaten the Packers any other way, the game would have faded into history as just another late-season NFL game. An offensive explosion by the Rams would have been excused away by the fact that the Packers seemingly had nothing to play for. Defensive heroics, such as a pass interception returned for a score, would have been unusual, especially against Lombardi's Packers, but not so rare as a blocked punt. The sudden change of emotion and field position that came from Guillory batting away Anderson's kick was a galvanizing instant. Coming as it did in the final minute of a must-win game played in front of a hometown crowd against the defending world champions, the victory over Green Bay was probably the highlight of Allen's tenure in Los Angeles. The many victories still to come, the disappointments and dramatics of future years and

8. Back to the Playoffs 73

the mystique that Allen was creating in less than two complete seasons never dimmed the thrill of the sudden victory that day in the closed end of the Coliseum.

Sudden reversals of fortune late in a home game are not rare in sports history. The blocked punt was electrifying for the Rams and their fans. However, some fans had left early and were either walking to their cars or already sitting in their cars when Guillory and Crabb converged on Anderson to save the Rams' 1967 season. Among the early walkers was journalist Bud Furillo, who was quoted by *Washington Post* columnist William Gildea as lamenting, "I was making a left turn off Figueroa onto 11th when it happened."[15]

Joe Doherty was an eight-year-old Cub Scout attending his first professional football game and he noticed the early departures. "I definitely remember the feeling that the game was lost and that that was the reason that they were leaving," Doherty remembered in 2021. "I remember watching across the stadium as people were leaving out the peristyle end and then the cheers started going up and then people trying to get back in to see it. ... I thought that was pretty funny because we stayed put."[16]

Since playing the Rams in Baltimore, the Colts had tied the Vikings, beaten the Redskins, Packers and Cowboys in close games and dispatched the remainder of their schedule rather easily. Between games against the Rams, Baltimore out-scored opponents 219–73. This undefeated Colts team, led by the incomparable Unitas and young head coach Don Shula, was tremendous. In fact, as the Rams and Colts faced off in the season finale, the teams shared the best record in the NFL. When the playoffs began a week later, the Colts had a better win-loss record than three of the playoff teams and an identical record with the fourth team. But the Colts did not earn a playoff berth; Allen's Rams did.

The Packers game was not broadcast on television in the Los Angeles market. League rules in that era allowed teams to blackout home games in the belief a free game on television would render harm to ticket sales. Rams fans who did not attend the game depended upon the Rams' radio play-by-play man Dick Enberg's call for the news as it happened. The same would be true the following week, when the Rams and Colts would play for all the marbles. So huge was the interest in the Colts game, one of the television stations in Los Angeles announced that it would broadcast the game via tape delay late that Sunday evening. In an era when the family telephone was the only social media, some fans were able to avoid the radio and television news and stay off their telephones long enough to watch the Rams play the Colts hours after the game was completed.[17]

The Rams beat the Colts 34–10. Baltimore led early in the game, 7–3, but the Rams led 17–7 at the half and dominated play the remainder of the way. The Rams' defense limited Unitas to completing 19 of 31 passes for 206 yards. Unitas threw a scoring pass but was intercepted twice. The Colts rushed for just 104 yards on 27 attempts. Gabriel bested Unitas by clicking on 18 of 22 passes for 257 yards and three touchdowns. Baltimore's tough, veteran defensive unit held the Rams to just 71 rushing yards on 27 tries.

Allen's Rams were the champions of the Coastal Division. Their reward was a trip to Wisconsin to play the Packers at Milwaukee County Stadium. The frozen tundra was typically a tough place for any visiting team, but during Allen's tenure in Los Angeles, the Rams had a 4–3 record against the Packers overall and were 3–2 in games where Hall of Fame quarterback Bart Starr started for Green Bay.

In a book he wrote shortly before he started his two-year tenure in the United States Football League, Allen wrote that Starr "was technically perfect as a quarterback. He executed plays with precision. He had the touch of a fine surgeon and he cut defenses apart. ... My teams did well against Green Bay over the years because we gave it the extra effort it needed. One time we defeated the Packers by intercepting Starr four times. That was very difficult to do. But he could come back the next game and beat you by passing perfectly."[18]

The Packers had a little extra material to study before their playoff game with the Rams. Kramer wrote in *Instant Replay* that Bears owner George Halas still held a grudge against Allen and the Rams. "We've watched a few extra reels of the Rams in action, sent to us courtesy of the Chicago Bears," Kramer wrote. "Halas wants us to whip the Rams. He hates the Rams because their coach, George Allen, used to be one of his assistants and broke his contract to take the job in Los Angeles."[19] Allen did not break his contract, as we have seen. The court upheld that Allen remained under contract with the Bears and it was Halas who dismissed Allen as soon as the Bears won their case. But Halas' hostility toward his former pupil and the team that hired him were well-known around the league. The Packers had played the Rams less than two weeks before Vince Lombardi and his staff began preparations for the playoff game and it is questionable whether the Packers coaching staff needed the extra game films for study. But it is instructive to see how angry the Bears' leader remained nearly two years after Allen departed Chicago for the West Coast that Halas would send film to Green Bay, the Bears' divisional rivals.

The weather was always a factor when Green Bay played in Wisconsin in late December. Pro-football-reference.com lists the temperature for the Rams-Packers playoff game as 13 degrees at game time with a wind chill of minus three. The playing surface was listed as grass, but it was really ice

8. Back to the Playoffs

and the Rams did not adjust. Gabriel hit Bernie Casey for a 29-yard scoring pass in the first quarter for the first points by either team, but the Rams were blanked the rest of the way and the Packers won 28–7.[20]

Deacon Jones recounted a conversation he had with Allen on the flight home in which Allen blamed himself for the shoes the Rams used during the game, saying that the Rams staff did not supply shoes that could cope with the condition of the field at game time. The shoes might have made a difference, Allen said. In *Headslap*, Jones quoted Allen as saying, "We should have asked ourselves, 'How far will the Packers go to win the championship?' In other words, 'What options are available to them?' We know we are playing on their field. 'What might they do to nullify our advantage in speed and quickness?' We should have figured that gridiron would be like a skating rink. With the temperature near zero anyway, nobody would question it. The spikes on those special shoes we made up were too short and there weren't enough of them. I know it now. We could have invented something with longer spikes, kept our edge and won the game for sure."[21]

Just as he had designed a pad to protect Max Fields' shoulder at Whittier in the 1950s, Allen felt he could have evolved a type of footwear that would have given the Rams extra traction on the frozen tundra at Milwaukee in 1967. Players, coaches and administrators who talked about Allen, whether they liked him or not, eventually made one point over and over again—Allen never ceased looking for an edge. He was so determined to out-work and out-smart other coaches and organizations that he was accused of sending spies to somehow observe the practice sessions of opposing teams and determine the other teams' game plans from watching practice. The same man who learned to grow potatoes in the basement to help his family as a boy was still looking for a chance to improve himself and those around him decades later. It was something he never quit doing.

In *Headslap* Jones said, "We played our first playoff game in Green Bay on a treacherous, slippery field. I was double-teamed by Forrest Gregg and Marv Fleming, but the real secret was that they nullified my—all of our—speed and quickness with the playing conditions. Sure, nobody can change the weather, but to this day, I'd really like to know if the weather alone beat us or just exactly how they prepared that field."

Despite his stunning turnaround performance with the Rams in 1966, Allen was overlooked for the Coach of the Year Award. Dallas' Tom Landry got the nod instead. In 1967, Allen was finally recognized.

The losers of the NFL conference championships, the Rams and Cleveland Browns, met in a meaningless postseason game in Miami. On January 7, 1968, the Rams beat the Browns 30–6. It was a nice start to a tumultuous year for the Rams. The season began with the NFL players striking and ended with most of the Rams roster threatening to quit. Allen's relationship with Rams owner Dan Reeves, already uneasy in 1967, worsened in 1968.

But that stuff was in the future. One week into the new year, the Rams were undefeated.

9

Out of the Playoffs and Into the Fire
The 1968 Rams

In a letter to his players prior to the 1968 NFL season, George Allen wrote that one factor would be the most important for the Rams to improve their 1967 finish. Allen wrote, "We must improve our concentration. We must have a practice program that is as close to game conditions as possible. Our practice attitude last year was very good, but this is a vital area where we can easily let up and take for granted. We must have concentration ON THE FIELD and IN MEETINGS with a seriousness of purpose. Only in this manner can we be ready and prepared to play championship football every week."

By the end of the season, there were distractions, among them the likelihood that Allen would be fired by owner Dan Reeves.

The 1968 season ended with dramatic controversies on the field and off, but as of April of that year, Allen considered tinkering with the unit his Rams teams were best-known for, his defensive line. The Coastal Division championship was powered at least in part by the dramatic and dominating play of the Fearsome Foursome: Deacon Jones, Merlin Olsen, Roger Brown and Lamar Lundy. Tackle Roosevelt Grier, a member of the Foursome until his injury in 1967, was trying to come back and Allen floated the idea of a Fearsome Fivesome with Grier playing nose tackle in the middle of the four guys who were already raising havoc around the league.[1]

In a *Pro Football Weekly* story that ran in April of 1968, veteran reporter Bob Oates disclosed that Allen was considering experimenting with running a 5-2 defensive scheme, putting two linebackers behind the five down linemen. The alignment had been popular in the league in previous decades, but few teams ever had five linemen with the potential talent and experience that the Rams would have with Grier in the middle. Oates wrote that Jack Pardee and Maxie Baughan would be the linebackers and the defensive backs would play a zone backfield orientation.

Oates quoted Allen as saying, "We're definitely going to a five-man line in the preseason. How much we use it depends on how well it works. I have a hunch it will be pretty exciting. We're not throwing out the 4–3, of course. We'll use everything we used last year, plus this."[2] Grier was unable to comeback from his injury and retired. The idea of instituting the 5–2 defensive front was never put into use. Still, the idea of adding the defensive look featuring five down linemen shows how Allen never stopped looking for advantages. There was nothing new about the 5–2 defense, but few teams used the scheme in the 1960s. On the other hand, few NFL teams in 1968 had the potential skill levels of Lamar Lundy, Roger Brown, Rosie Grier, Merlin Olsen and Deacon Jones.

By this time, Allen was a popular figure in Los Angeles. The Rams games were carried by Los Angeles radio station KMPC in 1968 and *The George Allen Show* aired immediately before the start of each game. Allen was paid $2,000 for expenses for June 1, 1968, through May 31, 1969, and an additional $3,000 salary by the station.

Allen's Rams had great hopes for the 1968 season and they started with six straight wins, including a tough week five 16–14 squeaker over the Packers in Milwaukee. Phil Bengtson had replaced Lombardi, who had retired as the Packers head coach. Zeke Bratkowski started in place of Starr, who was hurt. Los Angeles collected a 27–14 victory over the Falcons for the Rams' sixth straight victory and rolled into Baltimore leading the Coastal Division.

The Colts had kept pace with the Rams before suffering a week five loss to the Cleveland Browns. The 1968 Colts featured a defense some observers believed was among the best in NFL history but there was a major difference on offense. Unitas, the measuring stick against whom all quarterbacks of the era were tested, was not playing. He had injured his throwing arm during the preseason and could not throw with his customary zip. Unitas remained on the Colts roster but starting in his place was Earl Morrall. Morrall was a journeyman quarterback, having played for the 49ers, Steelers, Lions and Giants since 1956. He was a winner for the Colts in 1968.

In their first meeting in 1968, the Rams scored first on a 19-yard field goal by Gossett in the opening quarter, but the Colts scored a touchdown later in the quarter and never trailed again on the way to a 27–10 victory. Neither the Rams' Gabriel nor Morrall had particularly effective games. Gabriel connected on 16 of 29 passes for only 116 yards and a touchdown, with two interceptions. Morrall connected on just 11 of 27 attempts, but his passes netted 211 yards and two touchdowns. The Rams intercepted the Colts' passer three times that day.

In *Headslap*, Deacon Jones wrote that the Rams had not earned their money that week, at least the defense hadn't. "We were unhappy with the loss, of course, stunned and angry at ourselves. But we didn't recognize the importance of the game. With the season barely half over, we would play catch-up to Baltimore the rest of the way. And, though we didn't know it at the time, with Baltimore heading for a record of 13–1 on the year, our season was already all but over for us."[3]

The loss to the Colts put the Rams behind Baltimore in the standings. They had the same record, but the head-to-head competition was the tiebreaker and this time it was in the Colts' favor. The Rams came home to beat the Lions 10–7, then went on the road and beat Atlanta 17–10 before heading up to the Bay Area to play the pesky 49ers at Kezar Stadium.

In his five seasons with the Rams, Allen coached regular season games against San Francisco 10 times and each time the starting passer for the 49ers was John Brodie. Allen's Rams finished ahead of the 49ers during each season of Allen's tenure in LA, but the 49ers gave the Rams fits. For all of Allen's success at the head of the Rams, his teams swept both games against the 49ers just once, in 1969. It was Brodie and the 49ers who handed the Rams their only regular-season loss in 1967 and, as the Rams were fighting to keep pace with the Colts in 1968, Brodie and the 49ers tied the Rams 20–20 in week 10. The Rams out-passed Brodie and his mates 284 yards to 174 and the Rams had fewer turnovers, 3–4, but Gabriel had to rally the Rams to score 10 unanswered points in the fourth quarter to salvage the tie.

In his book, Deacon Jones and co-author John Klawitter were critical of the field conditions at Kezar, accusing the 49ers of creating a slick, mushy field in order to slow the Rams pass rush. Jones could have blamed another source for the sloppy conditions. The San Francisco area had experienced rain on Thursday of the week before the game and the field had not dried. Jones quoted himself and Merlin Olsen as telling the media after the game, "It is unfair to NFL teams to play on this field. It is as bad for the 49ers as it is for the others. The field is pure dirt. You can't play football here; and I think it is up to the commissioner to legislate some minimum standards." The book quotes *Los Angeles Times* reporter Mal Florence as describing the mess as "a miserable river-bottom field which chained the defensive linemen of both sides in their tracks." Jones wrote that he and Olsen planned to urge the Rams management to protest the conditions at the stadium to the league. Kezar was not a popular destination for any NFL visitor and Allen also criticized the field while talking to reporters after the game.[4]

"The end zones are like quicksand—and the way they're painted, they ought to sell them to the hippies," Allen said. "We lost two touchdowns there. Bernie Casey sank in the quicksand and fell over. Jack Snow was inbounds on his catch—but there's so much paint on those hippie end zones that the officials couldn't tell. I blame the painters, not [the officials]. Are we in the paint business or football?" He also said the Kezar Stadium field was "a disgrace to the league," and that the field was the "worst I've seen in 20 years as a coach." Asked whether an artificial playing surface, which was new in 1968, might be the answer in Kezar, Allen quipped, "I'd rather play on the grass the good Lord gave us. I wish they'd plant some."

The drama was just beginning. According to Deacon Jones, Allen took the players complaints about the field at Kezar to Reeves during the week following the game. A few days later Reeves, the Rams owner and the logical man for Rams players to ask for help in approaching the league about the conditions at the 49ers home field, was quoted as saying his coaches and players should not make alibis for losing. The players and coaches might have expected a different level of support from their organization, but they didn't get it. Jones wrote in *Headslap* that Reeves' alibi comment was the cause of what happened next.[5]

The following week's game was against the New York Giants and quarterback Frantic Fran Tarkenton in Los Angeles. Tarkenton, who scrambled his way into the Pro Football Hall of Fame, was ranked 12th among the all-time quarterbacks by Allen in his book about the 100 greatest players in NFL history. Allen wrote, "I don't think he liked it that he was best-known for scrambling, but because of it he was extremely difficult to defense. He was one passer you tried to keep in the pocket instead of trying to chase him out of the pocket. ... He was tough and durable and through sheer longevity wound up with many of the major passing records."[6]

It was a rough game. The Rams trailed 14–0 at the half before winning 24–21. Jones wrote that Giants coach Allie Sherman had his offensive linemen hitting Jones late, even after plays had ended, in an effort to slow the Rams pass rush. Willie Young, an offensive tackle for the Giants, was ejected from the contest after a late hit on Jones.[7] Tarkenton was sacked twice for 19 yards in losses—sacks were now an official league statistic—but he completed 14 of 28 for 146 yards and two touchdowns. The Rams intercepted Tarkenton twice. Gabriel completed nine of 20 throws for 154 yards and a touchdown, tossing two interceptions. Gabriel also scored on a 19-yard run. Gossett won the game for the Rams with a fourth-quarter field goal that broke a 21–21 tie.

In the winning locker room Allen was conversing with

9. Out of the Playoffs and Into the Fire

newspaper journalist Melvin Durslag when Reeves arrived. The Rams owner approached Allen, intent upon shaking hands with his head coach. Reeves said, "No problem with the field today, right George?" or words to that effect. Allen would not shake hands with his employer. He told Reeves (approximately), "You shouldn't criticize me in public, Dan. You embarrassed me and my family. Here I am working 16 to 18 hours a day, trying to build our team into a winner and you make a fool of me," before turning his back and walking away. Reeves reportedly walked after Allen and called out to him to no avail.[8]

Deacon Jones wrote later that he was standing next to Allen as Reeves approached Allen in the locker room after the victory over the Giants. From *Headslap:*

> Reeves was speaking in a loud, arrogant way, and the smell of liquor was heavy on his breath. "The turf conditions were a little better today—right, George?" Reeves asked, a silly grin plastered all over his face. It may have been his contorted way of congratulating his head coach on a thrilling victory, but it didn't come out that way. It sounded like a taunt. Allen's face purpled, and for a moment, it looked like he was going to yell at his boss. But he managed to control his temper, and after glaring at Reeves for a moment, turned on his heel and walked away. Reeves stuck his hand at the departing coach. "Hey George, don't walk away—I just wanted to congratulate you." But Allen's distaste of drunken conversation had kicked in, and he continued on his way. Reeves ran after him and grabbed his shoulder. "You don't walk away from me when I'm talking to you! Nobody on this team walks away from me like that! I own this team!" Allen spun around, his eyebrows lowered and face grim. "Dan, look—of course you own this team. Right now, you've had too much to drink. We'll talk later."

According to Jones' account, the argument continued. Allen said Reeves had failed to stand up for the team over the Kezar mess and that Reeves "alibi" comment was bad for team morale. The *Headslap* description of the event has Reeves' friends leading him away from the confrontation after Allen turned his back a second time.[9]

Durslag wrote several weeks later, "For this writer and for Bud Furillo, *Herald-Examiner* sports editor who had walked in, the situation was sticky. Here was a juicy scandal. It is, however, a point of ethics in this business that one doesn't take advantage of owners, coaches or players who have been drinking, no more than a gentleman takes advantage of a lady who has passed out. We choose at that time to protect Reeves, only an abridged version of the story leaked out three weeks later in a Hollywood paper."[10]

The victory over the Giants and the extraordinary Allen-Reeves clash happened on November 24, 1968. The Rams were still in the hunt to make the playoffs at 9-1-1. Allen's overall record with the Rams at that moment was 29-9-3. He was the winningest coach in franchise history and would be fired in a month's time.[11]

A week later the Rams beat the Vikings in Minnesota, 31-3, improving to 10-1-1. They trailed the 11-1 Colts in the standings but still had a path to the Coastal Division title with two games remaining in the season. The Rams had to beat the 6-6 Bears and then win their showdown with Baltimore. Both games would be played in the Coliseum. It felt like a repeat of the previous year's heroics were in order, except that the 1968 Bears were hardly the 1967 Packers. Coached by Jim Dooley, the Bears had three quarterbacks start games in 1968 and finished the season tenth of the 16 NFL teams in points scored. Even the Bears defense, long the team's strength, ranked only 12th in points allowed. On paper, it was a game the Rams should have won before gearing up for another all or nothing brawl with the Colts.

The Rams didn't beat the Bears and the story of the crazy game had more layers than a millionaire's wedding cake. Mac Percival opened the scoring with a 20-yard first quarter field goal for the Bears. Gabriel was knocked out of the game in the first quarter and was relieved by back-up Milt Plum. Halfback Willie Ellison scored for the Rams in the second quarter on a one-yard run and, with the conversion, the Rams led 7-3. On the ensuing kickoff, linebacker Dick Butkus fielded the ball at the Bears 12 and handed off to return man Clarence Childs, whose back foot touched the 10-yard stripe. Childs started up the right hashmarks, then weaved to his left, broke out of a tackle at the Bears 35 and made it all the way to the Rams 2-yard line before wide receiver Wendell Tucker tackled him. Brian Piccolo, later immortalized in the film *Brian's Song* for his fight against cancer and friendship with Gale Sayers, scored on a two-yard run.

In his book about special teams, Allen wrote about the importance of good tackling and said, "Clarence Childs returned a kickoff 90 yards for a touchdown, as the result of a missed tackle by Vilynis Exerins."[12] The big return had an impact on the game and an even bigger impact on professional football, as will be seen.

The Bears led 10-7 at halftime. Jack Concannon, the Bears quarterback, rushed for a four-yard touchdown in the third quarter to make the score 17-7 in the third quarter, but the Rams' Dave Pivec blew in to block a Bears punt out of the end zone to make the score 17-9, still in the third quarter. Tony Guillory, who figured so prominently in the dramatic victory over the Packers in the second-to-last game of 1967, chased after the blocked punt but the ball went out the back of the end zone before Guillory could get to it. Of such small things are seasons decided; had the blocked punt been recovered in the end zone for a touchdown rather than giving

9. Out of the Playoffs and Into the Fire

the two points for a safety, things could have turned out differently for Allen and the Rams.

In the fourth quarter, the Rams' Willie Daniels blocked yet another Chicago punt, putting the Rams deep in Bears territory. Gabriel was back in the lineup and he scored on a three-yard run to get the Rams within a point at 17–16. Later, with time running out, Gabriel tried to rally the Rams again and was in Bears territory when a holding call went against the Rams on a first down passing play. The pass fell incomplete but the Bears accepted the penalty in order to move the Rams further away from a potential field goal attempt. The mark off began at the point of the foul, which was marked six yards behind the line of scrimmage. The next play after the penalty should have been ruled a replay of first down. But somehow, in the excitement of the moment, nobody noticed that the down marker on the field was never changed back to first down. Thus, the Rams had the ball at the Bears' 47 yard-line; it was second down and 21 yards to go.

The Rams did not need to gain a first down to get Gossett into field goal range. A few short completions to move the ball just a few yards beyond the original line of scrimmage would have sufficed. But working with second down rather than first down, Gabriel worked at a distinct disadvantage. Gabriel threw three incomplete passes, one of which was a deep ball for Tucker. Tucker had two steps on the Bears defense, but the ball was slightly underthrown and fell incomplete. The Bears took over on downs with a few seconds left in the game. The league suspended the officiating crew for the gaff a few days later, but that did not help the Rams. The lost down may have made a difference in the game, although it should be said that the Rams might not have been able to score the winning points, even if the yardage marker had been handled properly.[13]

The loss to the Bears made a difference to the Rams' season. The Rams could no longer catch the Colts in the standings, even with a win a week later. The Colts beat the Rams 28–24 to finish the regular season with an NFL-best record of 13–1, but how might the Rams have played if they still had a chance to reach the playoffs? As it was, the Rams completed their season at 10–3–1 and had a better record than two of the teams that advanced to the NFL playoffs.

In *Headslap,* Jones quoted Allen as telling the press after the Lost Down game, "We have no excuses, no alibis. We've drained ourselves dry. Three years of working, and everything is down the drain. We have an axiom here that nobody can beat the Rams; the Rams lose because they beat themselves. The headline of this game is: 'Too Many Mistakes.'"

The result of the Bears game also made a difference to Allen's career. He had angered the owner over the matter of his comments about the playing conditions at Kezar and his refusal to shake hands with Reeves after the Giants game. Then the Rams failed to reach the playoffs. Reeves had once fired his head coach one game into a season following a championship. Reeves didn't seem likely to worry about firing a coach who had narrowly missed the playoffs. The loss to the Colts occurred on December 15. On the day after Christmas, Reeves called the Allen home to fire his coach.

Much has been made through the years of Allen's relationship with Reeves leading up to the Christmastime dismissal. Allen's free-spending attitude was a stress point. The new practice facility in Long Beach and the new preseason camp location in Fullerton cost the ballclub money. Bringing Jack Pardee and Roman Gabriel back into the Rams' fold apparently went against Reeves' preference. Veterans cost more than draftees but, under Allen's direction, the veterans won games. Then there was the matter of Allen's complaints about the state of the playing surface in San Francisco, Reeves' "alibi" comment and Allen's refusal to shake hands after the victory over the Giants. It could be argued that Allen was insubordinate toward his employer.

But there is another possible reason for Reeves dumping his coach: He may have developed an itchy trigger finger. Of the 10 men who held the title of head coach of the Rams once Reeves became the principal owner before the 1941 season, only one—Sid Gillman—held the position for as many as five seasons. None of the other nine lasted as many as four years and the average tenure for a head coach under Reeves' ownership was only 2.6 seasons. Neither of the two coaches who brought Reeves championships lasted more than a season beyond their championships. Adam Walsh won the title in Cleveland in 1945 and was gone after the 1946 campaign. Clark Shaughnessy coached the Rams to the title game in 1949 and did not return for the 1950 season. Joe Stydahar got the Rams to the title game in 1950, won the championship in 1951 and was gone after the first game of the 1952 season. Bob Waterfield and Harland Svare did nothing but lose but they each coached the Rams for more seasons than did Stydahar or Walsh. When Allen completed his third season at the head of the ballclub, Reeves may have simply reached the limits of his interest in an individual head coach.

Jennifer Allen, George's daughter and his youngest child, recounted the December 26, 1968, conversation between her father and the Rams' owner this way: "'Merry Christmas, George,' Reeves had said. 'You're fired!'"[14] On the same page where she recounts the dismissal conversation, Jennifer Allen summed Reeves up this way: "Dan Reeves had once said, 'I'd rather *lose* with a coach I can drink with and have fun with than *win* with George Allen.'"

9. Out of the Playoffs and Into the Fire

George Allen's drive to coach a winner and his willingness to work extended hours during the season led to phone calls in the middle of the night and other activities viewed then as eccentric. His demands upon the Rams front office were heavy duty. Nowadays, most NFL coaches match Allen's pace but that was not the case in 1968. It was a grueling schedule and it was hard on Allen's family but the firing was worse. A week after the phone call from Reeves, Jennifer Allen wrote, the family sat down to eat dinner on New Year's Eve. "This was a rare dinner with Dad since he had taken the job as head coach of the Los Angeles Rams three years before. For my father, getting the Rams to the National Football League Championship meant drinking a tall glass of milk at the office for dinner, then spending the night on his office couch so that he wouldn't waste valuable work time driving home, eating with his family, and sleeping with his wife."[15]

The grind, Jennifer Allen wrote, came with a physical cost. George Allen lost 15 pounds during the 1968 season. He skipped meals, drinking milk and taking vitamin injections instead of eating. George Allen suffered from ulcers, Jennifer wrote, and consumed gallons of milk in the belief that the milk helped soothe the ulcers. George Allen preferred drinking milk to eating, since chewing was a distraction. It was an extraordinarily brutal regimen, especially unusual for a man who would later serve as the Chairman of the President's Council on Physical Fitness.

George Allen was popular with his players, both in Los Angeles and Washington. But in Los Angeles, he was not popular with many members of the team's front office. Melvin Durslag wrote:

> Allen was accused of high-handedness and of trying to establish complete autonomy. He also was said to be extravagant. He admits that his popularity wasn't staggering.
> "When you pick up a losing team," explains George, "and you try to get going, you can't have static. You must have control. Shula has it. Gillman has it, Sherman has it and Lombardi and Al Davis and many others have it. ... I demanded changes and I spent money, but only because we had it. If we didn't have the money, I wouldn't have spent it. ... Reeves has surrounded himself with his cronies, more or less asking for last place. When I fought this, I was accused of flaunting authority and I became the office villain."[16]

Jim Murray, the legendary syndicated sport columnist who eventually won a Pulitzer Prize for his brilliant writing, lent a voice to Allen's dismissal, too. Murray wrote on January 3, 1969:

> Daniel F. Reeves is a festive man. He is a New York Irishman, which means that he is (A) Stubborn; (B) Loyal; (C) Sentimental; (D) Tough. He has a biting wit, will take a second drink, and frequently finds mankind funny.
> George Allen is a football coach. This means his idea of festivity is being

thrown under the shower after a victory. He almost never smiles and has the dour outlook of a man who sees life as a series of intercepted passes.

Allen thought Dan wanted a championship, not a team. Dan figured he might as well buy minority shares in an Albanian railroad if all he was going to get to see his investment was through binoculars or on visiting days.

Dan is a man of uncompromising morality and it outraged him to be confronted with George Allen's ever-present air of faint disapproval. But Allen is the kind of man who would greet John the Baptist with faint disapproval unless, of course, John could block and tackle. George, you see, is that most unfortunate of people, the perfectionist.

George found the Rams a relatively morale-less, happy-go-lucky squad of losers....

George skillfully traded his way to a winner. The first thing he traded away was his sense of humor.[17]

Los Angeles Herald Examiner sportswriter Morton Moss wrote of the Rams, "There has been a neurotic inevitability about the Rams dismissal of coaches. This has become a cherished Ram tradition."[18]

After Reeves' call terminating Allen's employment, the jangle of the family telephone would elicit a consistent response from the jobless coach. Jennifer Allen described it: "My father would say 'uh-oh!' and refuse to answer the telephone. We knew the call would invariably be for Dad, but we still all sprang to answer it, saying, 'Hello? Allen residence. Hello?' and then we would force the receiver into our father's hand. It would usually be just another sports reporter calling to ask Dad about his 'uncertain future.' Our number was unlisted, yet every sports writer in the country seemed to have it in his Rolodex."[19]

Jennifer Allen added, "When Dan Reeves fired our father, he fired our whole family."

Etty Allen, George's wife, received a call from the Rams shortly after the firing. The Rams were sending someone to pick up the Oldsmobile Toronado the team had given the family for use while her husband was the coach. The family called the car the "Batmobile," according to Jennifer. After the phone call from the Rams was terminated, Etty Allen remarked that perhaps the Rams representative would drive off a cliff on the way to repossessing the car and that, until he arrived, the family would keep the car.[20]

It takes a strong person to be a coach's spouse.

Deacon Jones was in Florida, spending the holiday season with his mother, when he learned Allen had been booted. Jones and his wife returned to Los Angeles in the hope that he could make some kind of effort to save Allen's job. In *Headslap,* Jones wrote that he felt Reeves waited until the players were dispersed around the country for the holidays with their families before firing Allen. Reeves felt, according to Jones, that by the time everyone returned to Southern California for the 1969 training camp, Allen would be forgotten, a new coach would be in his place and things would continue as they always had for the Rams.

From *Headslap*: "Allen had fought for all the things that make a winner—better facilities, equipment, players. He had fought for the players, to get them more money, better playing conditions, whatever they wanted. With George, it was team first, and he took whatever hours and money it took to get the job done. Reeves, on the other hand, fought only for control of the team. He operated on the principle that if it was good for him, then it should be done."[21]

Gabriel said years later, "I think that George had a feeling for the player right through his soul, right through his heart. He knew that the people that were going to win football games were his players. As a result, he battled for you to have the most comfortable facilities that you possibly could. He battled to get us a universal [weight] machine, an Olympic set; a sauna bath. You started staying in nice hotels. You started flying charter flights. And he also went to bat for you, as long as you gave him loyalty, he would go to bat for you in trying to help you make more money in your contract."[22]

The media reaction to Allen's dismissal was all over the map. Some

The original Fearsome Foursome (from left), Lamar Lundy (85), Roosevelt Grier (76), Merlin Olsen (74) and Deacon Jones (75), during a 1966 game against the Packers (Vernon J. Biever photograph).

seemed supportive of Allen and his winning record. Others, such as *Times* columnist John Hall, wrote that Reeves owned the ballclub and could do as he pleased. Jennifer Allen wrote about her mother's reaction to a television sportscaster's comment that coaches were hired to be fired. "Rot in hell," Etty Allen remarked.[23]

Reeves did indeed own the team. He had hired and fired coaches before and, to that extent, George Allen was no different. Allen worked for the Rams. Reeves owned the Rams. Allen worked for three years of a five-year contract and got fired. Reeves could find another coach and life would continue. Reeves had hired and fired both winners and losers before. The one thing Reeves had not done before was fire a coach who had turned losers into winners. Even Gillman had one very good season, followed by mediocrity. The men who had played for the Rams during the Waterfield and Svare years or who had played for other organizations, came to the Rams in a trade and found themselves winning were not happy with the news that Allen was gone and the players reacted.

Many of the Rams players met at the Sheraton-West hotel in Los Angeles. Jones described the tone of the meeting in *Headslap*. The players in attendance included Jones, Maxie Baughan, Dick Bass, Eddie Meador, Charlie Cowan and Roman Gabriel. The result of the meeting was that a press conference was called for the next day at the same hotel and during the press conference those same players, plus Lamar Lundy, declared they would not play in 1969 if Allen was not rehired as the head coach. Other players requested a meeting with Reeves to discuss Allen's dismissal.

"It wasn't a hard decision to make," Gabriel said years later. "I mean, look where we'd come from and where we were. I think we all felt like we owed something to this man, George Allen, because of what he gave to us."[24] Gabriel also told the Associated Press, "If Allen goes—well, if I can't go with him or be traded, the Gabriel Travel Agency may have a full-time official. Allen was a player's coach, not a management coach."[25]

In the following days, newspapers were filled with reactions and comments from the Rams organization and from the players. General Manager Elroy Hirsh was quoted by the *Times* as saying Allen's only interest was his personal goals while Reeves' only interest was integrity. A letter and signature campaign started among fans who wanted Allen to return.

Between the NFL and AFL, seven teams hired new coaches for the 1969 season: the Redskins, Eagles, Giants and Steelers in the NFL and Patriots, Bills and Raiders in the younger circuit. Of those hires, three coaches later became members of the Pro Football Hall of Fame: Vince Lombardi (Redskins), Chuck Noll (Steelers) and John Madden (Raiders). The Eagles hired Jerry Richardson, Alex Webster signed with the Giants, Clive Rush took over the Patriots job and Buffalo hired John

Rauch. Buffalo's Ralph Wilson apparently contacted Allen after the Rams fired him. Of the other positions, the possibility of Allen coaching for the Raiders and owner Al Davis, whose motto was, famously, *Just win baby*, is intriguing. Both men were driven and both were winners. Davis, obviously, was happy with Madden, who coached the Raiders to a Super Bowl victory. But if anyone ever wrote a what-if fiction book about professional football, an early subject story line suggestion might be what if Al Davis hired George Allen to be his head coach in 1969.

On that New Year's Eve, as the world whirled toward the birth of 1969, Jennifer Allen "hoped that maybe what one reporter predicted would come true: that Dan Reeves would change his mind and reinstate my father as head coach of the Rams. More than wanting Dad at home, I wanted to see Dad happy. He just seemed so unhappy to be home with us."[26]

George Allen himself doubted it would happen. Durslag wrote, "'I doubt it,' says George. 'I think he will make it stick. Reeves is a charming man and he has fooled the press, which protects him more than it should. For years writers have blamed Ram failures on everyone except the owner.'"

At this stage of the proceedings, Dr. Jules Rasinski stepped in. Rasinski was the Rams team doctor and he was friendly with both Reeves and Allen. It was Rasinski, more than public opinion and more than the threats by star players, who was able to get Reeves to reinstate the winningest coach in franchise history.

Jennifer Allen wrote, "Dr. Rasinski was the main man responsible for convincing Dan Reeves to hire Dad back at the Rams. The players' strike had been influential in making Dad's firing a national sports headline. But it was Dr. Rasinski who convinced Reeves to take my father back. A few days after the firing, Dr. Rasinski drove up to Dan Reeves' Bel Air estate to try to talk him into hiring George Allen back. That little talk turned into Dr. Rasinski spending the entire night hopping from bar to bar all over Los Angeles with Reeves, matching him drink for drink, trying to convince him that Allen was the most devoted coach he would ever find in the National Football League. Reeves wanted the recently retired Vince Lombardi to replace Allen. Dr. Rasinski convinced Reeves that Allen was his man. The night ended, near dawn, where it began: Reeves's [sic] home lounge for one last drink. Later that day, Reeves telephoned Dr. Rasinski and said he'd meet with Allen, but only if Dr. Rasinski came."[27]

In a January 7, 1969, *Los Angeles Herald Examiner* story, sports editor Bud Furillo largely confirmed what Jennifer Allen wrote about Rasinski's role in Reeves rehiring George Allen.

The meeting led to Reeves reinstating Allen and on January 7, 1969, a press conference was called to announce that Reeves would allow Allen to return. Allen's original five-year contract remained unchanged. Allen told reporters that he was back because the players stood up for him. Reeves said the two would communicate more frequently in order to avoid misunderstandings. Reeves, who was fighting cancer, spent much of his time in New York and that made communicating more difficult. Remember, email and cellphones were still decades away in 1969.

Allen had not been completely away from football since the firing. He coached the West team to victory in the NFL's Pro Bowl all-star game in the Coliseum prior to his reinstatement, but now he was back fulltime.

Some observers have written that the 1969 season represented the first of two opportunities for Allen to win a world championship and keep his job with the Rams beyond his contract. That seems unlikely. Reeves retained Joe Stydahar for one league game beyond winning the 1951 championship and Adam Walsh lasted one season beyond winning the 1945 title and the Coach of the Year Award. More likely, the 1969 and 1970 seasons were simply the final years of Allen's time with the Los Angeles Rams.

The final year had already come for Elroy Hirsch, the Hall of Fame receiver for the Rams who had served in the Rams front office since his playing days ended. Hirsch left his job as the Rams' general manager to become the athletic director at the University of Wisconsin.

Finally, one is left to play the "what if" game and consider the botched ending to the Bears game in the penultimate game of the Rams' season.

What if ... the officials correctly changed the down marker to give the Rams a first down after the penalty on the Rams final possession? Gabriel still needed to gain enough yards to get Gossett within field goal range and in the actual event, the Rams ended the game with three incomplete passes. But say the Rams got the needed yards with enough time for a successful field goal attempt and won the game.

What if ... the Rams beat the Colts the following week? Sportswriters at the time called the Baltimore defense one of the best in the history of the professional game but nobody said that about the Baltimore offense. In the actual event the Rams had nothing to play for, but running back Willie Ellison burst through the great Colts' defense for a 52-yard touchdown in the fourth quarter to tie the game at 21–21. The final score was 28–24. So, for the sake of "what if," say the Rams beat the Colts at the end of the season again and advanced to the playoffs. The Colts beat the Vikings and Browns to advance to their Super Bowl date with the New York Jets. The Rams never had much luck against the Vikings, especially in the playoffs, so assume the Rams then lost to Minnesota.

Then, would Dan Reeves had fired George Allen in December of 1968? Reeves had a long history of dismissing championship coaches and siding with assistant coaches to enhance team intrigue. He and Allen had sparred publicly over the issue of complaints by Allen about the playing conditions in San Francisco. But would Reeves have fired Allen after consecutive playoff appearances? The answer is probably yes but we'll never know for sure. Reeves gave way to public pressure and unfired Allen after two weeks anyway.

The final note for the 1968 season started with the loss to the Bears. When all the drama concerning Allen's firing and rehiring was completed, Coach George Allen got to work analyzing the 1968 season. Clarence Childs' long kickoff return stuck out as the key play to the season, Allen felt. Childs' return was not the only long one against the Rams in 1968. Detroit's Lem Barney had returned a kickoff for a touchdown as well and Allen was determined to put a stop to those big plays. The solution to the problem would cost his ballclub money and it would change the way professional football teams were coached from that moment until the present day.

Allen wrote, "I realized, after analyzing that play and our overall special teams play for that entire season, that the fault for the loss, and the abrupt end to an otherwise fine season, was as much in our approach to coaching special teams as it was in Ezerins' missed tackle. Because of Ezerins' lack of tackling fundamentals, we never should have placed him in that position; he was not the right man for the job. It was then that I decided a special teams coordinator was needed! ... I convinced Dan Reeves ... that a special teams coach was a necessity and would pay dividends in victories. Mr. Reeves asked how I was going to keep this new coach busy, and I told him that the special teams coordinator will be the busiest coach on the staff—and I was right."[28]

10

Out of the Fire and Into the Playoffs
The 1969 Rams

Between the draft, free agent signings and trades, pro football teams add new personnel constantly. That's one of the reasons they sell programs at the games, the continuous roster changes. Also new for the Rams was the signing of young Stanford University assistant coach Dick Vermeil to coach the special teams or kicking teams. If Vermeil was not the first NFL assistant signed specifically to coach the kicking game, he was certainly one of the first. It was Vermeil's first professional coaching assignment and he didn't believe the phone call with the job offer actually came from George Allen.

Vermeil told the author that he was on a recruiting trip for Stanford when Allen contacted him. Vermeil was staying at a friend's home and somehow Allen got the phone number where Vermeil was staying. Vermeil told the author, "I thought someone was playing a trick on me. I used to get phone calls and people would say, 'This is Bear Bryant and I want you to come coach for me.' I said, 'Who is this really?'" Allen somehow knew Preston Jones, the track coach at Stanford, and Jones recommended Vermeil to Allen.

"When I went there I was in my early thirties," Vermeil said. "I was learning the game. I was learning something every day. When I went to coach for George Allen he was far ahead of anyone I'd been around in terms of breaking down the scheme that [opposing teams] were running. It was a huge education for me." Vermeil added, "George Allen recognized the importance of special teams being coached. No one else had done it before. Howard Schnellenberger really helped. I had coached special teams as a high school head coach and as a junior college head coach. Howard Schnellenberger had worked for Bear Bryant at Alabama and they always had a strong kicking game."[1]

"I wasn't in my new office 10 minutes before George came in and outlined some studies he wanted me to do in preparation for the 1969 season," Vermeil wrote in Allen's book on special teams. "The first one was to grade each player on all the kicking teams in all 14 games and report to him the findings. ... Another study George had me do was evaluate the top-ranked special teams in each area and report to him *what* the teams were successful at and *why*—was it design, personnel, or good fortune? ... George was never too busy to drop into my office and inquire about the findings of these different studies."[2]

Vermeil added in the book, "If there was one thing that helped improve our special teams, I would have to say it was George allowing me to upgrade the coaching tempo for the kicking game. At first the players thought I was crazy. Who is this guy running up and down the practice field yelling 'Faster! Quicker! Tougher! More intensity!' ... The players gradually found out that an enthusiastic approach to preparation was fun and reflected as a real benefit on Sunday afternoon."

Vermeil also wrote that he shied away from Allen on game days, when possible, because the head coach frequently asked questions that were difficult to answer. Allen did the same thing during games sometimes. "What he was doing," Vermeil wrote, "was stimulating me to make sure every possible detail had been covered."

What better training could a young coach receive?

According to Deacon Jones' account in *Headslap*, the 1969 Rams were a traveling hospital ward. Starter after starter missed games, or parts of games, due to injury. Yet, somehow, the Rams came out of the gates like a racehorse on its favorite track. The Rams opened with 11 straight wins, 17 straight if you count the undefeated preseason. Los Angeles looked like the team to beat in the NFL.

Allen's NFL teams had a tradition. Each Tuesday the coach handed out prizes for good play. The Tuesday prizes went beyond the game balls handed out in the victorious locker room and none of the awards were associated with clauses in the players' contracts. There were stereos, televisions and cases of beer or wine handed out. Some prizes were bigger, some smaller but all recognized a contribution to the previous week's victory. If a Rams player blocked a punt, knocked the opposing punter out of the game and fell on the ball in the end zone, that player could look forward to a raucous greeting during Tuesday's prize ceremony. Jones wrote in *Headslap* that Allen paid for some of the prizes out of his own pocket. Certainly, if Allen's spending habits were a source of friction between himself and the Rams front office, not to mention owner Dan Reeves, it seems unlikely that the team paid for too many of the bigger items. George Allen was a master at gathering community support and some of the prizes may well have been donated by local businesses. Whatever the source, the prizes were a source of pride for the players and played a role in building the camaraderie that Allen's teams became known for. For 11 weeks in 1969, the Rams rolled and the Tuesday prize-day meetings were a lot of fun.

The Rams opened the regular season in Baltimore against the Colts. The two teams were the winningest pair in all of pro football the previous two seasons and yet neither of them had a Super Bowl championship to show for it. In 1967, when the Rams advanced to the NFL's Western Division playoffs, the Colts' regular-season record was better than either of the teams who advanced to the playoffs in the Eastern Division. In 1968, when the Colts advanced to the playoffs, the Rams' 10–3–1 record was better than the eventual Eastern Division champion Browns, who were 10–4 in the regular season. On January 12, 1969, the Colts famously lost to the AFL's New York Jets, 16–7, in Super Bowl III. The Colts, if anything, were better in 1969. Johnny Unitas' throwing elbow had recovered from the injury he suffered at the end of the 1968 preseason and Unitas was ready to go.

Rams kicker Bruce Gossett opened scoring with a 29-yard field goal but the Colts scored a touchdown to lead 7–3. Gabriel hit tight end Billy Truax for a short touchdown pass to put the Rams ahead 10–7, but the Colts tied the score before the half. The Colts went ahead in the third quarter when Unitas hit Jimmy Orr for a 41-yard touchdown pass but the Rams rattled off three scores on a pass from Gabriel to running back Willie Ellison, a 15-yard field goal by Gossett and a pass from Gabriel to Wendell Tucker to build a 27–17 advantage. The Colts got another field goal but the Rams won 27–20. Gabriel finished the game hitting 20 of 33 attempts for 268 yards and three scores. He was not intercepted. The Rams rushed for just 87 yards on 28 attempts, but the Rams defense held the Colts running game in check, allowing just 54 yards on 20 carries. Unitas threw for 297 yards and two scores, but he was intercepted three times and completed only 20 of 47 passes. It was a masterful performance by the Rams on the road against a great team.

There was also a changing of the guard for the Rams at Baltimore. Dick Bass, the running back nicknamed The Scooter and the franchise's all-time leading rusher, carried once for one yard against the Colts. It was the final carry of Bass' stellar career. Allen protected Bass during the preseason, playing the veteran enough to get his timing for the coming season but little further. But, after playing for 10 seasons, 112 NFL games (90 as a starter), 1,218 carries for 5,417 yards, 204 pass receptions for 1,841 more yards and 41 total touchdowns, Bass did not record another carry. Rookie Larry Smith and veteran Lester Josephson got the most carries and gained the most yards in 1969.

The Rams won home games against the Falcons and Saints before

10. Out of the Fire and Into the Playoffs

traveling to beautiful Kezar to play Brodie and the 49ers. The Rams fumbled five times against the 49ers but did not lose any. Still, the game was in doubt late. San Francisco led 21–13 in the final quarter but Gabriel and veteran running back Tommy Mason each scored on one yard runs and the Rams won 27–21 to improve to 4–0.

The Rams built a 20–0 lead in their next game against the Packers in Los Angeles, before winning 34–21. The Rams sacked Green Bay quarterbacks Don Horn and Bart Starr six times in that game. The next game was a narrow 9–7 victory over the Bears in Chicago. The Bears led 7–6 at halftime before Gossett supplied the winning points with a field goal in the third quarter. Los Angeles sacked Bears quarterback Bobby Douglas seven times. The Rams thumped the Falcons 38–6 in Atlanta before coming home to play the 49ers again.

The Rams were undefeated after eight games. San Francisco was struggling at 1–6–1, but their victory was against the mighty Colts in week six. The 49ers could bite, as Allen and the Rams knew. Early on, it was a Rams show. Gabriel hit Tucker for a 93-yard pass play in the first quarter and then Josephson caught a 35-yarder and the Rams led 17–6 at the half. Meador returned a pass interception 38 yards for a score and the Rams led 27–9 in the third quarter. But Brodie and his mates closed to within 34–30 in the final period before Gabriel ran in for a score from nine yards out, making the final score 41–30. Brodie connected on 25 of 42 attempts for 356 yards and three touchdowns. He also threw two interceptions and was sacked twice. Gabriel hit on 13 of his 23 passes for 319 yards and three scores without an interception.

The next three games were against teams from the Eastern Conference and the Rams scored narrow victories in each: 23–17 over the Eagles in Philadelphia, 24–23 over the Cowboys in Los Angeles and 24–13 over the Redskins in Washington. The Rams were 11–0, the best start in franchise history. The Colts, despite the return of Unitas, were struggling with a Super Bowl hangover and had lost four games. With three games remaining in the regular season, the Rams had clinched the Coastal Division championship. They were locked into the playoffs. But they also knew that even though they had the best record in the entire NFL at that moment, they would not be playing the first round of the playoffs at home. The Central Division champions had the home game, based upon the then-rule of alternating home sites for the opening round of the playoffs. In both of George Allen's playoff runs as head coach of the Rams, his teams played on the road in the postseason.

The next game was against the 10–1 Minnesota Vikings in Los Angeles. Coached by Bud Grant, the Vikings built leads of 14–0 and 20–6 before winning 20–13. The Rams rushed for just 61 yards in that game and Gabriel connected on 21 of 37 passes for 186 yards and a touchdown. He also threw an interception, just his fourth to that point of the season. Gabriel was previously picked off once by the Bears in week six and twice by Dallas in week 10. By the end of the Vikings game, Gabriel had passed for 23 touchdowns.

The following week was a shocking 28–0 loss to the Lions in Detroit. Gabriel threw two interceptions before Allen rested him and the Los Angeles defense did not stop the 8–4–1 Lions. A week later, in Los Angeles, the Colts gained a small measure of revenge with a 13–7 win over the Rams. After their glorious start, the Rams headed for the playoffs on a three-game losing streak.

The Vikings played their home games outdoors in those days at the old Metropolitan Stadium. According to pro-football-reference.com, the temperature at kickoff was 11 degrees with a windchill of minus one. The Rams led 17–7 at halftime and 20–14 as late as the fourth quarter but lost 23–20. Gabriel hit 22 of 32 passes for 150 yards and two touchdowns. He was intercepted once. The Rams out-rushed the Vikings 126–97 and the Los Angeles defense intercepted Minnesota's Joe Kapp twice, but the Vikings won the game.[3]

Vermeil remembered: "[The Rams were] a world championship-caliber team but we got beat in Minnesota in the deep snow. We went to Minnesota early and tried to get used to the conditions and that might have been a mistake. If that Rams team played that game in LA, the Rams win. Roman Gabriel could have been Roman Gabriel. He was a great football player. He was the MVP [that year], but in those kinds of conditions, it's really hard for the skilled position players to play. I remember [both teams] were on the same sideline and it was cold and miserable."

In *Headslap*, Jones listed several questionable penalties called against the Rams, penalties that Bob Oates took issue with in the *Los Angeles Times*. The two toughest for the Rams were a late hit call on linebacker Jack Pardee and a late-game safety. The late hit call came after a Vikings ball carrier went down, then got up and ran again. Pardee, unsure whether the offensive man was downed by a defensive player, tackled the runner. The safety came near the end of the final quarter when Gabriel was trying to rally the Rams one more time. Minnesota's Carl Eller hit the Rams passer and drove him into the end zone and tackled him. The ruling was a safety, though the Rams felt the initial contact was outside the end zone and the ball should have been spotted at about the one-yard line.

Jones wrote that the loss took "some of the heart out of me as a player." He also wrote, "The low level of officiating was and remains one of the biggest blights against football. With twenty-two men on the field, it is the most complicated bigtime sport. There's a lot going on in the same split seconds. In those days the refs could and did commit unforgivable acts and get away with it."[4]

Statistically, both the Rams and Vikings were whistled for four penalties. The Rams lost 37 yards and the Vikings lost 36.

After watching the game from their home in Los Angeles, Allen's children and Etty had the sad duty of dismantling the Christmas celebration they had planned for George's return from Minnesota. Jennifer Allen wrote, "We knew the last thing Dad would want to do was to have to celebrate Christmas with us." She wrote about listening as her mother played the piano later that night "composing a slow, funereal end-of-the-season dirge."[5] Despite the loss to the Vikings, George Allen was named the NFC Coach of the Year for 1969.

The Rams had another game to play, the Playoff Bowl for first round playoffs losers. It was the tenth and final edition of the Playoff Bowl. The Rams played the Cowboys and beat them 31–0. That victory over Dallas on January 3, 1970, was the last time the Rams would play in the postseason until December 23, 1973, when they lost to the Cowboys, 27–16, in Dallas. Between those two games against the Cowboys, the Rams changed head coaches twice.

Vermeil left the Rams after the 1969 season to become the offensive coordinator at UCLA. He returned to the Rams a year later as an assistant coach for new head coach Tommy Prothro. Vermeil remained with the Rams until 1974, when he returned to UCLA to become the head coach of the Bruins. In 1976, Vermeil became the head coach of the Philadelphia Eagles and he brought with him some advice from Allen.

"George had a philosophy about the NFL," Vermeil recalled. "He said no one gets tenure in the NFL. He told me, 'Someday you're going to be a head coach in the NFL if my projection about you is correct. You have to do it your way. If you do it the owner's way or the general manager's way, you're going to get fired anyway, so you might as well feel good about it.'"

Vermeil was named the Philadelphia Eagles' head coach in 1976 and coached against Allen's final two Washington Redskins teams. Allen's Redskins won all four of their matchups. Vermeil would eventually coach the Eagles into Super Bowl XV, where Philadelphia lost to the Oakland Raiders, 27–10. Decades later, Vermeil was the St. Louis Rams' head coach and won one of the most exciting games in Super Bowl history, 23–16, over the Tennessee Titans in Super Bowl XXXIV.

11

Lame Duck
The 1970 Rams

The 1970 Los Angeles Rams began their season with an owner fighting cancer and a lame-duck head coach. Dan Reeves was fighting Hodgkin's disease and living in New York, but his time was running out. It was the final season of George Allen's five-year contract and the two men had not patched up their differences. With Reeves on the other side of the continent, Allen and other members of the organization's front office banged heads because there was no clear leader.

It was an open secret that Dan Reeves would soon fire George Allen again. As early as September, Alfred Wright wrote of Allen in *Sports Illustrated*, "The people in his world are divided into Rams and non–Rams and the Rams are subdivided into front office types who work in Los Angeles and players, coaches, trainers, etc. who work in Long Beach, 30 miles away. Allen has as little as possible to do with management, which is the main reason he's going to get canned. He and Dan Reeves, the Rams' owner, are not compatible."[1]

Deacon Jones, who was a loyal George Allen man, did not hold back his opinions. Jones wrote in *Headslap*, "Those same people who showed up with champagne and celebrated the last time George was fired were all still there, yipping and snapping like snarly little dogs. ... By now, Dan was a very sick man and living in New York, with all he could do to fight cancer. He'd always tried to operate like his own general manager, but now he had to delegate more and more. Unfortunately for those who saw themselves rising in power within the organization, George Allen had taken over much of the decision-making process from the very start of his tenure with the Rams. He didn't need all these hangers-on and losers telling him what to do. He was obvious about it, and this did nothing to endear the Rams head coach to his enemies in the Rams camp."[2]

Between seasons, Allen lost an important member of his coaching

11. Lame Duck

staff when special teams coach Dick Vermeil was hired to become a key assistant to UCLA head coach Tommy Prothro. Vermeil contacted Marv Levy, at that time the special teams coach for the Philadelphia Eagles, and suggested that Levy contact Allen. Vermeil had recommended Levy to Allen. After some phone calls between them, Allen hired Levy with the stipulation that Levy could be in Los Angeles by the following Friday. Levy and his wife got packed and moved in less than a week and arrived at the Rams' offices by 8 a.m. on the date demanded. A secretary arrived nearly two hours later to open the doors. That secretary told the Levys that coach Allen started a two-week vacation that day. Thus began an association between Levy and Allen that continued a very successful aspect of Allen's Rams and Redskins teams, the kicking game.[3]

Allen was aware that he was likely starting his final season as the Rams' coach. Levy related in his autobiography that Allen said he could only offer Levy a one-year contract with the Rams. If the Rams failed to reach the Super Bowl, Allen and his entire staff would likely be fired by Dan Reeves. Levy, who was born in Illinois but had coached in California earlier in his career, accepted the job with the warning because both Levy and his wife were happy to return to the West Coast.

"I knew we would win," Levy wrote, "and I also knew that I wanted to work in the type of program that George ran. Even if he were fired, there would be many other teams clamoring to hire him, and if I did the kind of job I believed that I would do, George would very likely put me on his new staff."[4] Levy was right. When Allen and his staff were fired by the Rams and Allen was hired to coach the Washington Redskins, Allen took Levy with him to the nation's capital.

Levy wrote, "George had many attributes, and not the least among them was his ability to find outstanding staff members and his willingness to utilize their creative thinking. ... You would think that every head coach would have the appetite to capitalize fully on the talents of his assistant coaches, but too frequently they don't. Many are fearful of hiring men who might possess greater expertise in certain areas of the game than the head coach himself. That was an insecurity that did not plague George. In fact, I never saw him display any self-doubt."

"Directing the kicking teams for the Rams and later for the Redskins was the most enjoyable coaching experience I have had in my career," Levy added. "Once George determined that he had confidence in a staff member, he allowed that man to handle his assigned responsibility without standing around peering over the guy's shoulder. It wasn't that George ever lost touch or interest in any department of play, because he remained fully abreast of what was happening. He'd inquire frequently about what you were doing, and it is to his credit that the most often asked question he directed at me was a positive one: 'Marv, what can we do to make our kicking game better?' He wasn't asking that question merely to appear interested. George listened intently to the answer and he weighed carefully the validity of any proposals. Most importantly, he acted upon sound recommendations, pursuing implementation of good ideas to fulfillment."[5]

The league's configuration changed for 1970. The National Football Conference now consisted of three divisions: the East, West and Central. Somehow, the NFC West included the two California teams, Los Angeles and San Francisco, plus the Atlanta Falcons and New Orleans Saints. The teams advancing to the playoffs in each conference would be the three divisional champions and the second-place team with the best record. As well as Allen's Rams had played even during seasons when they failed to reach the playoffs, that seemed to indicate that a postseason berth was in the offing, one way or another. The other piece of good news for Allen and the Rams was that the Colts were no longer in the same division. The bad news was that another challenger was rising to make life difficult for Los Angeles.

Jones felt that there was a key rule change, but not one that was written down. He wrote in *Headslap* that, by 1970, NFL referees were starting to throw penalty flags when he used his signature move, the headslap, on offensive linemen. Jones would come out of his stance and slam his massive hands against the helmet of the man in front of him, frequently two shots or even three, as quick as a boxer throwing a punching combination. If the lineman was not knocked unconscious, his helmet was torqued enough to make it hard to see which way Jones had gone. Quick as Jones was, the headslap was a devastating way to gain an advantage. Nor was he the only Ram slapping heads. Merlin Olsen, the Hall of Fame tackle who spent much of his professional career lining up next to Jones, also used the headslap at times.[6] Jones may have made the move famous but Olsen used it effectively as well. Eventually, the headslap was outlawed. Several decades after Jones retired, football organizers at all levels began legislating against blows to the head. A lot of former Rams opponents probably wished the move was outlawed earlier.

George Allen and his LA Rams defensive teams are widely credited with inventing an extremely popular term. That term was later recognized as an official NFL statistic, Quarterback Sacks. In his autobiography, Levy recalls the exact moment, prior to a game against the Dallas Cowboys, that Allen invented the term.

Levy wrote: "One of George's most memorable pregame orations came during my single season with the Rams. Before one game, without even knowing it at the time, he was responsible for giving birth to a term that is now an integral part of football's lexicon. ... The Dallas sportswriters were boasting that the Cowboys quarterback.... Craig Morton, would leave the field with a clean jersey after the game." Levy continued, "Groping for some final words of inspiration as our team prepared for kickoff, George pointed across the field and blurted out, 'Today we are going to take that *Morton Salt* and pour it into a sack!'" Levy then wrote that the Rams sacked Morton eight times.

The Rams did not play the Cowboys in a regular season game in 1970, but the teams met on August 15 of that summer in a preseason contest in the Coliseum. It was the second week of the NFL's preseason schedule for both teams. The Rams won that game, 17–10. It does not seem likely that Dallas coach Tom Landry would leave his starting passer on the field long enough to get sacked eight times in a game that meant nothing, and it is equally improbable that Allen would leave his defensive starters in the game that long. But Levy's memory is specific about the Dallas quarterback—it takes Morton to make *Morton Salt*—and that the game in question was played during his only season as an assistant with the Rams.

The Rams did not sack any individual quarterback eight times in 1970. The ferocious Rams pass rush, led by Deacon Jones, sacked St. Louis Cardinals passer Jim Hart six times in week one, Buffalo's Dennis Shaw four times in week two, San Diego quarterbacks John Hadl and Marty Domres a combined 10 times (for 73 yards) in week three and got New Orleans throwers Billy Kilmer and Ed Hargett a total of five times in week seven. Atlanta's Randy Johnson and Bob Berry went down six times altogether in week 10 and Detroit's Greg Landry was sacked five times in the 13th week of the season.[7] In 1971, Morton started the week three game between the Redskins and Cowboys and split time under center with Roger Staubach that day. Morton was sacked once that day and he did not play against the Redskins in their week 10 game. Morton went the distance against Washington in the first meeting between the clubs in 1972's week six meeting and was sacked three times but he was not sacked at all when in the week 13 rematch. Staubach started and went the distance when the teams met in the playoffs that season. Staubach was sacked three times. The Redskins sacked Staubach seven times in their week four game in 1973 and twice more in their week 13 meeting.

Determining the exact moment the phrase "quarterback sack" was first coined is a little like trying to guess where Amelia Earhart crash-landed her plane in the Pacific Ocean in 1937. We know where she was trying to fly the plane to. We know roughly where the plane crashed into the sea and approximately when. But exactly where Earhart ended up remains a mystery. So, too, with the quarterback sack. George Allen is largely credited with linking the words to create the term during his tenure with the Los Angeles Rams, where he coached the Fearsome Foursome.

We know that Jones, Merlin Olsen, Lamar Lundy, Rosie Grier and later Roger Brown, Coy Beacon and Diron Talbert all served as the lightning rods for Allen's linguistic creation. We just don't know when Allen said it.

The Rams opened the regular season with three straight wins, beating the St. Louis Cardinals in Los Angeles in the opener. Levy's kickoff defense squad got off to a poor start, allowing the Cardinals to return the opening kickoff for a touchdown. Levy wrote that Allen turned to look for the Rams' new kicking coach but Allen couldn't find his assistant because Levy was hiding behind the massive form of Deacon Jones.[8] Los Angeles went on to beat the Bills in Buffalo and the San Diego Chargers in the Coliseum before hosting the troublesome 49ers in week four. San Francisco and John Brodie had a 10–6 lead at the half and put the game away with a 59-yard pass play to Gene Washington in the third quarter. Bruce Gossett, who by then kicked for the 49ers, booted two field goals and a pair of extra points against his old mates. The loss dropped the Rams into a tie with the 49ers, the new challenger for the divisional crown, at 3-1. The Rams had three straight road games next and their week five victory over the Packers briefly put them back ahead of the 49ers, who tied the Saints in the Bay Area on the same day. Then the 49ers rattled off four straight wins and the Rams struggled. Allen's team lost to the Vikings again, beat the Saints and tied the Falcons in as many weeks. The Rams lost a game they were expected to win against the Jets (who started Al Woodall at quarterback in place of the injured Joe Namath) in Los Angeles and then beat the Falcons in Atlanta before heading north to play in the 49ers in the sloppy confines of Kezar Stadium.

Gabriel completed just seven of 21 passes against the 49ers and the Rams gained only 70 yards through the air, but Les Josephson, Larry Smith and Willie Ellison each gained 50 yards or more running the ball and the Rams won 30–13. Jim Nettles intercepted Brodie twice. The victory left both clubs with records of 7–3–1 with three games remaining in the season. The teams had split their two head-to-head meetings and were tied for the division lead.

The Rams beat the Falcons the following week but then ran into trouble in week 13. The Lions were an improving team and were running neck and neck with the Rams and 49ers for the second-place playoff berth. The Lions had blown the Rams out a season earlier and it was unlikely that the Rams would look beyond the game for any reason. They needed to win to stay even with the 49ers and gain an edge on the Lions in the race for the playoffs in case San Francisco won the West. Gabriel passed for 334 yards and two touchdowns in the showdown against Detroit, but the Rams never led and finally lost 28–23. Los Angeles rushed for just 47 yards in the game, partially because they played from behind for most of the time, forcing

11. Lame Duck 103

Gabriel to throw 47 passes. The Rams hosted the Giants in week 14 and beat the New Yorkers, 31–3. That gave the Rams an edge over the Giants in the race for a playoff berth because the Giants finished second in the East at 9–5. The 49ers won their final three games and finished at 10–3–1 to win the West. The Lions grabbed the fourth playoff berth in the NFC with their record of 10–4. Two losses at home, to the Namath-less Jets (who finished the season at 4–10) and then to the Lions, left Allen and the 9–4–1 Rams out of the playoffs in 1970.

The Lions game may have been determined by a penalty against the Rams on a punt return in the second half. The Rams' Dick Evey was flagged for tripping. The call eliminated a good punt return by the Rams Alvin Haymond and changed the game's momentum. Recalling the lost down game against the Bears two years earlier and the late hit call against Pardee in the Minnesota playoff game the previous season, some of the Rams felt they were snake-bit.

Allen's final victory as head coach of the Los Angeles Rams came, ironically, in New York on December 20, 1970. The phone call from Reeves came on New Year's Eve. Jennifer Allen wrote, "Reeves told my father he couldn't talk long. He was calling from a hospital bed. 'It was a cold conversation,' Dad told us kids after he hung up the telephone. 'No gratitude, no appreciation, no thanks for what I've done.'"

Marv Levy wrote that losing the Rams job agonized Allen, who had wanted to remain with the club, "intensely." Allen had wanted to build the Rams into the kind of dynasty that could rival Vince Lombardi's Packers and felt that he was on the verge of doing so.[9]

In her book, Jennifer Allen said her father did not speak to Reeves all season long in 1970. That seems to make sense, given Reeves' health issues. The likelihood that Reeves would end Allen's association with the Rams at the end of the season hung over the Allen family all season long. Jennifer Allen wrote, "All I could do [during the games] was look at the game clock—first quarter, second quarter—waiting for the time to tick away to tell us it was over and our Rams years had ended. Some games, when I couldn't bear to watch the clock, I'd look through the program at the many local advertisements. One moving company ad pictured a football player carried off the field on a stretcher. The slogan read, 'We'll carry you anywhere!' It was the same moving company we used when we left the Chicago Bears. For a moment, I'd imagine my entire family on that stretcher, being carried away to another team, another town, another owner. For another moment, I'd imagine that my entire family was being carried to the grave."[10]

While Reeves was fighting cancer in New York, the power struggle within the Rams organization might have impacted any chance George

Allen had to remain in LA, but it probably did not. Allen did not spend a lot of time making friends with the Rams senior administrators, but his biggest problem was with Reeves. Baring a Super Bowl berth, Allen's days with the club were numbered from the moment Reeves rehired Allen after the player protest in 1968. Allen knew it and his staffers knew it. Levy, as we have seen, had been warned when Allen offered Levy the kicking teams job.

The 1970 firing was the third time Allen was canned by the Rams but the franchise wasn't done with Allen yet.

The Rams did not spend a lot of time interviewing candidates for their vacant head coaching position and perhaps they should have. They hired UCLA head coach Tommy Prothro, who had never coached or played at the professional level. In two seasons, Prothro's Rams went a combined 14–12–2 and never reached the playoffs. Reeves was not around to see how Prothro fared and so we'll never know whether Dan Reeves would have had more fun losing with Prothro than winning with Allen. Reeves passed away shortly after Prothro was hired.

It has been written and said that Allen's tenure left the Rams devoid of a future because of Allen's preference for veteran players. But is that true? Allen was still a member of the Chicago Bears staff when the 1966 draft was conducted, so he had nothing to do with the Rams' selections in that draft. In fact, he had a great deal of input on the Bears' picks. But Allen was with the Rams when they selected Willie Ellison in the second round of the 1967 draft. Ellison was a Ram for six seasons and finished with eight NFL years to his credit. The Texas Southern running back set a professional football record for yardage gained in a single game when he gained 247 rushing yards for the Rams on 26 carries on December 5, 1971, against the Saints in the Coliseum. USC defensive back Nate Shaw was a fifth-round pick that year, spending two seasons with the Rams and starting five games. The Rams did not have a first-round choice in 1968 and after a disastrous decision to select Heisman Trophy-winning quarterback Gary Beban of UCLA in the second round, they had a successful draft.[11] Guard Mike LaHood was selected from Wyoming later in the second round and spent four seasons with the Rams, starting 10 games over that time. Notre Dame's John Pergine, a linebacker, was picked in the 11th round and played in 90 games over seven seasons with the Rams and Redskins. The 1968 draft's star for the Rams was Jackson State receiver Harold Jackson. Jackson played in 16 NFL seasons with the Rams, Eagles, Patriots, Vikings and Seahawks. Jackson's stints with the Rams totaled six seasons, five of which came after Allen became the Redskins' coach. Jackson finished with 10,372 career receiving yards.

Los Angeles had three first-round selections in the 1969 draft. Running back Larry Smith of Florida was the eighth overall selection that year.

He played five years for the Rams and another with Allen in Washington. Smith averaged 4.0 yards per carry with the Rams and had more than a thousand yards in receptions. USC tight end Bob Klein was another first round selection that year and he played 11 seasons, eight for the Rams. He started 81 games for LA and scored 23 touchdowns. Pat Curran, another tight end, played 10 NFL seasons, six with the Rams. The Lakeland College product started 66 games for the Rams before finishing his career with the Chargers. After his playing days ended, Curran worked in the Chargers front office. Grambling State defensive back Roger Williams played two seasons with the Rams, mostly returning kicks. He recorded two starts with the Rams.

In 1970, Allen's final draft with the Rams, Jack Reynolds, a linebacker from Tennessee who was said to have used a saw, in a fit of anger, to cut his vehicle in half after losing a college game, was the Rams' first round pick. Nicknamed "Hacksaw," Reynolds played 15 NFL seasons, 11 with the Rams. Reynolds lost a Super Bowl with the Rams and later won one with San Francisco. Oregon State defensive tackle Bill Nelson was picked in the seventh round and played five seasons with the Rams, starting 47 games. Center Rich Saul was a great haul in the eighth round. The Michigan State lineman played 13 seasons with the Rams.

The Rams benefited from each draft during Allen's tenure as head coach. During that period, the franchise proved especially adept at scoring hits in the middle and later rounds, as Harold Jackson's and Rich Saul's careers would attest. Allen acquired for the Rams a long series of proven veterans through trades during his time there. That's how he turned the franchise into a winner in such a short period of time. But if he is to be blamed for creating an older roster, then Allen must also be credited for selecting college players such as Reynolds, Klein, Curran, Jackson and Ellison, men whose careers extended far beyond the day Reeves fired Allen for the second time. Allen also solved the most vexing problem the franchise had in the field of play when he installed Roman Gabriel as the starting quarterback. Gabriel played through the 1972 season with Los Angeles before he was traded to the Eagles and played five more seasons in Philadelphia.

George Allen, for all the problems he had with owners during his NFL career, was a shrewd judge of playing talent. That ability to judge talent and project a player's ability to perform in a specific system is a rare commodity. Allen was a player's coach and a motivator, but his greatest skill came in talent recognition. He had worked for Sid Gillman and George Halas, undoubtedly learning important lessons from each man, but the instinctive ability to evaluate talent is not something which can be taught. Either you have it or you do the best you can without it. George Allen had it.

Allen recognized more than just playing talent. He also scored when judging assistant coaches, especially young ones like Vermeil and Levy. In his book, Levy summed up the experience of working for Allen this way: "Working for George was fun. You didn't always know it at the time, but it was. If you were interested in leisure time, however, you were on the wrong coaching staff. With George, you might work until 3 a.m., and that included Christmas Eve if your team was in the playoffs."[12]

But Allen, Levy wrote, took the occasional vacation and liked to keep those vacations secret. The head coach of the Rams and then the Redskins enjoyed his reputation for working long hours and didn't want to lose it.

When Allen moved on to Washington, that reputation remained secure.

12

Ascension
The 1971 Redskins

The Washington Redskins franchise had struggled through a difficult decade in the 1960s, suffering through unproductive seasons that produced a cumulative record of 38 wins, 68 losses and six ties between 1961 and 1968. Vince Lombardi, who found himself unhappy in his role as General Manager of the Packers, returned to the sidelines as coach of the Redskins in 1969 and produced a winner with a 7–5–2 record. It looked like the old Lombardi magic was about to build another winner, but Lombardi died of cancer in September of 1970. Bill Austin was named the interim head coach and Washington went 6–8. Austin was not retained after his season in charge and the coaching search began for the Redskins.

There is a saying among coaches that you don't want to be the coach who replaces a legend. You want to be the coach who replaces the coach who replaced the legend. Austin, who had been an assistant for Lombardi in Green Bay and in Washington, was the guy who replaced the legend. Allen was the guy who replaced Austin.

Jennifer Allen wrote, "I was coached not to let on to anyone how much we hated Lombardi. I had never met the man, yet I was coached to not like any coach who had preceded my father at any job. That was our main enemy: not the opposing team, but the previous administration."[1]

It is impossible to over-emphasize the length of Lombardi's shadow when George Allen became the Redskins' coach. Lombardi's 1960s Packers teams were so dominant that no coach since his passing, with the exception of New England's Bill Belichick, has come close to establishing the respect around the league that Lombardi had. Under Lombardi's guidance, the Packers went from decades as an also-ran franchise to a decade of dominance and they did it just as professional football began captivating America's sporting interest. From 1960 through 1967, Green Bay won five titles and lost a championship game. The Packers won the first two

Super Bowls, which were not yet officially named the Super Bowl, and the championship trophy was eventually named for Lombardi. Then, in his only season on the Redskins' sideline, he produced a winner again.

When Austin was called upon to replace the stricken Lombardi, it equated to replacing Bear Bryant at the University of Alabama or taking the reins from UCLA basketball coach John Wooden. Neither Ray Perkins nor Gene Bartow are lovingly remembered by the respective fan bases of the schools involved. Neither, in fact, is the other guy who had to replace Lombardi, Phil Bengston, who took over when Lombardi retired from coaching the Packers after the 1967 season. Lombardi's style was loud and abrasive. He pushed and pushed his men, verbally whipping them to improve their effort and their results. Austin was less demanding, verbally, and got results that were not as good as the Redskins hoped. That created the opening that Allen filled.

Allen had to emerge from Lombardi's shadow. The differences between the two coaches were plain to see, some players said. Halfback Larry Brown said of Allen, "He's not like Lombardi. He doesn't pressure you. He gives you the opportunity and if you don't take it, then it's too bad."[2]

The new boss. Allen on the Washington sideline on November 7, 1971, against the Eagles at RFK. Number 73 is Paul Laaveg (Alamy).

12. Ascension

Edward Bennett Williams, the principal owner of the Redskins, said, "While Vince Lombardi reigned, Allen collaborates. He believes in creating intense personal relationships with his players, converting each of them to buddies, because, 'You've got to find out what makes your players tick so you can get the most out of them.' He has this unusual ability to get along with his players. ... Many of them just won't take the tough, spartan discipline some of the coaches today are handing out. It's true, he doesn't have much in common with them ideologically, but he recognizes that to get one hundred percent out of his players he has to have a good relationship with them and he strives to get it. ... At the most basic level, Allen gets along by refusing to raise his voice."[3]

Allen and the Redskins eventually agreed to a deal worth a lot of money, for the era. The seven-year contract was worth $125,000 per year in base salary and a $25,000 bonus for signing the deal. The club would pay the Allens $150,000 towards the purchase of a home, incentives worth $5,000 for reaching the divisional playoffs, $10,000 for a berth in the National Conference championship game and $15,000 for an appearance in the Super Bowl. Allen would run the football side of the operation. The team would provide Allen with a car and driver, a life insurance policy worth a quarter of a million dollars and a hefty expense account. He was granted travel expenses for visiting his family while they were still in Los Angeles and hotel expenses in Washington from the start of the contract until June of 1971; also, the team would pay for the family's move east. Finally, a point which came to matter later, the team gave Allen the option to purchase five percent of ownership stock for a price of half a million dollars.[4] When the Redskins reached the Super Bowl at the end of the 1972 season, Allen earned $155,000 in base salary and incentives.

Allen brought Rams assistant coaches Ted Marchibroda, LaVern Torgeson, Marv Levy and Joe Sullivan with him to Washington. The coaching staff included Boyd Dowler, Ralph Hawkins, Mike McCormack, Charlie Waller and Charley Winner.

Sullivan, Levy would later write, was Allen's key man. "The most valuable assistant George had, however, had no specific position assignment, but he was as important to George Allen as Gracie Allen (no relation) was to George Burns. ... I take nothing away from George when I declare that he would not have been as successful as he was without Joe Sullivan. Who? He was George's 'special assistant,' that's who. So what, you say, all these big-time coaches have special assistants, don't they? Not like Joe Sullivan, they don't. George was Mr. Ideas, Joe was Mr. Details. There has never been a more persistent, thorough, loyal, tireless presence in the game than Joe. George's teams didn't need a business manager, a traveling secretary, a film breakdown man, a manager of facilities, a trade negotiator, a waiver wire specialist, a contract negotiator, a legal expert, or any of the other impressively titled employees usually required for this myriad of responsibilities. Joe could handle all those tasks before the morning coffee break."

Allen also brought along his driver from Los Angeles, a former policeman from Long Beach, California, named Ed Boynton. In Washington, Boynton was named the team's chief of security and his primary job was to prevent other teams from spying on Redskins practices. Boynton roamed the practice fields on a bicycle, checking the trees beyond the fences to be sure he foiled any clandestine operations aimed at gathering information on the Washington game plan or, perhaps, to determine which Redskins might be injured worse that the team admitted in official reports to the league office. The Associated Press termed Boynton "a one-man secret service for George Allen. Boynton also toured the practice facilities, both for the Rams and Redskins, to be certain that there were no minor openings in the fencing that surrounded the practice fields that a spy, or even a newspaper photographer, might use to get a look at the goings on."[5] The Associated Press story quoted Boynton as saying that Allen preferred not to drive because the act of driving was a distraction and a waste of time that Allen could be spending reading up on the next opponent. During the Rams years, Boynton was nicknamed Double-O by one of the players and the title traveled to the nation's capital when Allen did. Even Allen's family called Boynton Double-O.

Allen was both the Redskins' head coach and general manager. In Los Angeles, he had one title and usurped the responsibilities of the other. Allen and the Redskins inked the deal on January 6, 1971, giving him both titles in Washington, and he got to work quickly. He sent eight draft choices away on a busy January 28, making trades that ultimately brought a host of former Rams east. The Redskins did give up one player, linebacker Marlin McKeever. McKeever returned to the Rams for his second stint with the club.[6] Newspapers quoted Allen as saying that defensive lineman Diron Talbert, one of the Rams who moved east with the coach, was better than a first-round draft pick because Talbert was already a star in the league and, at 26 years of age, was still a young player.[7]

Allen found himself in a spot of hot water shortly after arriving in Washington when he said he did not want his players to be distracted by regularly hosting radio or television shows. Allen had the club issue a press release in May saying that he, Allen, would not make himself available for such opportunities. Three returning Redskins, Chris Hanburger, Sonny Jurgensen and Jerry Smith, had profited from media work the previous season. Jurgensen's television show was taped on Mondays, which was an off day for players. It was the beginning of Allen's testy relationship with

12. Ascension

the Washington press corps. Allen had been on better terms with some members of the Los Angeles press corps, but even during those years he saw them as the enemy. Tom Mack, the offensive guard who played his first five seasons with the Rams under Allen, said, "George was always telling us the press was against us."[8]

Once he was hired, Allen convinced Redskins owner Edward Bennett Williams to build a facility where the team could practice, lift weights, get treatment for injuries and hold meetings. The facility would have coaching offices, too. Most NFL teams have a similar complex now, but it was something new and state-of-the-art for the time. The site that was eventually selected was largely said to be in the middle of nowhere, which was Allen's desire. In fact, the six-acre site was very close to Dulles International Airport and only twenty-seven miles from RFK Stadium, where the team played its games. The media, which was not allowed to enter the facility, dubbed the place "Fort Football," among other names.

The compound was surrounded by trees on three sides, trees which Allen eventually had labeled, and was patrolled by security guards. It included two football fields, one with natural grass and the other with an artificial surface. The fourth side of the complex included a two-story building which was windowless on the first floor and housed a sauna that could accommodate 12 players, two gymnasiums, a dressing room (the dressing room was carpeted, which seemed like a big thing at the time), weight room, trainer's room, doctor's office and rooms for film sessions and meetings. The second floor had windows and was where the coaching offices were located, including one for Williams and some for general office use.

Allen felt that moving everything football-related to one location reduced distractions for the players. The practice fields did not allow for distractions either, since having the trees on three sides and the building on the fourth eliminated the ability to see anything other than football activities. In her book, Jennifer Allen described a day when she went to the complex with her father. They were the only people there, she wrote, and she was free to explore the place while George Allen worked in his office. She did so. For a youngster, it must have seemed like heaven. There were no distractions.

George Allen brought lots of changes to the Washington Redskins. He brought new players, new offensive and defensive schemes and even a new preseason camp location. The players who pre-dated Allen with the Redskins had adjustments to make. Even the players who re-joined Allen from the Rams had to adjust to new surroundings and new teammates. It might not be too surprising, then, that the Redskins lost their preseason opener to the Chargers, 19–10. It marked the first time in his career that an Allen-coached team lost its preseason opener. The Redskins endured lengthy practices after losing to San Diego and some of them may not have understood the message behind all those extra wind sprints. Prior to a 17–14 victory over the Denver Broncos in the second preseason game, Sonny Jurgensen, Billy Kilmer, Larry Brown and Charley Haraway snuck out of the team hotel and were not present when Allen and his coaches conducted the room-by-room bed check. Each player was fined $500.

One thing did not change with Allen's relocation: The weekly awards. In Washington, Allen handed them out on Monday during the regular season. Levy wrote, "These awards were not just lollypops and bubblegum, either. The outstanding player in the game would receive a set of golf clubs. Color television sets were bestowed upon the most valuable players on the offensive and defensive teams, while the standout performer from the kicking game units won a new suit of clothing. Interceptions, sacks and big plays of any sort were all richly awarded, as well. After we moved to the Redskins, anyone on the kick coverage teams making a tackle inside the opponents' 20-yard line became the recipient of a 'Garfinkel' [actually Garfinckel]—a $50 gift certificate from Garfinkel's department store located in downtown Washington. The NFL frowned on such awards, but our players didn't." Allen also cobbled together ticket packages for local automobile dealerships that would then make cars available for Allen's assistant coaches. In 1971, this was unusual.[9]

As the 1971 campaign began, the Washington Redskins did not have a rookie on the active playing roster. Allen's trades brought in so many former Rams that some reporters took to calling the team the "Ramskins." Allen later referred to his deal with the Rams as his "Brink's job." The Redskins obtained star defensive lineman Diron Talbert, linebackers Jack Pardee, Maxie Baughan and Myron Pottios, backs Jeff Jordan and Tommy Mason, offensive lineman John Wilbur and safety Richie Petibon.[10] The "Skins" gave away McKeever and draft picks in the first, third, fourth, sixth and seventh rounds. Allen later acquired the playing rights to Boyd Dowler, an assistant coach with the Redskins whose playing rights still belonged to the Green Bay Packers. Dowler cost Allen a fifth-round pick but Allen saw Dowler as a player coach.[11]

Another important addition was defensive end Ron McDole, whom Allen aggressively pursued in trade talks with the Buffalo Bills. McDole, dubbed "The Dancing Bear" by a teammate in one of his previous NFL stops, turned out to be a key acquisition for Allen. McDole was a veteran with plenty of gas left in the tank, and his tenure with the Redskins was a year longer than Allen's. McDole had been playing for the Buffalo Bills, but the 1970 season was a disappointment after a long run of success for the team. McDole recounted, "In Buffalo we had great success at the beginning of the AFL. We were involved in the championships and stuff. They changed coaches that year [1970], they got the Oakland coach [John Rauch] and brought him in and so we played one more year and he tried to change everybody. We had all this success in Buffalo and he tried to change everybody and make them to a different system. It wasn't going very well."[12]

From Washington, Allen worked the phones as he tried to make a deal to get McDole. According to McDole, Allen nearly drove Bills' owner Ralph Wilson to distraction.

"[Wilson] called me and said, 'George Allen is driving me crazy. He's calling me at three o'clock in the morning. He's trying to get you [in a trade].' He [Wilson] says, 'You're one of our better players and I don't know with the way things are going here now, I don't know how long this thing is going to last,' and he says, 'I know you're getting toward the end of your career.' ... I said, 'No, if it's going to help the team, trade me.' ... When George made the trade for me, that's the greatest thing that happened to me. When George got me on the phone [later] ... he says, 'How does it feel to be with a winner?'"

By McDole's account, General Manager George Allen did not try to get players for cheap contracts. McDole said, "He was a hard man to control from the front office. You know what I mean? In other words, he didn't give a hoot about who owned the team. I mean, he had to. Socially you'd see them together very rarely. ... He paid everybody well. The players made good money. ... I said, 'I could use a few incentives,' and he said, 'That's no problem, I'll give you some incentives.' He said, 'You're making $35,000, I'll double that and give you $75,000 and then I'll double that again the next season.' I said, 'Oh, okay.'"[13]

Years later Allen left McDole off his list in *Pro Football's 100 Greatest Players*, but he did mention McDole in the book. Allen wrote, "I've left off my list some real personal favorites I could have picked, like Ron McDole."[14]

McDole agreed with Vermeil about Allen being ahead of his time in terms of game planning. "Oh God, yes. ... He was constantly trying to come up with something new, new ideas. ... George was kind of way ahead of his time. We were running stuff that they try to do now back then. Everybody had a job. Jack Pardee was the captain but we used to call him the General. He ran everything on the field. He was the outside linebacker. He called all the plays. The plays didn't come in from the sideline. Occasionally they did but other than that, Jack Pardee was the general and everything he said, we did. If we wanted to run a stunt, I could run a stunt with the defensive tackle or other linemen. Jack would call the defense and we had options off of those that you'd be doing on your own with the guy next to you. For example, I could run a stunt with the defensive tackle.

When [Pardee] called something [as a defensive audible after the team had lined up], you had to run it. If you had something, you had to void that and run what he wanted to run."

In the NFL Films highlight film for the 1972 Redskins, narrator John Facenda described Pardee thusly: "He is to Allen what Bart Starr was to Vince Lombardi in Green Bay: The coach's physical extension on the field. His intuitive and acquired knowledge of pro football is unequaled and it seems as if his prairie-tough thirty-six-year-old body has conquered age as well as disease." The script might be hyperbolic, but it was also accurate in terms of Pardee running the defense.[15]

In *Headslap*, Deacon Jones described the way he and Merlin Olsen frequently ran tricks between themselves within the framework of the overall defensive call while Allen coached the Rams. The freedom to make those decisions on the field was something the players enjoyed and it was one of the reasons Allen wanted veteran players. In order for the coach to give that kind of freedom to players, the coach had to know the players understood what they were doing.

Of course, making split-second decisions can be difficult, even for veterans. McDole recalled an instance when things did not work out so well between himself and fellow defensive lineman Bill Brundige: "[Brundige] said, 'Okay, this is what we're going to do. I'm going to call one number and then I'm going to call another number and then I'm going to call another number.' And I said, 'Okay, I can handle that.' Then we got on the line and I asked what I was going to do and he said, '[Brundige would] call a number and then another number and another number and then you add the third number and that's the direction I want you to go.' And so I get down and he starts to call the numbers. I'm looking for five, six, something like that. And he goes '33, 17.' I'm trying to multiply and divide and I got knocked flat on my ass. I said, 'I can't handle all this. Get me something I can add quicker.' I'm looking for all these small numbers. I had to divide the last one, add the first two."

"The philosophy behind creating the Over the Hill Gang, everybody thought he was crazy in Washington at the beginning," said McDole. "But he [Allen] didn't pass anything up. He studied the game. Unbelievable. He would bring in a college coach, for example, in training camp, who was running something that [Allen] wanted to run and they would tell him the best way to do it that. He said, 'I don't have time to teach somebody how to play the game, to do this or do that.' That was part of it, he wanted a very veteran team that could play the game already. His coaching staff was the same way."

One of the players Allen acquired from the Rams on draft day, outside linebacker Maxie Baughan, is an example of Allen's process for filling

12. Ascension

in weaknesses on his roster. It was the second time he'd used a trade to acquire the veteran. Allen ranked Baughan among the best linebackers of all time and wrote, "I brought Maxie to L.A. when the Eagles thought he was losing a little something. But I love those experienced players who know how to perform, and I think all they need is the opportunity to prove they can still play. I had a lot of confidence in Maxie, and he responded to it by having five more great years. I have to admit he was one of my personal favorites."[16]

The acquisitions of the former Rams and big-name players like McDole got most of the attention and rightfully so. But another player Allen traded for before the 1971 season gives an insight to Allen's ability to judge talent and project how a player might fit on a roster. That player was Mike Hull, a running back for the Chicago Bears.

Hull was the Bears' top draft selection in 1968 after playing his college ball at the University of Southern California. At USC, Hull played with two Heisman Trophy-winning backs, Mike Garrett and O.J. Simpson. The Bears' offense was led by Hall of Famer Gale Sayers at that time and Hull was projected to be a good prospect to block for Sayers. Hull started nine games in three seasons for Chicago, gained 202 yards on 73 carries and scored a touchdown. Hull's time in Chicago had soured him on football and he was considering retirement when the Redskins acquired him from the Bears.

"During my first meeting with George in early 1971, his whole focus was on my 'desire to play,'" Hull wrote in 1991. "He did not concern himself so much with how much I weighed, how strong I was or how fast I ran the 40; he was more concerned with whether or not I wanted to play. Clearly, he wanted a <u>thinking</u> ball player who, for one reason or another ... might be a problem for another team."[17] Hull wrote that he carried the ball about five times during the 1971 preseason games and had played well on special teams. On the last day before the first week of the regular season he learned that he was about to be cut from the squad and was told Allen wanted to meet with him.

> He greeted me as a distinguished professor would a humble student, or as a senior player would greet a troubled freshman; he was very aware of what I was going through, as he had seen that my spirits had risen during the course of training camp and that I was beginning to enjoy football again.
>
> What is particularly revealing about George that I learned from my fateful meeting with him is that he took the time to discuss with me, for approximately two hours, our common views on <u>life.</u> We talked about each other, what was important to us, and our essential outlooks on life (not just football). We shared our views of what had happened with the Chicago Bears, we were 1–13 the year I was traded, and the fact that the Bears' image promoting

the mentality of the "Monsters of the Midway," "Black and Blue Team," was not his approach. We agreed that the view that football as a bruiser, tough guy, bar-busting bad boys' game was outdated and primitive. He wanted a more sophisticated, thoughtful, yet disciplined and relentless approach to the game. Fantastically, after that meeting, George said that he was going to reconsider his position and that he would be in touch with me that evening or the next day. The next morning, while packing my bags, and not knowing how else I could make a living, I got a call from George. He told me that I had been reinstated to the team. He had made a decision to release another player instead of me. ... He didn't re-time me in the 40 or see how much I could lift; he simply talked with me.

Hull played for Allen and the Redskins for five seasons. Every year, Hull was cut near the end of training camp and then re-signed. Mike Hull was not just some guy George Allen liked. Allen did not keep players on his roster who could not contribute to winning games. Special teams coach Levy evaluated Hull this way after the 1971 season: "Excellent speed. Plays with a lot of recklessness. Has a knack for making big plays. Excellent attitude and spirit. Outstanding on kickoff coverage. Still doesn't have full concept of what our plan is designed to accomplish but I feel he can develop into one of the premier special teamers in the NFL."

Allen's ability to recognize useful talent went beyond the obvious skills of great ones like Gale Sayers or Dick Butkus, whom he had scouted for George Halas and the Bears. Allen's insight allowed him to find lesser-known talents like Mike Hull. It was the ability to judge talent and project a fit for that talent that separated George Allen from other coaches. He saw talent, understood it and knew what to do with it. NFL Films voice over announcer John Facenda said in a film about Allen's Redskins that Allen "assembled a group of strangers and taught them the meaning of togetherness. He brought in the disillusioned and the disaffected, the abandoned and the aged. He made them all winners. He made football fun again."[18] Mike Hull's story confirmed the film's hyperbole.

The team was in Allen's mold. As the general manager, he could make it so and he did. By wearing both hats, Allen could be sure things would be done his way. That did not work well for every player. Years later, Jurgensen said that he and Allen were not a good match. The fact that Allen wore two hats—head coach and general manager—made it hard for Jurgensen, who was a fan favorite, to get his way. "We had instant problems and I couldn't win the power struggle," Jurgensen said.[19]

Allen's way was to settle on a quarterback as soon as possible but the matter was taken out of his hands when Jurgensen was injured during the preseason making a tackle after throwing an interception against

12. Ascension

the Dolphins in Miami. Allen chose as his new starter journeyman Billy Kilmer, recently acquired from the New Orleans Saints. Sonny Jurgensen was popular with Redskins fans. Regarded by some as the best pure passer of his era, Jurgensen was in his 15th NFL season. When healthy enough to play, Jurgensen remained a great passer of the football. Jurgensen had played in all 14 regular season games in both 1969 and 1970 after missing two games in 1968. But as the 1971 season got going, Jurgensen was expected to be sidelined for about five games. Jurgensen's injury may have actually made things easier for Allen. Allen hated turnovers and did not like taking chances. His quarterback in Los Angeles, Roman Gabriel, had been productive, even brilliant. Gabriel did not take needless chances and seldom threw interceptions. By comparison, Jurgensen was a gunslinger. Jurgensen had 236 scoring passes to that point in his career, compared to 173 interceptions. Playing mostly for losing teams, he had tossed 20 or more scoring passes seven times. In the previous three seasons, under three different head coaches, he completed 62 scoring passes and been intercepted 36 times, nearly a two-one good-to-bad ratio. Kilmer had come into the league four seasons later and, like Jurgensen, spent most of his career playing for losers. To that point, Kilmer had 49 career touchdown passes and 71 interceptions. He was slightly better than that in the previous three seasons, with 41 scoring passes and 51 interceptions. Jurgensen got off to a good start in the preseason games but once he suffered the shoulder injury, Kilmer was elevated to the starting spot. Jurgensen would be available later but Kilmer started the season under center.

According to Hull, Kilmer did not make it easy for Allen. In his *Tribute*, Hull told of a pregame meeting the day before the opener for which Kilmer was not at his best. "When [Allen's] star quarterback showed up staggering drunk for the pregame meeting right before the 1971 opener, George's first game as a Redskin head-coach, George simply grabbed the bill of his cap, rubbed his chin (as always) and said, 'I sure hope you can play football tomorrow.' ... Lesser coaches or, at least, most coaches would have suspended or benched the guy. But George knew the temperament of his 'gang,' and our backgrounds, and brought us along cleverly, by example, not by punishment."[20]

Kilmer completed six of 17 attempts for just 65 yards against the Cardinals. But one of his completions was a scoring pass and he threw no interceptions. The Redskins played solid, conservative football and beat the Cardinals 24–17 in St. Louis. Kilmer went the distance at quarterback and the Redskins won the game. Whether it is fair or not, quarterbacks and coaches are judged primarily on their win-loss record and the Redskins started their season at 1-0. It was the sixth consecutive year that an Allen-coached team won its NFL opener, but it was just the fourth time in 14 seasons that Washington won in week one.

Marv Levy wrote in his book, "To the credit of George [Allen], Sonny Jurgensen and Billy Kilmer, we never had a quarterback controversy in Washington. Both players were magnificent competitors with egos that winning quarterbacks must have, but their regard for each other, combined with George's deft touch in handling them, gave us the NFL's best combination at that position."[21]

According to McDole, the players didn't worry too much about who the starting quarterback would be, at least the defensive players didn't. He said, "Sonny and Billy got along real well. We did not know who was going to start sometimes. Sonny was starting to have trouble staying healthy. Billy and I were the same age. We played against each other in college a couple times. Towards the end there, [Allen] had a lot of pressure about they wanted him to start [someone else], who was going to start and who shouldn't start. Then [a few seasons later] we had [Joe] Theismann out there. It wasn't our choice anyway, so it didn't really bother the players. We'd perform for whoever we had to perform for. If they threw Bill in the game or if they started Sonny, it wasn't a big problem."

It was especially not a big problem a week later when the Redskins beat the Giants 30–3 in New York. Kilmer lit up the Giants defense for 309 passing yards, connecting on 20 of 32 attempts. He had two scoring passes and was not intercepted.

Over the next three games, Washington out-scored opponents 62–29. Kilmer's numbers were not dazzling but he was effective, completing 24 of 48 passes. Over that span he threw one touchdown pass and one interception. All three games were Washington victories. Over the next five games, things did not go so well. The Redskins lost three, won one and tied one. Their record stood at 6–3–1 and the offense was struggling.

By then, Jurgensen was able to play and was the holder on place kicks. Allen looked for a spark and used both Jurgensen and Kilmer over the next three games, losing to the Bears and Dallas before beating Philadelphia. Over those three games, neither quarterback was really effective. Kilmer connected on 37 of 59 attempts for 385 yards with one touchdown and no interceptions. Jurgensen hit on 14 of 28 for 170 yards and two interceptions without throwing a scoring pass.

With three weeks remaining in the season, Kilmer went under center as the starter against the New York Giants but he was injured early in the game, according to a story related by both Jurgensen and Kilmer. Jurgensen related in an NFL Films interview, "We're playing the Giants. Billy got his bell rung on the opening drive and George came over to me. It was third down on about the twenty-yard line. He said, 'Go in there and run

12. Ascension

a draw play and we'll kick a field goal.' So I go in the huddle and I said, 'The hell with him, I'm gonna throw it.' I threw a touchdown pass. I came to the sideline and he wasn't happy. He said, 'I thought I told you to call a draw play,' and I said, 'I called a draw play ... but when I went to the line of scrimmage, they [the Giants defenders] were hollering, 'Lookout for the draw, look out for the draw ... so I audibled to the pass.' He said, 'Good play.' I said, 'Get me down there again, I'll get you another one.'"

Kilmer said in the same NFL Films piece that he, Kilmer, was re-inserted into the game.[22] The production showed Jurgensen throwing a short scoring pass as Jurgensen related the story. The NFL Films piece leads the viewer to conclude that the incident occurred during the 1971 season, after Jurgensen recovered from his injury but it did not happen, at least not the way Jurgensen told the story. The author checked the box scores for every season that Jurgensen played for Allen and found no game in which the story related by Jurgensen could have happened. There was an instance on October 9, 1972, when the Redskins played the Giants in Yankee Stadium. Kilmer started that game and Jurgensen did come in to throw one pass, a 13-yard completion, that did not go for a touchdown. Still the story illustrates the issues between the pass-happy Jurgensen, who was among the best pure passers the game has ever seen, and Allen.[23]

During the five-game span at mid-season, the Redskins won just once, lost three and tied once. A similar pattern hurt Allen's first season with the Rams, when Los Angeles and its new coach won four of the first five games before losing four straight. That Rams team rallied to win four of its last five games. In 1971, according to Levy, Allen rallied his troops again.

"George, however, was at his best when his back was against the wall," Levy wrote. "There was no surrender in the man. When he spoke at times like those, the true toughness and tenacity of his spirit became manifest. His coaching skills would become sharpened, and his feelings of care for the people with whom he worked were laid bare. It was when George's teams were rolling along successfully that he became fearful that his charges would let up and in those instances he would cloak the real person he was in a mantle of cute tricks. Eight games into the 1971 season the Redskins were reeling, and George pulled us back together."

The week 13 game in Los Angeles against the Rams was the ABC television network's Monday Night Football offering. George Allen brought his new team to the West Coast to play his old team in a game the Redskins needed to win. It was high drama. Tommy Prothro's Rams were 7-4-1 by then and still had a chance to advance to the postseason. The players left over from the Allen era had something to prove. Before the season started, Rams quarterback Roman Gabriel predicted that Allen might leave Los

Angeles with a football in his mouth after the game. Sportswriter Dave Brady wrote before the game, "Who would have dared … to submit a scenario that would have called for Allen, fired by the Rams, to oppose them for a playoff spot in the 13th game of the season. And to be played out in the Coliseum, where Allen's vindication will be more dramatic."[24]

"It's another Civil War," Allen told *Los Angeles Times* reporter Bob Oates during the week before his return to Los Angeles. "I guess there's never been a time in the NFL when so many good football players were friends one year and enemies the next."[25] Allen was generally complimentary of Prothro, the new Rams coach, during the lead up to the game, but he talked about Prothro's fondness for what Allen called, "gadget" plays. Allen did not like gadget plays.

Petitbon, the safety who played for Allen in Chicago, Los Angeles and Washington, told reporter Bob Oates, "Let's just say we're somewhat more intense this week. … On the [practice] field today it seemed to me the team was more alert."[26]

Talbert, the defensive tackle, said Rams players had to make the playoffs to earn as much as players on other teams and linebacker Pardee said he had told the Rams that he would not play another season for them.

The former Rams were not the only players talking. Gabriel said Allen had called Gabriel after taking over in Washington to say that he, Allen, would try to make a trade to get Gabriel. Gabriel said that he had heard later that Allen had no intention of working a deal to get Gabriel because, Allen supposedly said, Gabriel had too many personal problems. "I felt he was insincere as a person. … He's so tied up in football he's not aware he hurts people sometimes. Like maybe telling two ballplayers both of them would start," Gabriel told the *Washington Post*. But Gabriel also said, "I give him credit. He's the guy that taught me the importance of fundamentals. I've got a great deal of respect for him."[27]

Football is a game played by humans, coached by humans, between teams owned by humans. And those humans each have families. Jennifer Allen wrote that when she sat down in the Coliseum that night, she felt as if she had come home. She was conflicted at the idea of cheering against Roman Gabriel and Deacon Jones, men her father wanted her brothers to emulate and whom she later named her two sons after. The same fans who had cheered her father and his teams for five seasons now held up signs which said "Go home George!"

"On the Redskins' first drive, when the Rams intercepted a Redskins pass, I jumped up and cheered. I had forgotten who we were. We were the Redskins, not the Rams. My mother yanked me down in my seat. 'Are you out of your mind?' she screamed."

The daughter of the Redskins' head coach was not the only person in

12. Ascension

the Coliseum to get confused that night. Linebacker Jack Pardee, who was playing in the game, said the same thing happened to him.

"After the first scrimmage play, I looked up to the Rams bench and I almost forgot which team I was playing for," Pardee said later.

The interception that so confused Jennifer Allen came on a third down with six yards needed for a first down. Kilmer threw to a spot where he thought tight end Jerry Smith would be, but Smith got tangled up with Ken Geddes, a rookie linebacker for the Rams, while running the pattern and Rams defensive back Kermit Alexander caught the ball and raced 82 yards for a touchdown. But Kilmer came back on the next Redskins possession to throw a 69-yard bomb to even the score. The Rams kicked a field goal on their next possession to lead 10–7. Curt Knight booted a 52-yard field goal early in the second quarter to draw the game even. Later in the second period the Rams drove deep into Redskins territory twice and got nothing from the drives. Once they eschewed the field goal and failed to convert on fourth down. On the second opportunity, the Redskins' Ted Vactor blocked an attempted field goal. On the ensuing Redskins possession, Kilmer hit Clifton McNeal for a 32-yard touchdown pass. The Rams fumbled the Redskins' kickoff and Vactor recovered at the Rams' four-yard line. The Redskins punched the ball in on fourth down from inside the Rams' one-yard line to lead 24–10 at the half. Kilmer hit Roy Jefferson on a five-yard out pattern for a touchdown early in the third quarter to make it 31–10. Gabriel hit tight end Bob Klein for a score late in the third quarter. Willie Ellison punched the ball in from the one early in the final quarter to get the Rams within a touchdown at 31–24. In the final minute, Gabriel had a chance to drive the Rams for a tying score but Washington defensive back Speedy Duncan returned an interception for a touchdown to make the score 38–24. For some reason, the Monday Night Football crew of Howard Cosell, Frank Gifford and Don Meredith refused to call Rams defensive end David Jones by his nickname, Deacon. Instead they called Jones "Dave" or "David" Jones. Cosell mentioned the nickname during the broadcast but said the announcers would call him "David" instead without explaining why. Early in the game, when Gabriel had missed his first six passes, Gifford mentioned Gabriel's comment that Allen might leave Los Angeles with a football down his throat, then Gifford said that at that moment, Gabriel probably couldn't hit him.

Jennifer Allen wrote in *Fifth Quarter* that she was saddened after the game as she watched Jones walk off the field. She wrote that three individuals sitting behind her mother and herself were former Rams administrators, Reeves loyalists (she called them Reeves flunkies), and their alcohol-aided cheers quieted when the game ended. Etty Allen, Jennifer wrote, confronted the three after the game. "'Was Dan Reeves your friend?' my mother asked. The three slowly lifted their heads. They looked up at my mother. 'I'm sorry Dan Reeves is dead,' she told them. 'I'm sorry Reeves isn't alive to see this.'"[28] Jennifer Allen added: "'That game was the greatest game of my life,' my mother maintains to this day. To me, that game was the saddest game of my life. That game I learned that loyalty and love and friendship lasted only as long as a coaching contract."[29]

The victory put Washington in the playoffs, despite a 20–13 loss to the Cleveland Browns a week later. The turnaround for the Redskins was less dramatic than the Rams' 1966 season had been. The Redskins had started winning under Lombardi and were closer to success at the beginning of the 1971 season than the Rams had been when Allen started in Los Angeles. Still, the Redskins qualified for the playoffs in Allen's first year in the nation's capital, something the Rams had not done in 1966.

However, when the world spins around it frequently spins things into a complete cycle and waiting for Allen's new team was an old nemesis, John Brodie and the San Francisco 49ers. As his Rams teams had done in their playoff appearances, Allen's Redskins jumped off to a good start, leading 7–0 at the end of the first quarter and 10–3 at halftime. Brodie hit Gene Washington for a 78-yard touchdown in the third quarter to tie the game at 10–10 and the 49ers led 17–13 at the start of the final quarter. San Francisco locked the win away when the 49ers' Bob Hoskins recovered a Redskins fumble in the end zone to make the score 24–13. Kilmer got Washington closer with a 15-yard scoring pass to running back Larry Brown, but the game ended 24–20 and San Francisco advanced. Brodie passed for 176 yards and the two scores, hitting on 10 of 19 passes. Kilmer completed 11 of 27 attempts but gained just 106 yards. He tossed two scoring passes and was intercepted once.

In his 1982 book, *Pro Football's 100 Greatest Players*, written with Ben Olan, George Allen did not rank Brodie among the top 14 quarterbacks of all time, but if the book's title had been, *My Greatest Coaching Headaches*, Brodie might have been the quarterbacking leader. He gave Allen fits when he was under center. Allen mentioned the San Francisco passer in his book. Allen wrote, "John Brodie was another one of the fine pure passers of all time. But John forced the ball a little too much and threw a few too many interceptions. And he never came up with a title."[30]

After the playoff loss, Allen spoke to his players and his voice was thick with emotion. He told them, "We've still got a hell of a lot to be thankful for and, uh, we're all proud of you guys. We made too many mistakes to win but I know damn well that we're gonna have a championship football team next year."[31]

12. Ascension

While it is true that Allen wanted to win immediately, that he believed that the future was immediate, it is also true that the first year of any coach's tenure is a transitional season. The playbook changes, as does the language. Numbering systems are different and the players must adapt to the new coach's way of doing things. The Redskins were playing for their fourth head coach in as many seasons, except those who had been brought over from the Rams. Despite all of that, Washington advanced to the playoffs. They'd lost their playoff game—Allen was 0–3 as a playoff coach at that point—but they'd played well enough to earn a playoff berth and in a city starved for gridiron success, that was big news. Even Lombardi had not produced a playoff season.

The most recent postseason game for the Redskins before Allen became their coach was the 1945 NFL championship game, played on a cold day in Cleveland. In those days, the only playoff game at the end of the season matched the Eastern and Western conference champions in the NFL title game. The Redskins lost that championship game, 15–14, to the Cleveland Rams. During the contest, Sammy Baugh, the immortal Redskins quarterback, threw a pass from his own end zone that hit one of the goalposts. At that time, the goalposts were positioned on the goal line. Under the rules of the day, the play resulted in a safety for the Rams and proved to be the difference maker in the game. The next Washington Redskins quarterback to lead the franchise to the NFL championship game would also throw a goalpost pass.

By making his trades and then coaching his team to the playoffs, Allen might have accomplished something beyond pointing another franchise in the right direction. Vince Lombardi's giant shadow will never be removed from the National Football League but Allen pulled himself out of the shade Lombardi created in Washington by putting his own stamp on the club and then winning immediately. Linebacker Chris Hanburger, who had played through the Redskins' coaching carousel and was one of the really good defensive players the Redskins had when Allen arrived, said in 1978 that Allen impressed him. Sportswriter Bob Oates quoted Hanburger in *The Sporting News*, "There's no comparison between George and the others." Hanburger adds, "His system is the best, his practice program is the best, his training camp is the best. Now, don't quote me as putting down Lombardi. It's a rare privilege to have been coached by him. But George is the best organized coach I've ever been around."[32]

13

Checking the Angle of the Sun
The 1972 Redskins

Ron McDole told interviewer Warren Rogan that the 1972 season with Allen and the Redskins was the most fun season of his long pro football career.[1] He wasn't the only player to feel that way. George Allen's collection of veteran players, his brilliant defensive preparations, his collection of quarterbacks and his devotion to special teams play all came together for a season to remember. The Redskins' defense allowed 15.6 points per game, third best in the league. The offense scored 24 points per game, which was seventh-best in the NFL. Washington posted an 11–3 regular-season record, won two playoff games and advanced to the Super Bowl. The wins in the NFC playoffs were Allen's first playoff wins as a head coach.

Interestingly, the 1972 season presented two opportunities for the thing Allen hated more than anything for his players: Controversies that became distractions, one on the field and one away from it.

Early during his tenure in Los Angeles, Allen traded quarterback Bill Munson after deciding that Roman Gabriel would be the Rams passer, ending a quarterback controversy. But even after a year in Washington, Allen's quarterback situation was still debate fodder. Kilmer was the starter but Jurgensen remained with the team and started four games in 1972. The Redskins won all four games that Jurgensen started. Sam Wyche, a future head coach in the NFL, was the third quarterback that season.

Ted Marchibroda, Allen's top offensive assistant coach, wrote in his post-1971 report that Jurgensen had been a problem during the 1971 training camp and Marchibroda blamed the Redskins' coaching staff for allowing the problem to persist.

"I believe that Jurgensen should have been dealt with more severely in training camp," Marchibroda wrote. "Because of Jurgensen's attitude our QBs did not accomplish as much as they should have in training camp. This problem has been resolved and I know we will accomplish our goals in training camp this season." Marchibroda also wrote, "Jurgensen never will pay the price of winning a championship. His attitude has improved, but not to the extent needed to win." He completed his report with "To win the Super Bowl, we must improve our QB situation. A new QB is our answer."[2]

Marv Levy, the special teams coach who would later coach the Buffalo Bills to four consecutive AFC championships, also touched upon the quarterback situation. Levy wrote about Jurgensen, "We should decide whether we are or are not going to have him be our QB. If the answer is 'yes' we should recognize we're not going to change his life-style or his outlook or his temperament. In this instance we should put our confidence in him and capitalize upon his considerable abilities. If we can't 'live with him' we should make that decision. In any instance we are not going to reform him."[3]

McDole said the quarterback question did not faze the other Redskins players, but the uncertainty over who might be under center left things like the pentameter of the signal cadence and the spin of the ball off the quarterback's hand open to question. Every quarterback calls signals in a distinctive way and each passer's throws feel differently to receivers. Allen's veterans would have to adjust with each change at quarterback.

The other distraction came four games into the regular season.

The Redskins won 11 of their first dozen games in 1972. They beat the Vikings 24–21 in Minnesota in the opener. Kilmer passed for only 57 yards against Minnesota, hitting seven of 17 attempts. He did not throw a touchdown pass and was intercepted once. But Washington rushed for 146 yards on 31 runs, led by Larry Brown's 105 yards on 21 carries. Vikings quarterback Fran Tarkenton hit 18 of 31 passes for 233 yards. Minnesota rushed for 182 yards. But one of Washington's scores came on a Minnesota punt that was blocked by the Redskins and recovered by Washington special teams star Bill Malinchak for a touchdown. The Vikings briefly led 14–10 in the third quarter before the Redskins scored two straight touchdowns and built a lead the Vikings could not overcome.

The Redskins jumped out to a 14–0 lead in the second game, at home against the Cardinals, and went on to win 24–10. Kilmer hit 13 of 22 passes, good for only 97 yards. He threw two scoring passes and was not intercepted. Charley Taylor led Redskins pass catchers, gaining 39 yards on five receptions. Tight end Jerry Smith caught both of Kilmer's scoring passes and Larry Brown rambled for 148 yards on 26 attempts. St. Louis' running game gained only 79 yards. Hanburger and Rosey Taylor each had an interception for the Redskins.

Washington lost the week three game on the road against the New England Patriots, an oddball contest where the statistics looked as if the Redskins won. Washington led 14–0 early and the special teams managed to block another punt. Kilmer tossed three scoring passes and Brown rushed for more than a hundred yards. And yet the Redskins lost. New England quarterback Jim Plunkett hit 17 of 33 passes for 255 yards and two scores and Patriot runners gained 127 yards. Late in the game Bill Malinchak blocked a punt for Washington. The Redskins were unable to recover the ball in the end zone and got a safety when the ball went out of the end zone. Had Washington recovered the ball before it went out of bounds, the Redskins would have scored a touchdown and could have won the game.

Next, Jurgensen started against the Eagles and passed for 237 yards. But he threw three interceptions compared to one touchdown pass. Jerry Smith led Washington receivers with six receptions for 58 yards. The Redskins' defense held the Eagles to 236 total yards and Hanburger had another interception. Washington won 14–0.

Hanburger was one of the linebackers Allen ranked among his all-time best in his book *Pro Football's 100 Greatest Players: Rating the Stars of the Past and Present*. Allen wrote, "Chris was a little light for a linebacker. He's another who didn't fit the mold. He was seldom knocked off his feet. He had real good balance and excellent agility. But quickness was his biggest asset. He could really rush the passer and he covered a lot of ground on pass defense. Chris was as important to my Redskins as anyone. He was smart. I think that's a quality all of the great linebackers have, because a player has so much freedom at the position and has to know what he's doing out there or he won't get the job done. ... He played the right side as skillfully as almost anyone I ever saw. I think the right side is the correct place for the lighter linebacker to be, and Chris certainly was the right man for the job."[4]

On October 10, 1972, between the games against the Eagles and Cardinals, George Allen and the Redskins issued a new set of rules for reporters covering Redskins' practices. For a man who disapproved of anything that could be distracting for his players and coaches, Allen had created a huge distraction. The new rules, as reported by *The Evening Star* and *The Washington News*, were "(1) The press will be free, as in the past, to meet at any time after practice hours with Redskins' coaches and players. Such meetings should be arranged through the Redskins publicity department. (2) The press is welcome to attend Redskins practice sessions on Tuesday, Wednesday and Saturday. Thursday and Friday practices will be closed to everyone but Redskins personnel. (3) On Mondays at 2 p.m., Coach Allen will meet with the press and, either at that time or on Tuesday or Wednesday, OFF THE RECORD, will detail any possible changes in personnel or tactics that he may initiate for the next game."[5]

You want to talk about a distraction, a controversy? There is no better way to create either in a media-rich town like Washington than to slap limits on what reporters can do. Allen tried to do exactly that. Did Allen's somewhat distant friendship with Richard Nixon impact his decision to attempt to limit media access to his players? Possibly. One thing was for certain and that was that the Washington newspapers were universally critical of what some called Allen's manifesto.

Columnist Tom Dowling wrote that Allen's "regime," lacked a sense of proportion and then Dowling lost his own sense of proportion by writing of the delayed release requirement, "This is like getting a Vietnam peace settlement briefing from Henry Kissinger under the condition that you can't use it until the war is over." Dowling added,

> For my part, I see no threat to the First Amendment in Allen's current tomfoolery, nor do I claim the public's right to know in regard to the Redskins. In all probability the public interest would be better served by hearing as little as possible about George Allen. For that matter too much is written about the Redskins themselves during the week. The Redskins are a small-bore private business and they have every right to hold fatuous "OFF THE RECORD" news conferences whenever the mood strikes them. But, they are fundamentally a business that thrives on public exposure. As such they depend on free media coverage to whip up fan fervor for the big Sunday game, just as department stores depend on paid media advertisements to generate consumer excitement for the big bargain sale. In that sense, the prospect of George Allen demanding free news coverage on his own bombastic terms strains my sense of proportion to the breaking point. He conceives of the trifling personnel shifts at Redskin Park as life and death propositions and is apparently doomed to persist huffily in this charade.[6]

The National Football League told the media the following day that it had been in contact with the Redskins over the matter. Allen never mended fences with Washington reporters.

The following weekend, Jurgensen started at quarterback and the Redskins plastered the Cardinals 33–3 in St. Louis. Jurgensen hit 13 of 18 passes for 203 yards. He did not throw a scoring pass but was intercepted once. The Redskin defense allowed just 151 total yards and intercepted the St. Louis quarterbacks twice. Mike Bass and Pat Fischer had the interceptions as Washington improved to 4–1.

Fischer was another of the players Allen ranked among his 100 all-time best. Allen wrote, "One of the most amazing athletes I've ever seen was Pat Fischer. He was short, but he could really leap.... Pat was a tough cookie. He was a real bump-and-run guy. ... I was happy to have him, I'll tell you that."[7]

Riding high, the Redskins next hosted the Dallas Cowboys at RFK. It was the first of three meetings between the two teams that season and the rivalry was becoming must-see television. Dallas coach Tom Landry used innovative offenses and defenses, built around great players, to develop a consistently winning franchise. While Allen was with the Redskins, the Cowboys had the other strong presence in the NFC East and their meetings produced drama. Division titles and playoff berths were frequently on the line. In fact, their final meeting in 1972 determined the NFC representative in the Super Bowl.

Jurgensen threw a touchdown pass and hit on 11 of 16 passes for 180 yards in the first game against the Cowboys. He did not throw an interception. Larry Brown rushed for 95 yards on 26 carries and caught seven passes for 100 yards. Brown scored twice, once running and once receiving. Fischer and Speedy Duncan intercepted Dallas quarterback Craig Morton twice as Dallas was limited to 174 yards and Washington won 24–20. The Cowboys jumped out to a 13–0 lead and led 20–7 in the third quarter before the Redskins rallied and scored 17 unanswered points. The victory pushed the Redskins to the division lead with a record of 5–1. Dallas slipped to 4–2.

Duncan's story is typical of the veterans Allen attracted during his NFL career. A three-time AFL All-Star during his years with the San Diego Chargers, Duncan also played in the AFL-NFL Pro Bowl as a Redskin in 1971. Undrafted out of Jackson State, Duncan intercepted 24 passes and returned three for touchdowns during his career in the AFL. Allen acquired Duncan for the 1971 season and the cornerback played his final four seasons in Washington. He intercepted three passes as a Redskin. But Duncan was best known as a return man and that was his primary role under Allen. He averaged 8.6 yards as a punt returner and 25.3 yards returning kickoffs. During his stint with the Redskins, Duncan fumbled a few kick catches. Though he played on a team with a head coach devoted to special teams play, it wasn't Allen or an assistant coach who cured the bad habit. Duncan said later that his wife noticed that Duncan shifted his feet just as he was about to catch kicks or punts. Duncan stopped shifting his feet as he waited for the ball and he stopped dropping punts. Between the 1971 and 1972 seasons, special teams coach Marv Levy evaluated Duncan this way: "Provided outstanding leadership. Did a superb job on punt returns, particularly after our first three or four games. A good coverage man and as an end on kickoff coverage and punt coverage his years of experience helped him perform very well. ... Lack of size and strength would make it necessary for us to concentrate on sideline returns if he is to be our main return man."

13. Checking the Angle of the Sun

Duncan split the return duties for both punts and kickoffs with Ted Vactor and Alvin Haymond in 1972.

On October 29, 1972, something bad happened to the Redskins. Jurgensen, who was 38, started against the Giants at Yankee Stadium. He completed his first pass but, without getting hit, injured his left Achilles tendon. Jurgensen had seemingly reclaimed the starting position and was playing on a team with a tremendous defense for the first time in his tenure in Washington but, in players' parlance, Jurgensen blew out his Achilles without getting hit and was lost for the remainder of the season. Kilmer stepped in and led Washington to a 23–16 victory over the Giants. Kilmer connected on eight of 16 for 114 yards and two scores. The Giants intercepted Kilmer once and out-gained Washington 258–127, but the Redskins did enough to win and improved to 6–1.

Kilmer told the *Washington Post*, "I'm really sorry about Sonny. I know he is very disappointed and so am I. I didn't want to win the job back like this. But I have to be ready. It's just like last year."[8]

Over the next five games the Redskins outscored their opponents 130–66. Washington did not score less than 21 points over that span and did not allow more than 17. Kilmer was efficient, completing 58 of 94 attempts for 900 yards and nine touchdowns. He was intercepted three times during those games. In an odd piece of scheduling, the Redskins played the New York teams for three consecutive weeks, beating the Giants twice and the Jets once. In the Jets game, Kilmer out-dueled future Hall of Fame passer Joe Namath. Namath threw for 148 yards and a touchdown but the Redskins defense intercepted Namath three times. Kilmer hit seven out of 16 attempts for three scoring passes, 222 yards and one interception.

The Redskins were rolling at 11–1 as they headed for a rematch with the Cowboys in Dallas. The Cowboys went into the game needing to win with a record of 9–3. At this stage of his career, Allen had had success against the Cowboys. Allen's Rams beat Dallas in their two regular-season meetings and Allen's Redskins split with the Cowboys in their two meetings in 1971. Add in the first meeting between the teams in 1972 and Allen was 4–1 overall against Tom Landry's team as they kicked off for the second time in 1972.

Dallas jumped out to a 21–0 lead and eventually won, 34–24. Dallas quarterback Craig Morton threw 17 passes and completed only seven. But one of Morton's salty completions was a touchdown pass and he was not intercepted. Kilmer hit on 14 of 29 attempts and had three scoring passes. But Dallas intercepted Kilmer twice that day and the Cowboys' defense also limited Washington to 143 rushing yards on 39 attempts. Conversely, Dallas backs Walt Garrison and Calvin Hill both had more than a hundred yards on the ground. The Cowboys improved to 10–3, while Washington fell to 11–2.

The final game of the regular season was forgettable, a 24–17 loss to McDole's former team, the Bills. The Redskins had already clinched their playoff berth but they dropped their final two regular season games. The same thing happened to Allen's 1969 Rams, except the Rams lost their final three games that year.

The 10–5 Green Bay Packers, revived under head coach Dan Devine, traveled to Washington for a Christmas Eve playoff game. The temperature at kickoff was 38 degrees and the humidity was 98 percent. Neither team passed the ball much. Green Bay quarterback Scott Hunter had better numbers than Kilmer did, completing 12 of 24 throws for 150 yards. But Hunter was intercepted by Hanburger and did not have a scoring pass. The Packers scored first on a field goal but did not get on the scoreboard again and the Redskins won 16–3. Larry Brown rushed for 101 yards on 25 carries and Curt Knight kicked three field goals to lead Washington's offense.

Between the 1971 and 1972 seasons, Allen's assistant coaches reviewed the Redskins and Knight got special notice from special teams coach Marv Levy. Knight was perfect on his 27 touchdown conversion kicks and successful on 29 of 49 field goal attempts in 1971, nailing two of three from beyond 50 yards. But Knight was successful on just three of 11 between 40 and 49 yards and was spotty from other distances at times.

Levy wrote in his 1971 review, "I feel Curt Knight will kick much better if we do not try to coach him so far as technique is concerned. There are things he can work on in the off-season and this should constitute the major part of his technique work. Other than that we should film him frequently and limit our technique discussions to the times when we review the film. We should allow him to be at ease mentally on the practice field and thereby develop rhythm and confidence."

Knight handled the placekicking duties in 1972 and it was one of the few times that Allen's faith in a veteran special teams player was not rewarded. Knight was successful on 14 of 30 field goal attempts in 1972, although he hit 40 of 41 conversion kicks and was perfect on field goal tries from within 20 yards.[9]

In the locker room after the victory over Green Bay, Allen told his players, "Great win. We beat them at their own game; we out-hit them. Now we bring on those God Damned Cowboys next."[10]

It was the first playoff game Allen ever coached on his home field. On New Year's Eve, Washington hosted Dallas as they played for the right to represent the NFC in the Super Bowl. The temperature at kickoff was 49 degrees. After a scoreless opening quarter, Knight hit on an 18-yard field goal and then Kilmer connected with Charley Taylor on a 15-yard

13. Checking the Angle of the Sun 131

touchdown pass. Dallas scored a field goal before the end of the half but the Redskins led 10–3. The third period was scoreless, but Kilmer and Taylor burned the Cowboys for a 45-yard scoring pass early in the final quarter and Knight added field goals of 39, 46 and 45 yards. The Redskins advanced to the Super Bowl with a thoroughly convincing 26–3 victory over the Cowboys.

Kilmer was very efficient against Dallas, completing 14 of 18 passes for 194 yards and the two touchdowns. He was not intercepted and the Redskins offensive line did not allow Kilmer to be sacked. Charley Taylor finished with seven receptions for 146 yards and halfback Larry Brown rushed for 88 yards on 30 carries.

Roger Staubach, who had not played in the previous Redskins games that season, went the distance at quarterback for Dallas and Staubach struggled. He completed just nine of 20 passes. He did not throw a touchdown pass and was not intercepted but Staubach had not by then refined the skills that made him a superb postseason quarterback. His passing gained Dallas 98 yards and he ran five times for 59 yards. Staubach was by far the leading rusher for the Cowboys that day. Washington's defense was so good against the Dallas running attack that Roger the Dodger gained more rushing yards than all of Dallas' other runners combined.

In *100 Greatest Players*, Allen ranked Staubach seventh among the best quarterbacks of all-time. Allen wrote, "Roger Staubach was the best passer-runner I ever coached against. He was a better runner than Terry Bradshaw and Fran Tarkenton. Roger was a great passer, but when he saw the place to run, he could really run. He ran straight ahead to daylight. ... Staubach was the key player who led [the Cowboys] to championships. They used a balanced attack, but he threw all the passes superbly. He was also the most difficult quarterback to intercept I ever coached against, and the best third-down quarterback I ever saw. At third and four or five, he came through consistently."[11]

In *100 Greatest Players*, Allen wrote that his Redskins beat Dallas more often than not, but that was inaccurate. While he was with the Redskins, Allen was 7–8 against Landry's Cowboys. In games during which Staubach appeared, Allen's Redskins were 6–7. Allen's Rams went 3–1 against Dallas (including the January 3, 1970, Bert Bell Benefit Bowl, the meaningless game between first-round playoff losers, which was better-known as the Playoff Bowl). Allen's teams played Dallas twice in the postseason, one a playoff game and once in the Playoff Bowl, and Allen won both of those games. Thus, Allen was 10–9 against Dallas overall. From 1966 through 1977, the years Allen was a head coach in the NFL, his teams compiled a tremendous 116–47–5 record. Dallas, under Landry, went 124–42–2 in the regular season during same period. Landry's Cowboys won two Super

Bowls and lost two in those years. Allen had to kick-start two franchises in that time and coached the Redskins to a Super Bowl appearance. Landry was the original Cowboys coach and was part of a strong organization that built the franchise into a winner after its birth in 1960. If they were different in their approach, the two coaches had one thing in common and that was that they coached winners.

And after winning the National Football Conference title that night, George Allen had another game ball. Center Len Hauss loudly told his teammates after the game, "Listen up, gang: Here's a ball for a guy that works real, real hard and he's been in a lot of these games before, but it took a lot of cast-offs, a bunch of Redskins and a helluva great group of guys to get him his second one."

Jennifer Allen wrote of the moments after the victory: "Redskins fans stormed the field. Fans bent the goalpost down onto the end-zone turf. They tore up bits of souvenir turf. My father was lifted high above all fans, transported like a king, on the shoulders of two mammoth Redskins. He was riding high, waving to all the fans who reached up to touch the man who had made Washington a winner for the first time in thirty years. His Redskins cap was ripped off his head. The Redskins band played 'Amazing Grace.'" Fans chanted, "Amen, amen, amen." How crazy was the mood? Jennifer Allen later wrote about someone asking for her autograph on a souvenir program. The autograph seeker asked Jennifer to sign it "George Allen's daughter," and she did so.[12]

Allen, Levy recounted, planned a New Year's Eve celebration for the coaches. Politicians of every stripe, cabinet members, news reporters and other members of the nation's elite showed up. The head coach led the gang in singing "Hail to the Redskins" and later led a conga line as it danced around the room. Those moments, surrounded by his coaches and the nation's power elite, would be memorable for a man who grew potatoes in the family basement to help his family eat as a youth and whose failing car wash put an exclamation point on his first foray into professional football.

Professionally speaking, it would be hard to find a more satisfying point in time for anyone. Allen had been *out of the game* in the late 1950s before his chance came along to help George Halas and the Chicago Bears. Allen, whose college players jokingly referred to as The Green Arrow, had been forced to fight his way to his first head coaching opportunity in professional football—by divorcing the Bears—and built the Los Angeles Rams into a winner. Then came two emotional firings by those same Rams with whom he was never able to win in the postseason. Now, not only had Allen finally won a playoff game, but he had also won two straight and coached the Washington Redskins, a team he had rebuilt with bold strokes in less than 24 months, within reach of a world championship. It was a

13. Checking the Angle of the Sun

heady night for Allen. He'd insisted on doing it all his way and was then within one game of the top of his profession's pyramid.

The 1972 Miami Dolphins team is considered by some observers to be the best NFL team of the modern era. The Dolphins were undefeated heading into their Super Bowl meeting with the Redskins. Their offense led the league in scoring that season with a 27.5 points per game average. Likewise, their defense, the so-called No-Name Defense, also topped the league by allowing only 12.2 points per game. For comparison, Allen's Redskins were third in scoring at 24 points per game and the defense was the third-most effective in the NFL, allowing 15.6 points per game.

"They played very well and they had great players," Ron McDole said. "There wasn't a weak spot on that team."[13]

The Dolphins' offense was led by a three-headed rushing monster made up of bruising fullback Larry Csonka, plus halfbacks Mercury Morris and Jim Kiick. Csonka and Morris had each rushed for a thousand yards or more during the regular season. The Dolphins rushing game was aided by the man who might have the distinction of being the most under-rated member of the Pro Football Hall of Fame, wide receiver Paul Warfield. Warfield caught 20 passes that season, gaining 606 yards for an average of 20.8 yards per reception. Warfield's mere presence on the field forced opposing defenses to stage their defensive backfield in such a way to respect the possibility of a deep pass, making it harder for their cornerbacks and safeties to crowd the line of scrimmage and stop the runners. Warfield had come into the league as a Cleveland Brown and initially performed the same service for immortal running back Jim Brown.

Allen rated Warfield seventh on his list of receivers in his *Pro Football's 100* book. Allen wrote, "Warfield was great. He was outstanding with both Cleveland and Miami. With Washington, I had to coach against him in a Super Bowl game. We double-teamed and triple-teamed him. And we contained him. But at a cost. Containing him made it a close game for us against a superior team, but loosened our defense just enough for the Dolphins to defeat us. He had sprinter's speed, good hands, super running ability. And boy, could he block! Some people may not remember that about him, but I do. The receivers who didn't block never got good grades from me. In my book, Warfield was strictly A-plus."

Miami's starting quarterback, Bob Griese, suffered a broken ankle in their week 5 game against the Chargers. Earl Morrall directed the offense while Griese was recovering from the injury. Griese played briefly in the Dolphins' final regular season game and then came off the bench to spark Miami's offense in the AFC championship game against the Steelers.

In the AFC title game, which was played in Pittsburgh due to the rules of the era, the Steelers broke a halftime tie by capping their first possession of the second half with a field goal that gave them a 10–7 lead. Morrall had not been especially effective in the first half, throwing both a touchdown pass and an interception. Miami coach Don Shula inserted Griese into the game on the following Miami possession and Griese directed two scoring drives. Miami won the game 21–17.[14]

"That was a great team," McDole said. "Our biggest problem was that we didn't know who was going to start the game, Earl Morrall or Griese. At that time Griese was banged up. So we trained for both of them, which we'd do anyway. We knew it would be a tough game."[15]

Allen spent the two weeks planning, coaching and warning the Redskins about the distractions. It was Allen's first Super Bowl, but he had coached and lived in the Los Angeles area for parts of two decades. Kilmer played his college ball in Los Angeles and all the former Rams knew the city as well. They might have even looked forward to some of the distractions Allen warned them about. One distraction came about at the Redskins' practice facility before the club ever left Washington: Richard Nixon, the President of the United States and a football fan, visited the team during a practice and even suggested a play for Allen's offense to try.

According to Levy, Allen told his coaches during a planning session that he, Allen, would cut off his right arm to win the Super Bowl. He kept saying so, offering to cut his arm shorter and shorter before finally saying, "In fact, I'd cut off my testicles to win this game!" Levy wrote that Dowler, who had already won two Super Bowls and five NFL championships with the Packers, all the while retaining his various body parts, told Levy, "Marvin, *maybe* my right arm."[16]

Much has been made of the fact that George Allen sent representatives to the site of the game, the same Los Angeles Memorial Olympic Coliseum where Allen had coached the Los Angeles Rams for five seasons, to check the position of the sun at the scheduled kickoff time and through the time the game would be contested. The pregame coin flip would determine which team would receive the opening kickoff and which direction the teams would face during each quarter. The sun's position at game time would determine which direction Allen would want his team to face at the start of the game but Allen probably should have known where the sun would be during the game after his five seasons as the head coach (not to mention his season as Gillman's assistant in 1957). It is true that he had not coached the Rams in the LAMOC in a January game, but he did coach the Western Conference team in the NFL Pro Bowl all-star game twice while still with the Rams. Super Bowl VII as played on January 14, 1973. Allen's Pro Bowl coaching assignments were on January 22, 1967 (he lost to Landry's East team, 20–10) and January 19, 1969 (the West beat Landry's East squad, 10–7). Allen should have been aware of the sun's path over the

13. Checking the Angle of the Sun

ballpark. Allen's Redskins were officially the visitors and one of his team captains could choose "heads" or "tails" immediately before the coin was flipped by a referee.

Everybody knew Kilmer would start for Allen's Redskins. Jurgensen was still recovering from his injury. Years later, Jurgensen sounded bitter about the way Allen treated him at the Super Bowl. "He didn't want me to be a part of it," Jurgensen said during the same NFL Films interview cited in the previous chapter. "I was sitting in a box for twelve people alone. He wouldn't let me talk to the coaches so I could help Billy. It was sad. I was down on the field before the game. I'll never forget Don Shula walked over and said, 'I know how hard you worked to be in this game,' and he said, 'It would be a better game with you in it. I'm so sorry for you.'"[17]

Griese started for Miami and went the distance against Washington. He completed eight of 11 passes for 88 yards and a touchdown. He was intercepted once. Still, the best-remembered attempt at throwing a pass from Super Bowl VII was not performed by Griese or even Billy Kilmer. It was one of the zaniest plays in NFL championship game history and it was brought about by George Allen's dedication to special teams play.

But more on that later.

Miami's defense, as referenced above, was tagged with the No Name Defense moniker, but middle linebacker Nick Buoniconti was inducted into the Pro Football Hall of Fame in 2001 and Allen included safety Jake Scott on his list of defensive backs in *Pro Football's 100*. Allen wrote that Scott "was another big-play, big-game guy who produced under pressure, a key man on one of the great teams of all time, the Miami Dolphins of the early 1970s. ... Jake lacked speed but he made up for it by playing smart. He read keys extremely well, anticipated developments, and always was in position to make the play he had to make." Years later, Allen brought Scott to the Redskins for three seasons. Buoniconti intercepted Kilmer once during the Super Bowl and Scott picked off a pair.

The Dolphins' offense had five future Hall of Famers that year: Griese, Csonka, Warfield and linemen Jim Langer and Larry Little.

Super Bowl VII was a defensive classic. The teams combined to produce 481 yards total offense and most of those yards came from rushing plays. The teams combined for 21 points but only 14 of those points were scored by an offensive team because one touchdown was scored on a special teams play. Both defenses intercepted passes in the end zone.

Miami scored first and seemed to be in control for most of the game. Yet, on the game's final play, Washington was one big play away from knotting the score and forcing overtime.

The game started at 3:50 p.m., the temperature was 64 degrees at kickoff and there was very little wind. Miami won the coin toss and elected to receive.

A special teams play seemed to give Washington a chance to score first when a muffed center snap on a Miami punt was recovered by the Redskins deep in Miami territory. But Washington was penalized for interfering with the Miami center's snap of the ball and, after a five-yard walk off, Miami punted again, this time without incident.

"Their center winds up [when he snaps on punts] and Harold [McLinton] slapped the ball," Allen explained later.[18] Levy, the kicking coach, had detected that Miami long snapper Howard Kindig had an unusual snapping motion. "I found that, in order to generate momentum, he lifted the ball off the ground for a fraction of a second before he sent it speeding back to the punter. Two of our players, Jimmie Jones and Hal McLinton, devised a technique for flicking the ball just as Kindig was about to release it. Every day for the two weeks leading up to the Super Bowl, Jimmie and Hal remained out on the field with me for 30 minutes after our regular practice session had ended in order to sharpen their ability to execute this technique. By game day they had mastered it." Levy continued, "Kindig lined up as their long snapper, and as he lifted the ball and hesitated for that split second, Jimmie got a piece of it just as it was being delivered. The ball dribbled back ... and one of our players fell on it at the Dolphins' 26-yard line."

The Redskins were penalized for interfering with the snap and the Redskins argued that the Washington defensive front had not moved until Kindig started his snapping motion. The defense, Washington's coaches said, was entitled to charge into the neutral zone between the opposing lines once the snapping motion started. The officials ruled otherwise and the penalty yardage allowed Miami's offense to get back to work. Skipping over the question of whether Kindig's mid-motion hesitation was a legitimate target or not, an outstanding piece of scouting and two weeks' worth of practice had been flushed down the drain.

Later in the first quarter, the Dolphins drove 68 yards on six plays and scored on a 28-yard pass from Griese to Howard Twilley.

In the second quarter, the Redskins got lucky when a 47-yard bomb from Griese to a wide-open Paul Warfield was nullified by an illegal procedure call against Miami. Late in the second quarter, Kilmer got Washington's offense moving and the Redskins crossed midfield. Kilmer, under pressure, had to throw as he was backing up and was intercepted by Nick Buoniconti. Worse, the Dolphins linebacker returned the ball 32 yards to set Griese up at the Washington 27 with a minute and 51 seconds remaining in the half. Kiick scored from a yard out with 18 seconds remaining in the half and the tone of the game was permanently changed. The turnover put the Redskins behind by two scores.

13. Checking the Angle of the Sun

Kilmer told reporters after the game, "The big play in the first half was Buoniconti's interception. That set them up for a 14–0 lead and then we had to start doing things differently. On that play, they [rushed] their strong side linebacker and I didn't have anybody to pick him up. I tried to get it to Larry Brown, but Buoniconti played it well."[19]

Then, in the third quarter, Washington's offense started moving the ball consistently. On their initial possession of the third quarter, the Redskins drove from their own 30 to the Miami 17. Kilmer's pass to Charlie Harraway at the goal line was inches too long, falling incomplete on second down and Kilmer was sacked at the 25 by Manny Fernandez on third down. The drive stalled and, worse, Curt Knight missed a 32-yard field goal, wide right.

Washington drove even deeper into Miami territory in the final quarter, reaching the Miami 10. On a second down and six play, Kilmer threw toward tight end Jerry Smith who was running open across the back of the end zone. Kilmer's pass hit a goalpost upright and fell incomplete. It was an amazing twist of fate that Kilmer's pass should strike the goalpost apparatus. As mentioned in a previous chapter, 27 years earlier, in the 1945 NFL title game, Washington quarterback Sammy Baugh's pass struck a goalpost and the play was among the most pivotal of the game, which Washington lost to the Cleveland Rams, 15–14. Kilmer's pass was incomplete, but the worst was yet to come. On third down, Kilmer was intercepted in the end zone by Jake Scott, who returned the ball to the Washington 48.

With just 5:08 remaining in the game, Miami seemed to have everything in hand. The Dolphins had a two-touchdown advantage and possession of the ball, in good field position, with one of best clock-draining running attacks in the history of the sport. It all seemed predictable as Griese and the rest of the Miami offense trotted onto the field. Then again, football is played with an oblong spheroid that can take funny bounces.

The Dolphins drove to the Washington 34-yard line and lined up to attempt a field goal with 2:38 remaining. Miami's kicker, Garo Yepremian, successfully booted 24 of his 37 field goal attempts in 1972. He was good on 17 of his 18 attempts from 39 yards and closer but his ratio of success dipped once he got beyond the 40-yard mark. He was good on just four of 11 between 40 and 49 yards. But Yepremian had scored on three of his eight tried from beyond 50 yards, so the 42-yarder in the final minutes of the Super Bowl was solidly within his capability. Passing the ball, on the other hand, was not.

"We worked on a blocked kick, which was about the only thing we did [right]," McDole told the author in 2019. "Marv Levy was our special teams coach. He studied the films all the time. I took a look at them. We did a lot of that kind of stuff because we had a coach to look at it. A lot of us would work on different things that we could do and he'd come up with how we could run a stunt."[20]

Bill Brundige broke through the middle of the Miami line and blocked Yepremian's kick. Ted Vactor charged in from the defensive left side and very nearly blocked the kick, but it was Brundige who blocked it. After that, things got a little crazy. The oblong spheroid bounced back and toward the defensive left where Yepremian, a five-foot, eight-inch native of Cyprus, scooped the ball up and tried to throw it as he ran. The ball fell off Yepremian's "throwing" hand and rolled down his chest, whereupon Yepremian batted the ball back up into the air. The ball was plucked out of flight by Washington's Mike Bass. Bass raced past Yepremian and down the left sideline for a 49-yard touchdown.

Curt Gowdy, the veteran NBC play-by-play announcer said, "What a kooky play that was."[21]

It was the only scoring play for the Redskins that day and, in a final twist of irony, Bass scored his touchdown in the same end zone where Bernie Casey caught Roman Gabriel's scoring pass in 1967 when Allen's Rams blocked the Green Bay Packers punt in the final minute to save the day.

"My mind went blank," Yepremian said later. "I just picked up the ball and thought I could throw it to somebody. I saw two teammates who were open, two white jerseys. But the ball—when I tried to throw—just slipped out of my hand. ... I was so scared. Scared maybe I could've lost the game. I should have just fallen on the ball. I should have ate it, but I made a mistake. Coach [Don] Shula told me the same thing when I got to the sideline. He told me, 'Next time, just fall on it.' Here we are ... we win 16 games in a row. And then if we had lost on that play of mine, some people would've said we were a fluke team. ... I know one thing. I won't ever try that again."[22]

Yepremian also said that he and Bass talked on the field after the game. The Miami kicker recounted, "He came over and said, 'What were you trying to do, tackle me? You know better than that.' I laughed and told him, 'You just ruined my big break.' Really, we're good friends—we were teammates at Detroit."

Jim Murray, the legendary sports columnist for the *Los Angeles Times*, wrote, "I don't know whether it was supposed to be a down-and-out, a post pattern or who the primary receiver was or whether Garo was bucking to be the backup quarterback next year, but this was the poorest forward pass ever seen in a Super Bowl. Even for an Armenian tie salesman from Cyprus, it was poor."[23]

Allen faced a difficult decision immediately after the touchdown:

13. Checking the Angle of the Sun 139

Whether to try an onside kick, hoping to get the ball immediately, or to kickoff deep and try to stop Miami's offense from getting a first down.

Allen elected to kick deep and said later, "There was too much time left [two minutes, seven seconds] to try an onside kick. You just try to kick deep, hold them, and maybe block the punt."[24]

Miami got one first down before it had to punt. Washington used all of its timeouts to stop the clock while the Dolphins had the ball and Allen's team got the ball back with 1:14 remaining. If ever a gunslinger like Jurgensen was needed, that would have been the time. But with Jurgensen injured it was Kilmer who had to go miracle hunting and it was not to be. Kilmer threw three incomplete passes and then was sacked, ending the game.

Miami used two defensive fronts during the season, a 4–3 look with four down linemen and three linebackers and a 5–3 front with five down linemen. Allen admitted the 5–3 front stopped Washington's running game better than he expected.

"Our problem was running," Allen said after the game. "We thought we could run, but couldn't. Miami used a controlled charge to stop our running. We had planned to throw some at [Miami defensive back Lloyd] Mumphord, but we had to run first to do it."

In the locker room after the game, Allen told his players that the Redskins would return to the Super Bowl. Jennifer Allen wrote that a few days after losing the Super Bowl her father visited Jack Kent Cooke, the owner of the Los Angeles Lakers and a part owner of the Redskins. Cooke had played a major role in Allen coming to Washington and Allen apparently had it on his mind to thank Cooke for the owners' faith in the coach. Jennifer tagged along with her father as he visited Cooke in the Inglewood Forum. She recalled the conversation this way:

"I just wanted to thank you, Jack," he told Cooke.
Cooke took a sip of his drink, swallowed slowly and said in a gravelly voice, "George, dear," He cleared his throat. Took another sip, and said, "Dear George, don't be ashamed of a thing. Be proud of what you have done."
My father had his head down. He looked as if he was studying the pattern in the carpet.
Then he lifted his head and said, "Let me just say one thing: we will be back."[25]

George Allen would never again coach a team to victory in a National Football League playoff game.

The Montreal Alouettes of the Canadian Football League hired Levy to be their head coach shortly after the Super Bowl. Levy would coach the Als to CFL titles in 1974 and 1977. Levy returned to the NFL as coach of the

Kansas City Chiefs for five seasons and then a dozen more as the boss man of the Buffalo Bills. Under Levy, the Bills famously reached four straight Super Bowls, only to lose them all. But Levy won two titles in Canada and then built two NFL franchises into winners. Very few men can say they coached NFL teams to four Super Bowl appearances. Levy was eventually inducted into the Pro Football Hall of Fame.

Levy wrote of Allen, "My hectic three years working for George ... [had] at times been sheer hell, but there had been other times when the ecstasy of victory made it all worthwhile. I hadn't slept for more than five hours a night during those three years. When you work for George, you don't live longer; it just seems longer. ... If my observations indicate that George had some quirks, I am sure that some other person can point out many of mine as well. George's attributes and his human qualities far outweighed his idiosyncrasies. He cared about the individuals who worked for him and who played for him. George was instrumental in helping many of his former assistants get head coaching positions. ... An association with George taught a person how to win and how to derive great joy from the preparation for winning. ... Someone once said to me that George was a genius. He wasn't. He just worked hard and had an indomitable spirit."[26]

14

Chasing the Cowboys
The 1973 Redskins

It is common for Super Bowl participants to struggle the following season. The phenomenon is sometimes called the "Super Bowl hangover." The Redskins did not exactly struggle in 1973, advancing to the playoffs, but they did not return to the championship game either.

Washington had used its top pick in the 1973 draft to acquire wide receiver Roy Jefferson. The draft choice eventually went to the San Diego Chargers. The most notable addition to the Redskins Roster for 1973 was troubled running back Duane Thomas. Thomas was a rookie with the Cowboys in 1970 and an important part of Dallas' offense. But a contract dispute with Dallas resulted in a trade, sending Thomas to New England. Thomas clashed with the Patriots so badly that the league office eventually voided the transaction, sending Thomas back to Dallas before the start of the 1971 season. Thomas put up good numbers again in 1971 and was an important part of Dallas winning the Super Bowl that season. So important was Thomas that Dallas traded him again, this time to the San Diego Chargers, before the 1972 season. Thomas didn't report to the Chargers, who eventually placed him on the injured list, making him ineligible to play in 1972.

Allen gave up two draft picks to get Thomas. Thomas had developed a reputation for moodiness and talent. He did not start a game for Washington in 1973, but he played in 13. Thomas rushed for 95 yards on 32 carries and caught five passes for 40 yards that year. He did not score a touchdown. He did not like talking to the media, a feeling he shared with George Allen. Columnist Shirley Povich wrote that Thomas' refusal to speak with Redskins beat writers during training camp might have pleased Allen. Povich wrote, "It has always been Allen's compliment to himself he can handle these great big problem children whose need for kindness and affection goes unrecognized by those other, mill-run coaches. Allen immediately lined up on Thomas' side at Carlisle, Pa. [site of training camp that summer], sheltering him from the questioning of football writers eager to interview the newest Redskin."[1]

Povich quoted Allen in the same column, "You don't understand our problem. ... The thing is to get him oriented. He's just made a big move, and you guys are worrying about where to put the dishes when you don't even have the beds in yet."

Thomas did not speak to writers at his previous stops in the NFL, although he did have a great one-liner prior to playing in the Super Bowl. "If this is the ultimate game," Thomas asked, "how come they're playing another one next year?" Povich compared Thomas' silence in the Redskins' training camp with that of the Great Sphinx of Giza, although the writer admitted the Sphinx had better than 4,800 years of practice by the time Thomas took the vow of silence.

Winning the NFC championship had its downside. Allen's assistant coaches and other members of the Redskins organization were popular candidates for coaching positions with other teams. Joe Sullivan, whom Levy wrote was very important to Allen's success, left Washington for a front office position with the Cardinals. Offensive line coach Mike McCormack became the head coach in Philadelphia. Charley Winner, who coached Allen's defensive backfield, became the head coach of the Jets and Levy went home to his native Canada to coach Montreal. Of the three assistants who became head coaches that season, Levy was the most successful. He coached the Alouettes to three Grey Cup appearances, winning twice.[2] Boyd Dowler, who coached Washington's wide receivers, went to Philadelphia with McCormack.

As an organization, the Redskins had internal problems. In a March 4, 1973, *Washington Post* story, *Post* writer George Solomon delved into the Redskins' financial situation and concluded that the team had an "incredibly poor financial condition." Solomon quoted owner Edward Bennett Williams as saying "as investors, we'd be better off putting our money in municipal bonds. None of the stockholders are making any money. ... I am gravely concerned about the economic aspect of our team." Williams went on to say the team needed RFK stadium to increase its seating capacity. Solomon's story showed RFK's seating limit at 53,039. Williams told Solomon that the Redskins needed to sell 60,000 tickets for each game in order for the franchise to survive. Allen's spending habits, in terms of the hefty player salaries, were a problem for the franchise, Solomon wrote.

And then there was that other problem. Jurgensen came back for another season and Kilmer was still there. It didn't matter too much in the opener at home against the Chargers. Kilmer started and went the distance as the Redskins rolled 38–0. Two of the scores came on fumble returns by Verlon Biggs and Brig Owens.

A week later, against the Cardinals, the Redskins were in trouble. Kilmer started the game and went 14 of 22 for 161 yards and a scoring pass without being intercepted. Jurgensen was inserted and he clicked on 12 of 18 for 140 yards and a score. It wasn't enough and the Cardinals won, 34–27.

The third week offered a game with more story lines than Leo Tolstoy's *War and Peace* because the Redskins faced the Philadelphia Eagles in Philly. Allen elevated Jurgensen to the starting spot. Mike McCormack, the recently relocated former Redskins assistant, was the Eagles coach and their starting quarterback was Roman Gabriel, Allen's former Rams passer.

Jurgensen went the distance for Washington, connecting on 16 of 29 passes for 195 yards and two scoring passes. He was intercepted once. The Washington offensive line did not allow the Eagles to sack Jurgensen. Gabriel's day, on the other hand, was a little tougher. He hit on 19 of 38 attempts for 266 yards (including an 80-yard touchdown pass to Norm Bulaich), but he was sacked eight times and intercepted twice. Washington's Ted Vactor returned an interception 34 yards in the fourth quarter to seal the 28–7 win.

Jurgensen started and went the distance again the following week when the Redskins hosted the Cowboys and it looked like Allen made the right call. Washington won 14–7 as Jurgensen completed 14 of 20 passes for 140 yards and a touchdown. Dallas' defense sacked Jurgensen five times but he did not throw an interception. Roger Staubach started for Dallas and Craig Morton played later. Dallas rolled up 269 total yards to just 174 for Washington. The Cowboys led 7–0 in the final quarter but Jurgensen completed a one-yard scoring pass to Charley Taylor to tie the game and Brig Owens returned an interception 26 yards for the winning score. Washington was not piling up the yardage or points, but the 'Skins were winning. Washington and Dallas were tied for the division lead with 3–1 records.

The Giants scored first the following week, but Washington scored 21 unanswered points, including an interception returned for a score by linebacker David Robinson. Jurgensen was not productive, completing eight of 13 passes for 52 yards. He did not throw a scoring pass.

The Redskins had scored 17 touchdowns in five games, but four of those scores were defensive and one came on special teams. Washington scored 128 points in those five games, but when you subtract the 35 points scored by the defense and the special teams, Washington had scored 93 offensive points, an average of 18.6 per game. The Redskins allowed 51 points over the same span of games, averaging a little more than 10 points per game.

Allen went back to Kilmer for the next game, against the Cardinals, and the offense responded with 31 points, winning 31–13 at RFK. Kilmer torched the Cardinals for 294 yards and two touchdowns, but he was also intercepted three times. Allen used both Jurgensen and Kilmer the following week against the Saints in Tulane Stadium, but neither passer could lead the offense to a touchdown and Washington lost, 19–3. The Saints improved their record to just 3–4 and the Redskins fell to 5–2. Kilmer went the distance the following week against the Steelers and Washington gained just 190 yards of total offense, losing 21–16 in Pittsburgh.

Over the next four games, Washington faced four teams with winning records and the Redskins rallied. Jurgensen played in two of the four games, but Kilmer carried most of the passing load and Washington won all four, scoring 20 or more points each week. The defense allowed just 47 points over that span of games. The rematch with Dallas loomed next. Washington was 9–3 and riding a handsome streak of wins. Dallas was 8–4 and the game would be played in Texas.

The Redskins and Cowboys played a game on that day in Texas, but it was not a contest. Dallas scored 27 unanswered points and won, 27–7. Washington's only points came on a blocked punt in the fourth quarter. Jurgensen went the distance and passed for just 114 yards. He was not intercepted. Washington rushed for just 59 yards. Staubach was intercepted twice but he completed 16 passes to his teammates (out of 25 attempts) for 223 yards. Dallas ran for 193 yards, led by Calvin Hill's 110.

Kilmer went the distance in the final game of the regular season, beating the Eagles again, 38–20.

The Redskins had to travel to frosted Minnesota to play the Vikings in their first-round playoff game. The temperature was 19 degrees at kickoff, with a windchill of seven degrees. Washington led 7–3 and 13–10 before losing 27–20. Minnesota quarterback Fran Tarkenton, that old Allen nemesis, passed for 222 yards and two touchdowns. The Washington defense intercepted the Vikings once and sacked Tarkenton once. Kilmer completed 13 of 24 for 159 yards and a touchdown, but he also threw an interception. Minnesota ran for 155 yards and held Redskins runners to 141 yards.

Washington finished the season at 10–4, second in the NFC East, and had lost in the first round of the playoffs. The quarterback situation remained unresolved, although the pairing of Jurgensen and Kilmer was more successful than is generally believed. In 1973, Washington passers threw 372 times, completing 209, gaining 2,358 yards. That was fifth-best in the NFL that season. Washington tied with Pittsburgh for fifth with 20 touchdown passes and tied Buffalo for the sixth-fewest interceptions with 14. Among the teams who finished the season with more points than

14. Chasing the Cowboys

Allen working the sideline during a 41–3 victory over the Saints, September 21, 1975, at RFK (Alamy).

Washington was the Denver Broncos. Denver's record was 7–5–2 and they finished third in the AFC West Division, not good enough for a berth in the playoffs.

Where Allen's offense really had problems in 1973 was rushing the ball. The Redskins were 25th out of 26 teams with just 1,439 yards, an average of 3.1 yards per running play. They scored just nine times on the ground. Larry Brown was the team leader with 860 yards and an average of 3.2 yards per carry. Brown scored eight touchdowns. Charlie Harraway was next with 452 yards, a 3.5-yard average and one score.

Even with the poor rushing results, Washington was sixth in points scored that season. The fans and media could whine about the quarterback situation, but the truth is that Allen's offense produced. The defense ranked sixth in points allowed, just 198 in the regular season, 14.14 per game. Playing in the NFC's toughest division, Washington won 10 games and tied Dallas for the NFC East title. The Vikings and Rams each won 12 games. In the AFC, only Miami won 12 games and both the Bengals and Steelers won 10. Thus, Allen's Redskins trailed three teams in games won and tied for fourth most victories with three other teams. Put another way, seven NFL teams won 10 games or more in 1973 and Washington was one of them.

15

"Follow me to the Super Bowl!"
The 1974 Redskins

Deacon Jones, who had been traded by the Rams to the Chargers and suffered through both bad team results and team controversies involving drugs in San Diego, was acquired by Allen and the Redskins prior to the 1974 campaign. Jones, who was then 36, would play on passing downs for the Redskins. He would spend the final season of his Hall of Fame career doing what he had always done best, attacking opposing passers. Jones had struggled in recent seasons with a sore foot but the opportunity to play one more season for Allen made Jones want to give himself one more season on the field.

Billy Kilmer, who had played against Jones in the past, said, "In his last year, Deacon didn't start; Ron McDole started, and was in on first downs and running plays. Deacon came in on passing situations. He was still effective. He never lost his ability to put pressure on the quarterback."[1]

The quarterback debate enlisted a new point of contention when the club traded a sixth-round draft pick to Miami for the NFL rights to former Notre Dame quarterback Joe Theismann. Miami had drafted Theismann in the fourth round of the 1971 NFL draft but the two sides never reached contractual agreement. According to Theismann's book, *Theismann*,[2] Dolphins management eventually agreed to Theismann's request for $35,000 in the first year, then $45,000 and $55,000, plus a $35,000 bonus spread over the three years. Dolphins owner Joe Robbie agreed except that he wanted Theismann to return the bonus for any year Theismann did not make the roster. Theismann's version is that the Dolphins eventually agreed to make the bonus his to keep. By that time, Theismann said he was disillusioned with the Dolphins. He had agreed to Miami's offer but had not signed a contract with them. The Canadian Football League's Toronto

15. "Follow me to the Super Bowl!" 147

Argonauts had already offered Theismann $50,000 a season for three years and "I had asked the Argonauts if their offer still stood. The money wasn't much more than Miami's offer, but, yes, it still stood and it hadn't changed. Toronto dealt straight with me and I felt Miami didn't."[3]

Theismann played for the Toronto Argonauts for three seasons. His Argos team lost the 1971 Grey Cup title game but Theismann was selected as a CFL Eastern Conference All-Star in both 1971 and 1973. His three seasons in Canada were productive. Theismann completed 56.3 percent of his passes (382 of 679) for 6,093 yards and 40 touchdowns. He also threw 47 interceptions but 21 of those turnovers came in his rookie season.[4] Three years later, Miami still owned Theismann's NFL rights. From *Theismann*, "In '74 Miami was off my list of prospective NFL teams because Bob Griese was still a young quarterback at the top of his game. The Washington Redskins, on the other hand, had Sonny Jurgensen, who was 40, and Billy Kilmer, 35. I figured I could spend a year or two learning from them and then get my shot."

"So I talked to George Allen, the Redskin [sic] coach. He took me into his office. I'd never met anyone so enthusiastic. Or so strange. He wrote down everything he was telling me on the back of an envelope. He listed

Allen on the Washington sideline at RFK during a 17–10 loss to the Cardinals, September 22, 1974. From left are linebacker Dave Robinson (89), Allen, linebacker Chris Hanburger (55) and offensive guard Fred Sturt (65) (Alamy).

all the reasons I would be the perfect Redskin quarterback. He said, 'I want you because you move around. You've got a great arm. You're young. You're durable. You're a winner.'"

"Wow, exciting. Me and George Allen, the great coach. He would trade a No. 1 draft pick to Miami for the rights to me. That was great. I'll do it, George, sign me up. I'll be here. This was it. The big time for little Joey Theismann. Jurgensen and Kilmer were getting old. In a year or two, I'd be the quarterback in the nation's capital."

"Yeah. Sure. Little did I know that when Jurgy and Billy went out drinking, it wasn't only from a Jack Daniels bottle. It was from the Fountain of Youth. The next two years were the toughest of my football life."[5]

Theismann came to the Redskins with three years of professional football experience, including experience in playoff football, but had not played 11-man football since his senior year of college ball, back in 1970.[6] He did not start a regular season NFL game and played only sparingly until 1976. Instead, Theismann played mostly as an emergency fill-in punt returner in both 1974 and 1975. Most of Theismann's returns came in 1974 but his two-season total came to 162 yards on 17 returns, an average of 9.52 yards a return, which compared favorably with any returner the Redskins had during Allen's tenure. Theismann's longest return was 44 yards. He did not score a touchdown as a return specialist. In his first two years with Washington, Theismann threw just 33 passes and completed 19 of them, good for 241 yards and two touchdowns. He was intercepted three times.

But rather than learn from the veterans in front of him and from his coaches, Theismann whined. He was a distraction as much as he was supportive of the team effort and he started his NFL career enraging virtually every new teammate he had. He wrote in *Theismann*, "When I moved to the nation's capital I made the mistake of bringing my mouth along." Here was a veteran team of rowdy desperadoes who'd been to the Super Bowl just one season earlier. They were called the Over-the-Hill Gang. Now here came this upstart from the Golden Dome who announced: "I'm not here just to be on the football team. I want to be the starting quarterback."[7]

Not bad by itself. Every player on every NFL team wanted to be a starter and saying so was not viewed as a sin. But, as training camp opened, Theismann gave the non-quarterback veterans a reason to dislike him or at least resent him when he crossed a union picket line.

"After alienating Jurgensen and Kilmer, I infuriated most of the other players by crossing their picket line to enter training camp."

Theismann wrote, "The Redskins were the closest, toughest, strongest union team in the NFL. Our center, Len Hauss, a growly, gruff Georgia guy, became the union president. The union went out on strike when training camp opened that year. To them, the strike was a statement of principle. To me, it was an opportunity. It never occurred to me that by crossing my teammates' picket line, I would make them angry forever. That wouldn't have stopped me, anyway, because I was thinking short-term. I wasn't a union member, I didn't have to strike. If Jurgensen and Kilmer were on strike, the quarterback job was open. ... All I wanted was the quarterback's job. I told [his teammates]: 'I've waited all my life to play quarterback in the NFL. I'm not going to miss this opportunity because of a picket line....' And when I crossed the picket line, they said, 'You'll live to regret this....' They never forgave me. I was forever an outsider with the Over-the-Hill-Gang."[8]

George Allen detested distractions. He planted trees around the Redskins' practice complex mostly to keep spying eyes off of his practice sessions but also to cut down on things outside the fences which could have momentarily capture the attention of the players. He limited the media's access to the team. The coach must have been happy to have his first-year quarterback in camp but he must have also been aggravated to have a high-profile player anger the rest of the roster before the rest of them even had a chance to practice with him.

Eventually the players' union and the league found common ground and the regular season started on time.

Jurgensen and Kilmer split the passing duties in the Redskins' 28–17 October 6 loss to the Cincinnati Bengals, dropping Washington's record to 2–2. The Redskins were never really in the game, although Washington's offense out-gained Cincinnati 337–231. Kilmer hit on 12 of 21 attempts for 148 yards and he was sacked twice. Jurgensen was pretty much the same, 12 of 20 for 104 yards, but Jurgensen threw two scoring passes without being intercepted.

A major test was next, the defending champion Dolphins. Miami had uncharacteristically lost its season opener and then rattled off three straight wins. The Dolphins still had basically the same team that beat Washington in the Super Bowl 21 months earlier and were expected to make yet another trip to the Super Bowl. But the 1974 meeting with the Redskins was played at RFK rather than on a neutral field and Don Shula finally got a chance to have a more interesting game because Allen made the decision to start Jurgensen against Shula's Miami squad.

Jurgensen was playing in his final season and he still had the swaggering confidence that captivated NFL fans throughout his career. Jurgensen told NFL films, "George came and he said, 'You know, a lot of coaches wouldn't do this, start a forty-year-old quarterback against the world champions.' And [the] smart aleck retort from me was, 'If you want to win, you'd better.'"[9]

Jurgensen delivered with a game for the ages, completing 26 of 39 passes for 303 yards and two scores. He was intercepted three times and sacked once, but he brought Washington back from 10–0 and 17–13 deficits in the second half. Trailing 10–3 in the fourth quarter, Jurgensen hit Roy Jefferson for a 37-yard score to tie the game. After the Dolphins scored on a touchdown pass by Griese, Jurgensen got the winner on a six-yard pass to running back Larry Smith. Washington's 20–17 victory improved its record to 3–2.

The game wasn't entirely the story of Jurgensen and the Redskins offense. The Washington defense limited Miami's powerful running game to just 107 yards on 39 attempts. Griese completed 11 of 24 passes for 139 yards and a score, but he was also intercepted twice and sacked twice. Miami gained just 233 total yards that day. Washington gained 325 total yards, although just 26 of those yards were gained on 18 running plays.

By the time Washington hosted Dallas in week 10, on November 17, the Redskins were 6–3 and Dallas was suffering through a rare season with an average record, 5–4. It was Allen and Landry again. Deacon Jones had another chance to attack the Dallas passing game and Billy Kilmer had to face the always terrific Dallas defense. George Allen always looked for new ways to motivate his players and prior to the unusually late first meeting of the season against their bitter rivals, Allen literally broke new ground in his zeal to enthuse his men.

He also broke his hand.

In *Strategies*, Allen wrote about how keyed up he got for daily meetings with his players. He wrote that he never arrived for meetings first because coaches lose their effectiveness when they stand around waiting for the players to straggle in. Then Allen wrote about a particular meeting during which he tried an outside-the-box method of getting his players enthusiastic.

Allen wrote, "One time after a loss, I brought Jhoon Rhee, a karate expert with whom I had been studying, and I broke two boards with my hand and five with my feet. The players all roared. I also cut my hand and broke a small bone in it."[10]

There are other versions of the incident but what seems consistent is that three assistants walked into the Washington locker room with some wooden boards. Allen shouted something that was anti–Dallas and kicked the first board, breaking it. His players cheered and reportedly laughed a bit. Allen attacked the second board with another Cowboy epithet and broke the second target with his left fist. Finally, he went a board too far and chopped the third board, cracking it. But he also broke his hand. Allen did not admit to the injury. He stuck his hand in a pocket and went out to coach the game. Years later, Etty Allen showed author John Klawitter a removable cast George Allen wore around the house while his hand healed. He wanted to hide the injury but Klawitter, who collaborated with Jones to write *Headslap*, wrote that George Allen eventually admitted to his wife, "I think they know," because the grip of his handshakes were not the accustomed firmness.[11]

Allen suffered through that Dallas game. But, had a soothsayer told him that a victory over the Dallas Cowboys would come with broken bones in his own hand, Allen would have immediately signed up for the victory. He had offered to do a lot more than that to himself if it would have meant winning the Super Bowl.

Jhoon Rhee owned a series of martial arts studios in the Washington, D.C., area and it was Rhee who instructed Allen on the fine art of board-busting. Rhee described the incident this way: "I was present when he gave his demonstration for his team, the Redskins. I remember it was a big success. But even I did not know he broke the bones in his hand; it would be like him to say nothing, even though it was bleeding a little. He was one with the ability to make strong men stronger, a leader among other leaders."[12]

Theismann told the story differently. His version had Allen breaking the boards prior to a practice in preparation for a game against the Cincinnati Bengals. Theismann did not cite a specific season, but the Redskins and Bengals played only once after Theismann came to Washington and before Allen was fired. That game was in 1974, the fourth game of the season, October 6, in Cincinnati. Calling Allen a "karate fanatic," Theismann's telling had Allen breaking a single board first, then two boards at once and finally striking three boards. During practice that day, Theismann said, Allen wore only a bandage.[13]

Deacon Jones played just the one season in Washington and his telling is specific about which week Allen went board-hunting in the locker room. Allen shouted that he hated Tom Landry. Allen had written anti–Dallas slogans on the boards he attacked, the *Headslap* version recounts. Theismann's telling has the boards embellished with the letter "C" for Cincinnati and he has Allen shouting things about Cincinnati coach Paul Brown. It doesn't matter how the incident occurred, who the Redskins played that week or even which season the head coach of the Washington Redskins made wooden boards feel his rage to win football games. What does matter is that Allen, being Allen, wanted his players to feel inspired. After all, he had two hands and, anyway, bones healed.

The record does show that Washington lost to Cincinnati and Paul Brown 28–17 in the week 4 game. The Redskins beat Dallas 28–21 in week 10. In Allen's telling, he gave the demonstration after a loss, but the Redskins did not lose prior to either of the Cowboys games or the Cincinnati contest. Washington's losses that year came in week 2 (prior to a week

3 game against the Denver Broncos), week 4 (Miami Dolphins), week 7 (Green Bay Packers) and week 12 (Rams). Jones' recollection is so detailed that it seems likely that Allen's bone and board-busting came a few days prior to a game against Dallas, which would mean that it did not happen during a week after a loss.

Two weeks after beating Dallas in week 10, with a 26–7 victory over the Eagles in between, Allen's Redskins faced Dallas again and seemed to have the game won. Washington led 16–3 in the third period and Dallas star Roger Staubach had been knocked out of the game with an injury. But Dallas rookie passer Clint Longley led a comeback and Dallas beat the Redskins 24–23 on a long pass to Drew Pearson with 35 seconds left. It was a gut-wrenching loss that made Allen admit, "This is the type of defeat that can stay with you for a while. It can take something out of your team if you let it."[14]

With two weeks remaining in the regular season, the Redskins played the Rams in Los Angeles and, while nobody broke any bones that time, another attempt to get the team fired up went offline. Washington was 8–4 and needed to win. The Rams were 9–3. It was a big game for both clubs. Deacon Jones would retire before the next season after a career that eventually catapulted him to the Pro Football Hall of Fame. Much of that success had come as a member of the Los Angeles Rams, playing in the same Los Angeles Memorial Olympic Coliseum where the Redskins and Rams would shortly go at it. Prior to the kickoff, Jones had emotions running through him at a fever pitch. In *Headslap*, Jones described screaming at his teammates and them screaming back. Finally, the defensive end who had ferociously led attacks on opposing quarterbacks and helped make it popular to talk about defense, knew he had his teammates fired up. He led the charge out the door bellowing the words "Follow me to the Super Bowl!" Unfortunately for Jones, Allen and everyone else on the Redskins roster, the Redskins were ensconced in the visitor's locker room at the Coliseum. The visitor's locker room was just like the home team locker room that Jones had used for so many years, except that everything was reversed. Instead of leading his enraged teammates out the door and into the tunnel that led to the field, Jones led them into the showers.

The Redskins won anyway, 23–17, and then beat the Bears 42–0 to finish at 10–4. Near the end of the Bears game, Jones made his career-long work habits pay off. The Redskins had scored 41 points after Washington's sixth touchdown of the game against the Bears and someone had to attempt a conversion kick to bring the total to 42. It was a measure of Allen's feeling for Jones that Allen sent the massive defensive end out to kick the final conversion of the afternoon in that victory over Chicago. Jones had spent hours each week of his career practicing conversion

15. "Follow me to the Super Bowl!"

kicks, determined to be the emergency kicker if his team ever needed one. Remember, Bruce Allen was shagging kicks for Jones at the end of a Rams practice before George Allen gave his son Jones as a model to emulate. After all those practice kicks, Jones went out to boot a conversion for real against the Bears.

"The Bears weren't used to being shoved around and it was late in the game and getting ugly and sloppy," Bruce Allen said. "Of course, they accused us of piling it on, and maybe we were, just a little bit. ... Deacon came up to my dad and said, 'I've been the back-up kicker in high school, in college, with the Rams, the Chargers and now the Redskins. Don't you think it's time somebody let me kick one?' So Dad sent him out there to kick the extra point."[15]

All accounts say the kick was an ugly one, including Jones' own description in *Headslap*. Jones wrote, "But that ugly little kick flew like the most beautiful bird.... I made it, and it made all those years of extra effort worthwhile, like the icing on a cake." Jones completed his kicking career with a perfect one-for-one record in touchdown conversion kicks.

Mark Moseley, who handled Washington's placekicking duties (except when Jones wanted to kick) was a little different from most of Allen's re-energized veteran players. Usually, Allen had to trade something to acquire a player but that was not the case with Moseley, who had kicked for Cleveland and then Houston. The Oilers cut Moseley one game into the 1972 season and he was out of football for the remainder of that season, plus all of 1973. But kickers are always in demand in the NFL. Moseley stayed in shape during the hiatus and eventually gained strength. He felt he was kicking better than ever and hoped he might get an offer to try out for a team. Kickers sometimes start missing field goals and lose confidence, which forces their team to bring in free agent kickers for a try out.

Moseley got a call from George Allen well in advance of the 1974 training camp, with an offer to try out for the Redskins. Moseley accepted. The kicker was so excited that he arrived at training camp an hour before he was due. Walking out on the practice field, Moseley heard someone call his name and learned it was Allen. The men had not met previously.

Moseley later recalled, "He said, 'You know why you're here.' I said, 'Yes sir, I want to be your kicker.' He said, 'Yeah, but the reason you're here is because in 1972, when you were with the Houston Oilers, you kicked four field goals against my Redskins in a driving rain storm.' He said, 'I am always going to have a great defense. All I need is three points. But I need somebody that can get me three points in any kind of weather and I think you're that guy for the job.' I said, 'Yes sir, thank you.' He said, 'Now all you've got to do is go beat out those other 12 guys that are here and the job is yours.'"

Moseley called Allen "a phenomenal motivator of men."[16]

The only time Moseley and the Houston Oilers played against Allen's Redskins was during the 1971 season, when Moseley booted field goals of 42 and 25 yards in a losing cause at RFK. Be that as it may, Moseley was still kicking for the Redskins after Allen left.

Like so many games that were important to Allen's career, the Redskins' 1974 playoff berth put them in Los Angeles to play the Rams again. Los Angeles had shed itself of Prothro's coaching and hired an Allen-like replacement, Chuck Knox. Knox's offense was so conservative that it came to be known as "Ground Chuck," but the formula worked well enough that the Rams went 10–4 in the regular season. The homestanding Rams drew first blood when quarterback James Harris hit tight end Bob Klein for a 10-yard scoring pass in the first quarter. The Redskins got a field goal and then a one-yard touchdown run from Moses Denson and led 10–7 at halftime. The Rams went back in front, 13–10 on the strength of two David Ray field goals.

Sonny Jurgensen played in 218 regular season games for the Eagles and Redskins, starting 147 times, but he never started a playoff game. Kilmer had started at quarterback against the Rams and he struggled, completing seven of 18 passes for 99 yards. He was not intercepted, but neither did he throw a scoring pass. Allen inserted Jurgensen and Jurgensen was intercepted three times. One of the interceptions was returned for a touchdown by Rams linebacker Isiah Robertson in the fourth quarter to seal the win for the Rams. Jurgensen's stats for the day were marginally better than Kilmer's; Jurgensen hit six of 12 passes for 78 yards. The Redskins gained just 218 yards from scrimmage against the excellent Rams defense in that game. The Washington defense surrendered only slightly more, 226 yards. The Redskins lost three fumbles in the contest which, added to Jurgensen's interceptions, gave Washington six turnovers, far too many giveaways to win a playoff game. The Rams were awarded the dubious honor of returning to Minnesota for another postseason game with the Vikings. With the wind chill hovering at 19 degrees, the Vikings beat the Rams again, 14–10.

A lot has been written about George Allen's way of handling Sonny Jurgensen after Allen became the Redskins' coach. As we have seen, Jurgensen and even Joe Theismann were critical of Allen's preference for playing Kilmer. But Allen did understand Jurgensen's value and ability to energize the Washington offense. Allen turned to Jurgensen in the 1974 game against Miami, for example, and went to the 40-year-old again in the playoff game against the Rams when Kilmer could not generate points. It is also a fact that Allen valued Jurgensen as a place kick holder. In his book *George Allen's Guide to Special Teams*, Allen listed Jurgensen among the three best holders of all time, along with Paul Krause of the Vikings and Richie Petitbon of the Bears.[17]

In his *Special Teams* book, Allen called St. Francis of Assisi "unquestionably the patron saint of special teams players," and Allen quoted St. Francis as saying, "To accomplish the impossible you must start with what is necessary; then you accomplish what is possible and, before long, the impossible has been done." Whether St. Francis truly is the patron saint for the men who play on football's suicide squads (as the kicking teams were known in Allen's time) or not, Allen and perhaps University of Alabama coach Bear Bryant could be considered the trailblazers among coaches who increasingly concentrated on developing more effective special teams.

Allen wrote that his Washington teams had the most successful special teams of his coaching career. His treatment of those players was significant. After games at RFK, Allen pulled his special teamers aside for postgame meetings in a small room. "After I talked to them about the game, I would get on top of a large table and start setting the special teams tone for the following week, telling them what we would do to the other team, getting them excited about their potential, and stimulating their enthusiasm to work hard during next week's practice." Allen further wrote that he frequently had players hand him wooden folding chairs that he hurled against walls. Allen wrote that his special teams players looked forward to those postgame meetings.

Then he wrote, "You have to find an approach to motivating your special teams that is unique to your personality and apropos to your coaching circumstance. But before any motivating tool or exercise can be effective, you must develop that personal rapport.... Without that, no amount of yelling, screaming, or breaking chairs can motivate anyone."[18]

For his *Special Teams* book, Allen wrote, "What has become more apparent since 1969 when I initiated the position of special teams coach is that it is tough to be a consistent winner with a poor or inefficient kicking game."[19] Allen's special teams, both with the Rams and Redskins, were consistent. In his dozen NFL seasons, Allen employed four kickers: Bruce Gossett and David Ray with the Rams and then Curt Knight and Mark Moseley in Washington. None will join Allen in the Pro Football Hall of Fame but the four had commonalities. All were effective field goal kickers from inside 30 yards, somewhat less so from 30–39 and mostly ineffective outside of 40 yards. Knight nailed the first 50-yard field goal for an Allen-coached team in 1971 when he kicked a 52-yarder. But even Moseley scored on just 11 of 25 attempts between 30 and 49 yards that season.

In his book *Where Else Would You Rather Be*, Levy revealed one of the reasons Allen's teams always had success with the kicking game. Allen, Levy wrote, made sure that his kicking game coach played a significant role in roster selection. In this way, Allen's teams might keep a back-up running back whose production as a runner was limited because the same running back was adept at punt coverage. A lineman who was a very good long snapper on punts might remain on the roster while another lineman who did not snap the ball at all could get cut from the roster. In this way, Allen's kicking teams were better because some of the players on the roster were kept specifically for their skills in the kicking game. As the NFL has allowed teams to have increasingly larger rosters, it has become easier to keep kicking team specialists. But during Allen's era, the roster limit was smaller and choosing players primarily for the ability to play on kicking downs was unusual.

Many coaches around the league did not devote the same roster space for long snappers or coverage men as Allen did at that time. One of the reasons Allen was able to turn floundering teams into winners quickly was his willingness to devote time and energy to kicking, punting and his return coverage teams. More than just serving the kicking teams by hiring highly energetic and intelligent assistants like Vermeil and Levy, Allen's NFL rosters were partially molded around the players needed to make that aspect of the game a strength. The selection of the kickers and punters was done differently, too. Allen valued hangtime—the length of time the ball floats in the air before a returner can catch it—above distance for both kickoffs and punts. The more time the ball spent in the air, the more time Allen's coverage teams had to converge on the unfortunate return man for the opposite team. A 38-yard punt that was kicked high in the air and needed a comparatively long time to fall back to Earth, for example, should be covered well and allow very little return yardage. A 50-yard punt that is lower and spends little time in the air would be out in front of the coverage team and give the return man space to maneuver and potentially break off a long gainer. Allen favored punters with quicker punting motions because those men would have fewer punts blocked. A placekicker whose field goal range was slightly shorter than others would be favored if his kickoffs had better hangtime.

Over the same period, Allen's teams allowed just two blocked punts, both against the 1967 Rams and punter Jon Kilgore. Kilgore, by the way, was a successful punter for the Rams. He had the NFL's second-best average yards per punt in 1966 at 42.8 yards. Kilgore was sixth in the league in 1967 but then he was replaced by the more versatile Pat Studstill, who Allen acquired from the Detroit Lions. Studstill led the NFL in punting in 1967 and also played wide receiver.

Allen proved that one of the keys to turning losers into winners was to instill a high-quality kicking game into the squad and to establish an *Esprit de Corps* among the players who manned those positions.

16

Chasing Dallas
The 1975 Redskins

For the second straight summer, the Redskins struggled in the preseason, splitting their six games. Jurgensen was retired. Kilmer remained the starter. A new add to the quarterback room was Randy Johnson, who had played eight seasons with the Giants and Falcons before his single season with Washington. Johnson had been a starter early in his career and was a classic George Allen reserve quarterback: a veteran and former starter who had seen plenty of enemy defenses during his career. Johnson had thrown many more interceptions in his career than he had scoring passes, by a nearly 2–1 ratio. But he had started his career with the then-new Atlanta Falcons franchise and things are never easy for quarterbacks in situations like that. Allen had coached against Johnson when Allen coached the Rams.

The Redskins opened the season by scoring 90 points in their first two games, whipping both the Saints (41–3) and Giants (49–13) at RFK. Kilmer had six scoring passes and two interceptions in those games, hitting on 28 of 50 attempts for 385 yards. Johnson played in the second game, hitting all of his six attempts for 77 more yards and a pair of scores. Redskins runners gained 304 yards in the two games combined. Kilmer was sacked six times in those wins.

It wasn't the same in week 3. Playing on the road for the first time that season, Allen's Redskins were handed a 26–10 loss by the Eagles in Philadelphia. Philly passer Roman Gabriel completed 11 of 20 for 182 yards and two scores. Washington's Dennis Johnson intercepted Gabriel, but that was about the only thing that went wrong for the Eagles. In the football vernacular, Philadelphia rammed the ball down Washington's collective throats, gaining 213 yards and a touchdown on 53 running plays. The Redskins led 10–9 at the half and did not score again. Philadelphia's rushing score was a one-yard sneak by Gabriel, the final score of the contest.

The Redskins finally got their running game going a week later when they beat St. Louis 27-17 at RFK. Mike Thomas led all rushers with 100 yards on 18 carries, scoring two touchdowns. As a team, Washington gained 158 rushing yards on 39 attempts. Kilmer threw for 168 yards without a touchdown or an interception, but Theismann was inserted in the third quarter, with the score tied 10-10 and he threw one pass, completing it to John Pergine, a 30-yard touchdown that put the Redskins ahead. The Cardinals later tied the score at 17-17 but Washington scored 10 unanswered points in the final quarter to lock the win away.

Washington was 3-1 and every win had come at home. Three very negative indicators repeated themselves the following week against the Oilers in Houston: Washington lost on the road again, its running game was non-productive and its offensive line allowed its quarterbacks to be sacked multiple times. In the 13-10 loss, Washington rushed for just 58 yards and allowed Houston runners to gain 121. Kilmer went the distance under center, completing just 12 of 29 attempts, throwing two interceptions and getting sacked three times. Washington's Mike Bass intercepted Houston quarterback Dan Pastorini once and the 'Skins sacked Pastorini three times. Houston's record improved to 4-1 and Washington dropped to 3-2. In the tough Eastern Division of the National Football Conference, a 3-2 start was grim news. Happily for Washington, the next game on the schedule was a road game against the Cleveland Browns, who were in the midst of a disappointing 3-11 season. The defense sacked Cleveland passer Brian Sipe three times and allowed just 200 total yards. The Redskins rushed for 190 yards and threw for 207 and beat the Browns, 23-7.

The Redskins were off to an inconsistent start. Allen's combative nature served him well in those situations. Joe Theismann described Allen's intensity in *Theismann*: "George would say that losing is worse than dying because if you die you don't have to think about the next game. He wasn't kidding. He'd die a thousand deaths if we lost. He had a chauffeur, and not because he was a big shot. George couldn't be trusted to drive, because he was always thinking about how to stop the Packers or Roger Staubach. If the man had to drive his own car, he wouldn't have lived five days. He'd be in a ditch or up a tree. ... Every minute of George's day was devoted to winning. On his desk he had a little sign that asked, 'What have you done today to make the Redskins a winning team?' ... George had a voice that always sounded hoarse. He talked almost in a whisper, like he was giving away national CIA secrets. He squinted his eyes into slits. The effect was comical, although he certainly meant to be dead earnest."[1]

Next for Washington was an earnest test: The Dallas Cowboys were coming to Washington. The Cowboys led most of the way, but Kilmer showed his toughness near the end of the game. Dallas defender Cliff

16. Chasing Dallas

Harris returned an interception for a 27-yard touchdown in the fourth quarter to put Dallas ahead 24–17, but Kilmer tied the game with a 7-yard pass to tight end Jerry Smith and then Kilmer, who was intercepted four times that day, won the game with a quarterback sneak in overtime. The final score was 30–24. The result was that both Dallas and Washington were 5–2 and Washington had a tie-breaking victory over its rivals.

With Johnson going most of the way against the Giants after replacing the injured Kilmer, Washington won its third straight. Johnson started again the next week and went the distance as the Redskins lost to the Cardinals. Kilmer returned and went most of the way against the Raiders at RFK, but George Blanda kicked a field goal in overtime and the Raiders won, 26–23. A week later, Kilmer brought the Redskins back from a fourth-quarter deficit to beat the Vikings at RFK, 31–30 and the Redskins improved to 7–4. The next week, the Redskins beat the Falcons in Atlanta on a 39-yard field goal by Moseley in the final quarter and improved their record to 8–4.

Then the Redskins had to go to Dallas.

Kilmer and Johnson were sacked three times and the Redskins got beat 31–10. Washington's offense gained just 222 yards from scrimmage when the yardage lost due to quarterback sacks was deducted. Kilmer threw for just 135 yards and a touchdown. Johnson completed two of eight and had two others intercepted. Dallas' stingy defense limited the Redskins to 81 yards on the ground. Washington's defense sacked Roger Staubach once and intercepted him once, but the future Hall of Fame passer completed two scoring passes. Where Dallas really hurt Washington was on the ground, where Allen's defense was gashed for 207 yards.

The loss dropped Washington to 8–5. In the final game, Philadelphia's defense intercepted Theismann and Johnson a combined seven times in a terrible 26–3 loss that finished the season at 8–6.

On average, Washington scored 23.2 points and gave up 19.7 per game. Its passers threw more interceptions, 29, than scoring passes, 28. The quarterbacks were sacked 27 times and the running game had not been consistently effective.

17

Coping with Quarterbacks
The 1976 Redskins

The 1976 season opened with a 19–17 victory over the Giants at RFK. Kilmer started and went most of the way. Theismann was sacked on a pass attempt, his only credited attempt of the game. In *Theismann*, he recounted his mounting frustration with Allen. Theismann, which rhymes with Heisman (as in the trophy), had been a star at every stop of his career, from high school to Notre Dame to Canada. He had been an afterthought for two seasons in Washington and, although he wrote that he thought he might have to sit and learn for a season or two after finally arriving in the NFL, he very quickly discovered that he didn't want to sit and learn. He volunteered to return punts on an as-needed basis. He wrote in his autobiography about running pass patterns in practice. What Joe Theismann did not do up to that point was play much at quarterback and that left him bitter.

Theismann wrote, "After those first two miserable years with the Redskins, all I wanted was out. I wanted to play. I begged George Allen to trade me. ... I decided to simply and totally defy George Allen. I did everything I could to infuriate him so that (1) he'd trade me just so he wouldn't have to listen to me anymore or (2) he'd say, 'Theismann, get in the game—and I hope you fall on your face.'"[1]

Theismann's attitude was very different from when he met Allen for the first time and said he thought he might be an understudy to Jurgensen and Kilmer for two seasons. That's exactly what he had been prior to the 1976 season. But if Theismann accurately described his actions during the first two seasons he played in Washington, he spent more time hoping to draw attention to himself than he did learning his position within Allen's offense.

Theismann described an incident when he and Washington linebacker Rusty Tillman made a public appearance and Theismann told the

17. Coping with Quarterbacks

assembled, "George Allen is a unique guy, and a winner. ... George Allen is also an egotist. He is unfair. He doesn't give players a chance to prove themselves. I play now because I enjoy the game. I don't play for George Allen."[2]

Theismann then wrote that he went first to Allen's home the next morning and then, upon learning that his coach was already at the team offices, met Allen there and apologized. He had done the same thing after similar transgressions with his coaches at Notre Dame and in Canada. He later did the same with future Redskins coach Joe Gibbs. Theismann's version of the meeting with Allen tallies well with other players' description of meetings with Allen. Theismann wrote that he said, "Coach Allen, I said some things I shouldn't have and I want to take full responsibility for it. I said them out of frustration, and I sincerely apologize to you for doing that." Theismann continued, "George never got mad. He surprised me by saying: 'I appreciate your coming in and telling me. But, Joe, I'm really disappointed. If not playing was bothering you so much, why didn't you take the time to come talk to me?'"

Theismann wrote that he was "dumbfounded" by Allen's reaction.[3]

"I was trapped," Theismann wrote, "a prisoner in the George Allen Retirement Home for Wayward Warriors."[4] As a result, Theismann made things as difficult as he could for his teammates. He later wrote, "Running the scout team, I did my own thing, not what was best for the Redskins. I tried to beat our defense, which served absolutely no purpose. I went full speed in half-speed drills and threw touchdown passes to wide receivers when the ball was supposed to go short."[5]

It wasn't uncommon to have a player unhappy about not getting playing time. That was a frequent event in team sports and has always been so. But it was unusual for a back-up to refuse to even practice properly for the betterment of the team. George Allen understood the importance of team chemistry very well and Theismann's refusal to put the team in front of himself was problematic.

Washington won its second and third games before losing 33–7 to the Bears in Chicago. Theismann accounted for Washington's only score of the day with a one-yard scoring toss to tight end Jerry Smith, but Theismann and Kilmer both struggled to generate just 48 passing yards, net, and only 119 total yards. Allen started Theismann a week later and Washington scored 30 points against the Chiefs at RFK, but the Redskins' defense suffered through a rare bad day and Kansas City won 33–30. Theismann completed 20 of 37 for 230 yards and two scores, but he also threw two interceptions as the Redskins fell to 3–2.

Theismann went the distance again a week later against the Lions. He was sacked three times and threw an interception, but he also had a scoring pass and Washington won 20-7. Theismann was sacked seven times by St. Louis the following week and Kilmer had a pass intercepted, but Eddie Brown bailed the Redskins out with a 71-yard punt return in the fourth quarter and Washington won 20-10. Allen's special teams had been decisive again.

Dallas was next at RFK but the Cowboys upped their record to 7-1 with a 20-7 demolition of the Redskins. Washington fumbled three times—losing two—and gained just 146 total yards while Dallas gained 253. Roger Staubach passed for 152 yards. Allen used Kilmer and Theismann, but Dallas sacked the Washington passers a total of seven times. The Redskins did not seem destined to reach the playoffs with a 5-3 record but they finally got things turned around the following week with a 24-21 victory over the 49ers at Candlestick Park in San Francisco. Theismann went the distance and threw for 302 yards and three scores. The 49ers intercepted him twice. Theismann went the distance again a week later and did not play poorly but Washington did not score a touchdown as the Giants beat the Redskins 12-9. It was New York's first victory of the season.

The situation was ripe for a disillusion of team chemistry. The Redskins already had four losses. Theismann was itching to play more and the offense wasn't scoring regardless of who was under center. Allen's defense was allowing more points than usual. But Allen's teams typically enjoyed very good team chemistry. One reason for that was the Five O'Clock Club, veteran players who met in an equipment shed after practice.

Allen told a story that when he coached the Redskins the players hated wearing their helmets during the week. Defensive players did not have to wear their helmets because they didn't hit. They wore hats instead, some of them goofy hats like a railroad engineer's cap. Allen said Kilmer, the quarterback, used to take defensive lineman Dave Butz's helmet, go to the training room, put ice and a six-pack of beer in the helmet and take it to the equipment shed for the Five O'Clock Club meetings after practice.

"Butz would be calling 'Where's my helmet?' and it would be icing a six-pack in the equipment shed," said Allen's Long Beach State assistant Chuck Hayes, recalling the tale. "This is George Allen telling the story. We would crack up, it was the funniest thing. He could be so disarming that way. He would tell little stories about that stuff."

The existence of the so-called Five O'Clock Club and the idea that defensive players did not hit much in practice, so much so that they did not need helmets much of the time, are examples of Allen's approach and how he came to be known as a players' coach. Football practice is vital for preparing for a game but it can also be drudgery, especially late in the season when the players are sore and worn. Any gesture toward understanding the situation can go a long distance toward helping players' attitudes. Allen understood that.

Three of the Redskins' final four games would be on the road. Their collective backs to the wall, Allen's men beat St. Louis again, 16–10. Kilmer started and went the distance and Washington improved to 7–4.

It was at this stage of the season that George Allen made the type of roster move that showed his genius. His offense was not scoring many points, leaving his defense in trouble far too often. Allen looked to his kicking game, specifically his defensive kicking game, for a spark.

Bill Malinchek had played for Washington as a special teamer from 1970 through 1974 and had been a tremendous boon to the club. Drafted by Detroit as a wide receiver in 1966, he had caught 34 passes for 496 yards and four touchdowns with the Lions before joining Washington. Once Allen got to town, Malinchek became a crucial part of the special teams effort as a punt blocker. But Malinchek had been out of football for all of 1975 and through the first 11 games of 1976, working as a commodity broker on Wall Street.

Then Allen called. The final game of the season would be against the Cowboys in Dallas and Allen thought that if the Redskins won their next two, they could go to Dallas with a chance to make the playoffs. A big special teams play here or there could change the course of the season.

Malinchek related later, "Knowing that George Allen had faith in me to come back and maybe make one or two big plays for him, I couldn't refuse."

Washington beat the Eagles 24–0 and the Jets 34–16,[6] setting up the season-ending showdown with Dallas. Early in the game, Dallas had to punt and Malinchek trotted out on the field. As he lined up, he noticed Dallas' linemen were pointing out to each other who would block which Washington player.

"I saw that the only guy I've got to beat is the upback," Malinchek recalled. "I've got a free run here because they were blocking down. I closed the gap and I ran in and I just had to jump a little bit over the upback there and I got my hand on the ball, was able to block it, luckily. It was just being observant, watching what the blocking scheme was. It wasn't called, I just took the chance once I saw the opportunity."[7] He added, "When you make a big play [blocking a punt], it's not for five yards. When you block a punt, then you've gained sixty yards. ... Any big play on special teams is big yardage, so George was always looking for a way to get that little bit of advantage that would win the game."[8]

Malinchek's success as a punt blocker had an interesting backstory. He had punted earlier in his career and felt his experience as a punter taught him how to aim his direction of attack when rushing a punter.

When he reached the point where he had to lunge at the ball, he spread his hands apart, roughly the width of a football, giving him a better chance to get a piece of the ball than others who kept their hands closer together. Allen never forgot Malinchek's unique ability to pressure opposing punters and, in true Wall Street style, the coach called and the player's response paid dividends.

Malinchek related, "The one thing that made us special back then was that George Allen had his hands on the special teams. He would always get the players and call them over individually ... and he would take me over, for instance, and he would talk to me about what I was expected to do playing on special teams, that I had to make a big play. ... And I think that at the end of the conversation I thought the game rested on my shoulders, and I think every other special teams player did too because they probably got the same speech, that we had to make a big play. When you do that on special teams, you just don't go through the motions."

The Redskins beat the Cowboys 27–14. Kilmer went the distance, passing for 199 yards and a score. He was intercepted twice and sacked three times. Dallas' Staubach completed just five of 22 for 91 yards. Staubach threw a scoring pass, but he was intercepted twice and sacked three times. Both teams had four turnovers but Washington out-gained the home team 359 yards to 203 and, with the win, advanced to the playoffs.

Washington finished the regular season at 10–5 and had to travel to play the 12–2–1 Vikings in Minnesota's Metropolitan Stadium in the first round of the playoffs. The Vikings jumped ahead early, led 21–3 at the half and won going away, 35–20. It as an ugly end to a season whose highs and lows rivaled a Richter scale tape measuring a California earthquake.

18

A Contract Offer
The 1977 Redskins

Allen started 1977 with a contract offer from the Redskins. He never signed the contract, which would have made him the best-paid coach in the NFL, because something was missing. His first contract with the team offered Allen the opportunity to purchase a small piece of the team. Allen had not taken advantage of the option as of the summer of 1977, although he certainly still could have as of the time the second contract was offered because Allen was still employed under the original Redskins contract. Allen's daughter, Jennifer, would later write in her book that her father did not read the contracts that he signed and history seems to make that likely. George Allen certainly did not pay attention to the three-year contract he had as an assistant coach with the Bears before he sought out an interview with the Rams for the head coaching position in Los Angeles. It is also possible that he did not realize, or at least that he forgot about, the clause in the first deal that allowed him to buy a piece of the Redskins. Jennifer Allen wrote that it was her mother, Etty Allen, who noticed that the chance to buy part of the team was not part of the new deal. Instead, the new four-year contract offered to Allen before the 1977 season (for the 1978–81 seasons) doubled Allen's salary to a quarter-million dollars a season through 1981.[1]

Money and the ownership option were not the only issue between George Allen and his employer. Allen wanted control of the football part of the team operation. Edward Bennett Williams, the president of the Redskins, was not willing to give Allen that authority. There was friction between Allen and his boss.

Joe Theismann signed his contract, however, and nearly doubled his earnings. Theismann reportedly went from $85,000 a season to $150,000. This may have been egged on by the Toronto Argonauts which, as media reports of the day stated, dangled a million dollars for Theismann to return to play quarterback in the frozen north.

Allen suffered a serious distraction in late August when his mother, Loretta May Allen, died a couple of weeks before the season opener. Things did not get much better for a while. The Redskins got off to a slow start and key players suffered season-ending injuries as time went on. Defensive back Pat Fisher went out with a back injury, running back John Riggins tore a knee ligament and reserve fullback Bob Brunet was out with a neck injury. In addition, linebacker Chris Hanburger, safety Jake Scott and receiver Charley Taylor all missed games during the first part of the campaign.

The week 5 game against the Cowboys in Dallas provided a glimpse at what Theismann could do for the Redskins. Kilmer started but struggled, completing just four of 15 attempts. He was not intercepted but neither did he throw a scoring pass. Theismann came in and, while his passing stats don't look much better (he completed three of 10 for 19 yards), he did throw a scoring pass to Clarence Harmon in the second quarter to draw the Redskins within a point at 14–13. Washington took a 16–14 lead in the third quarter before Dallas pulled away to win 34–16. Washington was in trouble with a 3–2 record. The following week, Kilmer went all the way against the Giants and passed for 217 yards but he did not throw a scoring pass and was intercepted once. The Redskins lost 17–6. Washington's record fell to 3–3 and the playoffs seemed to be a distant dream. The Redskins had scored 73 points in the first six weeks and allowed 91, a very rare stretch of games for an Allen-coached team.

Allen had been under pressure from the front office to play Theismann and finally, he did. Theismann recalled in his book, "Early in the '77 season Coach Allen told me, 'You're my number one quarterback.'"[2] Theismann wrote that he started eight games that season but he did not. Theismann started six games. There were eight games remaining in the season when he got his chance and Theismann played well. His first start, against the Eagles on October 30, was successful. He connected on 16 of 34 attempts for 218 yards and two scores, with one interception. From a distance, Theismann's performance is less inspirational. He completed fewer than half his passes and he threw the interception. The Redskins offense produced just a field goal in the second half. But the threat of Theismann's passing helped open things for the running game and Washington rushed for 118 yards against a good Philadelphia defense. Theismann himself was credited with four rushes—on scrambles—good for 21 yards. He had sparked Allen's offense and the Redskins' defense responded well to having points on the board by forcing four turnovers and limiting the Eagles to 281 yards of total offense.

According to sportswriter Len Shapiro, Theismann was a sort of whirling, one-man show. Theismann "put some fun, frolic and

18. A Contract Offer

flamboyance back into the Redskins' offense," Shapiro wrote in his lead sentence. Shapiro added later in the story, "There were many smiling faces and fluttering hearts in the crowd of 55,031 as Theismann quickly stamped his first start of 1977 memorable." Theismann, Shapiro also wrote, did "several joyful dances after each of his touchdown passes."[3]

A week later, the Redskins played the Colts at Baltimore. The Colts were 6-1 before hosting the Redskins and 7-1 when the game was over. Theismann completed just 11 of 27 passes for 168 yards. He was intercepted twice and did not toss a scoring pass. Washington fell to 4-4. Things were better the next week in Philadelphia against the Eagles. Theismann engineered two scoring drives in the fourth quarter for a come-from-behind victory. He completed 15 of 27 for 187 yards, two touchdowns and two interceptions. Washington got another low-scoring victory the next week, a 10-9 win over a Packers team that finished the year with only two victories. Theismann's numbers were not overwhelming; he added another scoring pass and interception to his totals. His fourth quarter touchdown pass to Mike Thomas was the difference in the game.

The next game was in Washington against the Cowboys. The Redskins were 6-4 and fighting to keep their momentum going. There was speculation in the media that Allen's job was in jeopardy. Dallas was sailing along at 8-2. Allen started Theismann again. Dallas won a tough game, 14-7. Theismann scored Washington's touchdown on a one-yard run, giving the Redskins a 7-0 lead and he completed 17 of 35 passes for 231 yards. He also threw another interception. For comparison, Dallas quarterback Roger Staubach competed 10 of 24 for 138 yards. He tossed a scoring pass for the Cowboys and Ken Houston grabbed an interception for the Redskins. Theismann started again the next week at Buffalo, the defense pitched its second shutout of the season and Washington won 10-0, improving to 7-5.

The Redskins were 4-2 with Theismann as the starting quarterback. Over that span of games, he averaged 13.5 completions out of 28.6 attempts and gained 179.6 yards. He threw six scoring passes and eight interceptions. Kilmer's performance in the six earlier games was marginally worse. The veteran averaged 12.2 completions out of 25.3 attempts and 153.8 yards. He threw five touchdown passes and the same number of interceptions. Neither passer had shown himself to be the best choice. Theismann's scrambling ability gave the offense an extra round in the chamber but Kilmer's vast experience in pressure situations was something Theismann had less of.

George Allen had always said that his job was to win games now, not to develop players during games for the following season. Allen felt the future was now, not some date further into the mist of time. He was getting paid to win the next game, not next year, he felt. But there was pressure from within the organization to stay with Theismann. The younger quarterback's play had energized the fans in RFK Stadium and been positively received by the media, two aspects of a head coach's job that Allen shrugged off.

Allen, according to Theismann, told Theismann that Kilmer would start the second-to-last game against St. Louis because Kilmer had a good record against that team. Kilmer started the last two games of the season (against the Cardinals and the Rams) and Washington won both, but they missed the playoffs anyway. Hindsight is always 20/20 and it is easy to say, with the knowledge the Redskins were unable to win even a wild-card berth in the playoffs, that Theismann should have played to get him ready for the future. Allen had no way of knowing what would happen over the last two weeks of the season. Further, the Redskins won Kilmer's final two starts that season and it is true that wins validate decisions. Kilmer's two-game passing production was acceptable: 26 completions in 49 attempts for 264 yards. He threw three scoring passes and had two intercepted, both interceptions coming against the Rams. Forty years later, those numbers would have been a good half for some NFL passers, but in 1977, they were respectable.

The penultimate game of the 1977 season closed a remarkable chapter in the careers of Allen and St. Louis Cardinals coach Don Coryell, who had succeeded Allen at Whittier. Both were highly successful but in very different ways. Allen's defensive preparation was ahead of its time and his work habits changed coaching at the NFL level. Coryell's offenses at St. Louis and later with the San Diego Chargers gave defensive coaches something to prepare *for*. The Air Coryell offenses on his San Diego teams that were powered by quarterback Dan Fouts years later were the stuff of legend. Both Allen and Coryell were later inducted into halls of fame. Neither ever won an NFL championship as a head coach but both men changed the way the game was played.

Allen's Redskins and Coryell's Cardinals were members of the same division and played each other twice each season. On December 12, 1977, in St. Louis, when they coached against each other for what turned out to be the final time, the temperature at kickoff was just six degrees, there was a 12-mile per hour breeze and the wind chill was minus 10. The game was played on an artificial surface at Civic Center Busch Memorial Stadium in St. Louis. The Redskins opened a 10–0 lead in the first quarter but the Cardinals rallied to tie the score at 10–10. Washington led 13–10 at the half. The Cardinals tied the game at 13 in the third quarter but Washington pulled away to win 26–20. Jim Hart, the Cardinals passer, completed seven of 26 passes for 156 yards and a touchdown. He was also intercepted three times.[4]

18. A Contract Offer

During the five years they coached against each other in the NFL, Allen and Coryell met 10 times. Coryell's team won three of their first four meetings but Allen won five of the last six and his teams out-scored Coryell's, 218–178 in those games. Both men coached two NFL franchises and reached the playoffs with both teams. Allen's regular season winning percentage as an NFL coach, 71.2 percent, is better than Coryell's 57.2 but Coryell's postseason record, 3–6, is better than Allen's 2–7. Only Allen coached a team to the Super Bowl. In retirement, both men lived in Southern California.

The final regular season game George Allen coached in the National Football League was the December 17 meeting with, who else, the Rams at RFK in Washington. Kilmer threw touchdown passes to Frank Grant (a 59-yarder) and Jean Fugett (three yards) in the first quarter and Moseley kicked a 45-yard field goal to give the Redskins a 17–0 advantage. The Rams had a quarterback controversy of their own and, after Pat Haden started but put no points on the board, Vince Ferragamo came in and got the Rams two touchdowns before the game ended with the Redskins ahead, 17–14.

Oddly, Ferragamo would play roles in Allen's final two bit parts in pro football history.

There is a misconception that Allen's tenure with the Redskins left the franchise without draft picks and lacking a future. While it is true that Allen traded away draft picks like the wind scatters pollen, ridding themselves of draft opportunities had become a franchise tradition for the Redskins. We have seen how the club sent Allen and the Rams Washington's first round pick for the 1969 draft in the Gary Beban deal. Similarly, Washington also sent away its first rounder for the 1970 selection process to the San Francisco 49ers in 1968. In 1978, *after Allen was gone*, the Redskins traded away their first-round pick in 1979. So Allen's dump-the-draft style was actually a good fit for the Redskins in that regard.

As for the bare cupboard idea, that isn't accurate. Allen had not used them much, but he left Washington with the lynchpins of their first Super Bowl run. Joe Theismann and John Riggins were the most obvious holdovers. Rick Walker, who was the starting tight end on the Redskins' team that won the Super Bowl at the end of the 1982 season, was drafted by Allen in the fourth round in 1977. George Starke, the starting left tackle in 1982, had been with the 'Skins since Allen drafted him in the 11th round in 1971 and running back Clarence Harmon, acquired by Allen in 1977, was still there as well. Defensive lineman Dave Butz, whom Allen controversially acquired from the St. Louis Cardinals in 1975 for two first round picks, was still the starting left defensive tackle in '82. Defensive backs Joe Lavender and Mark Murphy were Allen additions and Mark Moseley was still Washington's kicker.

It is hard, even now, to determine exactly which former Ram was acquired for which of Washington's 1971 and 1972 first round draft picks, although Allen felt defensive lineman Diron Talbert was the equivalent of his first-round picks from those years. The remaining first rounders from Allen's era are a little easier to examine. Allen traded his 1972 first-rounder to the Jets for Verlon Biggs in 1971 and sent the Redskins first pick for the 1973 selection process to the Colts in 1971 for receiver Roy Jefferson. Washington's first pick in the 1974 draft went to the Rams after the NFL office penalized Allen for trading a draft choice to the Rams that Washington didn't have anymore. One could argue that this was the worst of Allen's draft choice deals, but maybe it wasn't. As recounted in an earlier chapter, Allen sent a first rounder in the 1975 draft to the San Diego Chargers for Duane Thomas in 1973. The headaches that coaching Thomas brought on, combined with Thomas' issues with the press, made the deal non-productive. In 1974, the Redskins sent the Dolphins Washington's first choice in 1976 for Theismann and in 1975, Allen traded the first picks in 1977 and 1978 for Butz. While Allen did not use Theismann much, the deal that brought the quarterback to Washington was a winner from the vantage point of franchise history and the deal for Butz may have been the best of the bunch.

19

Dumped, Hired, Fired Again

George Allen was fired by the Washington Redskins on January 19, 1978. Perhaps it is more accurate to say that the Redskins announced on that date that Allen would not be retained. Allen had never autographed the contract extension offered by the Redskins the summer before. Basically, Allen lost a power struggle with his boss, team president Edward Bennett Williams. Williams was determined to have more say in how the club spent its money.

Williams told the *Washington Post,* "I thought we reached an agreement. Last Saturday was six months since we made the announcement [of the new contract]—with his approval—and nothing happened. ... I just reached the point where I couldn't wait any longer for George to make up his mind and have so advised him of our decision to look for a new head coach and general manager. Our negotiations with George Allen are concluded."[1]

Sportswriter Bob Oates wrote that Allen was among the most controversial figures in pro football at the time. Few people, Oates wrote, would color Allen gray. But Oates also wrote that most of those opposed to Allen were sportswriters in Washington, D.C., although Williams might have been included in that group after dismissing Allen. Remember back when Allen first arrived on the scene, he briefly issued a rule prohibiting players from appearing on their own television and radio shows, which were nice sources of income for those with shows. Allen abandoned that rule quickly when he discovered the scope of his players' involvement with broadcast media. Then there was the poorly conceived rule reducing media access to Redskins players. Allen violated the primary rule for public figures, which has always been to avoid alienating those people who bought their ink by the ton.

As in every argument, there was another side to this one. Allen was quoted by the *Washington Star* as saying of Williams, "He's devious and deceitful."[2] The Star later quoted Allen as saying, "All Ed does is paint a black picture. He always talks about big payrolls, old players, high ticket prices and criticizes the offense. Every time he raised the ticket prices he said it was because of George Allen. We don't have the highest payroll in the league. That's another of his fabrications. I'm proud of what we've accomplished here. There were never seven greater years.[3] But Ed Williams will now use the approach that they don't have any draft choices, the team is too old, and he's got to rebuild. That'll be his theme song, and that's not so."[4]

Sportswriter Dave Brady wrote about Allen's dismissal, speaking to Allen's executive assistant Tim Temerario. Temerario resigned when Allen was canned and Temerario told Brady, "Williams has been saying the Redskins have the highest payroll in the league and has criticized Allen's spending. ... But it was Williams who signed John Riggins [at a reported $1.5 million for five seasons], Joe Theismann and most of the other high-salaried players. We have been accused of busting the budget, but you can't bust the budget if you don't control the budget."

Riggins and Theismann would eventually become Super Bowl heroes for the Redskins but neither had produced much for the club by the time Allen was dismissed. Neither was happy to be playing for Allen by the time his stay in Washington ended.

Theismann told sportswriter Bob Oates, "I welcome the coaching change because I'll have a 50–50 chance to play now." Theismann became the starting quarterback in 1978, starting 14 of the 16 games. The team won half his starts as he tossed 13 scoring passes and 18 interceptions.

Len Hauss told Oates, "I think the only guys who really appreciate George are those who have had to learn what losing is like. I was here [in Washington] seven years before George came, so I can see better than some people what he's done for us. I sometimes think it takes a stretch of bad years to make a man appreciate the good."

Billy Kilmer, the man in the middle of the Great Redskins Quarterback Controversy, held a unique perspective on Allen's coaching. Acquired to give the 'Skins a veteran relief pitcher behind the very popular starter, Sonny Jurgensen, Kilmer eventually replaced Jurgensen and then played in front of Theismann. Asked whether Allen was devious in his treatment of his players, Kilmer said, "He has this burning desire to win. And if he told the full truth to all of his players, it would be harder to win. Suppose you tell a wide receiver you're sitting him down because he's no good. Then suppose your first-stringer breaks a leg on the first play. Now what do you do?"

Hanburger became the defensive signal caller when Pardee retired and he told Oates that Allen's problems with the media (termed "the press" in Allen's coaching years) were due to the fact that Allen had a different sort of personality from other coaches.

"He is different, you know," Hanburger said. "I've never met anyone in my life who's so determined to win. And you know, people who are 'different' irritate other people. ... I also think you'll have to agree that most people are negative-minded, and George is a natural for these people to dislike. He's a winner, and winners antagonize negative-minded people."

Allen did not remain unemployed very long. Incredibly, the Rams hired him again. Carroll Rosenbloom, now the owner of the franchise, hired Allen to replace Chuck Knox. Knox had turned Prothro's losers back into winners. Knox's Rams even won some playoff games. But, under Knox, the Rams never advanced to the Super Bowl. Knox had left the Rams to coach the Buffalo Bills.

For the first time in his career, Allen took over an NFL team that was accustomed to winning. The players were not looking for someone to lead them out of a losing morass and into the playoffs. In fact, many of the Rams players were unhappy to have lost Knox. Team chemistry, one of Allen's coaching calling cards, was in the wind. Further, Allen did not have the General Manager's title and was not free to build a roster to his liking. Don Klosterman, who was well-respected around the league, had that title. Rosenbloom said when he hired Allen that he wanted to see Allen work without the burden of responsibilities beyond coaching. That comment turned out to mean that Allen was on a short leash.

Allen got in trouble with the league in July, when he was fined $3,000 for "acrimonious and destructive statements" about the Redskins. Allen had made continued and direct personal attacks against members of the Redskins' front office, according to the league.[5] Four decades later, since the advent of social media, Allen's descriptions of his former employers seem tame. But in 1978 the National Football League was much more buttoned up, as the saying goes. The league's owners didn't like current or former players and coaches making negative comments and the commissioner worked for the owners. A few weeks later, Allen was free to say whatever he wanted.

Trouble brewed early in training camp. Some players—veterans— were unhappy with Allen's practice methods. Allen's rules regarding other aspects of training camp, which extended into the area of decorum in the dining hall, irritated players. A few walked out of training camp and then came back. Without the authority of being his own General Manager,

Allen needed the support of the Rams' front office, which he did not have. George Allen, long known as a player's coach, had a players' rebellion on his hands.

Then the Rams lost their first two preseason games and Rosenbloom fired his coach, replacing Allen with Ray Malavasi, the lone assistant holdover from the Knox era. Malavasi was popular with the players and his promotion went a long way toward soothing ruffled feathers.[6]

Rosenbloom told the media, "It is my feeling that I have made a serious error in judgement in believing George Allen could work within our framework."[7]

Allen told reporters, "I told him [Rosenbloom] what I have to offer is what the Rams need. There were several things he said, that he thought we wouldn't win if I continued as coach, and that I would work better in the framework of an organization where I'd be general manager and coach. ... All I know is that I did everything in my power, did it the way it should be done, did it my way. We worked hard and were committed to the program we've used successfully all these years and I could not change that if I was to live with myself."

Tom Mack, who was a rookie with the Rams in 1966 and was still playing in Los Angeles a dozen seasons later, was still among the best offensive guards in the league. He had played for Allen, Prothro and Knox. Mack said, "We have to vindicate ourselves. I think George will be back as a coach and a winner. He was replaced because the players didn't play well ... they're the ones who play football, not the coach."

Quarterback Pat Haden said he was surprised by the firing. "I was happy with the way things were going with George Allen. We had two bad games and I feel badly that I didn't play well. I didn't do a good job of directing the offense, maybe that's why this happened."

Offensive tackle Doug France said, "It was a shock. The man [Rosenbloom] just wants a Super Bowl and we want it too and if this is the best move, then we're for it. We played bad in those two games, it wasn't the coach's fault. We lost five preseason games last year."[8]

Allen had earned the rare distinctions of (A) getting fired four times by the same NFL franchise and (B) getting dumped by two different franchises within eight months. According to various media reports, the Rams honored their three-year contract, paying Allen $200,000 a year.

It is interesting to note here the differences between owners. When George Allen's Rams lost their first two preseason games and players grumbled about Allen's coaching practices in 1978, owner Carroll Rosenbloom fired Allen. After Rosenbloom's sudden death[9] in April of 1979 his widow, Georgia, became the owner and years later she hired Dick

Vermeil to become the head coach of the then-St. Louis Rams. Vermeil's Rams struggled for two seasons and there were player grumblings about the length of Vermeil's practices, among other things. By then married to composer Dominic Frontiere, Georgia Frontiere supported Vermeil and the Rams won the Super Bowl in his third season.[10]

THE 1980S: ALLEN'S ODYSSEY

20

Stranger in a Strange Land— Briefly

"You cannot control what people are going to do," George Allen wrote, "but I have always been able to control myself and my preparation. From a very young age, I was always busy; that was one of the choices you made when you were poor in the midst of the Depression. I've always had the feeling, no matter what I was doing, that I could be putting my time into something else as well. It bothers me to waste even a few minutes."[1]

As of the 1978 football season, George Herbert Allen was the winningest coach in the history of two National Football League franchises, the Rams and Redskins. He had been branded as expensive, eccentric and difficult to work with. His bizarre final chapter with the Rams, which could be argued was more about uncertainty within the Rams organization than it was about problems with the head coach, damaged Allen's image as a winner to the point where he wasn't wanted.

"I did not return to the NFL because I am incapable of being a puppet coach," Allen wrote. He went on, "In any job I ever accepted, starting with the first one at Morningside College, I knew instinctively that I had to make all decisions that related to what takes place on the field, just as Landry and Shula have done. I say this without conceit: I have always run the show because I know of no other way to make everyone give more of himself than he wants. And this is the essence of good coaching. Of good management. Of good leadership."

"I don't want this to come across as sour grapes. But today, in an era when TV revenues guarantee every owner a profit before they tee up the first kickoff, when the name George Allen is mentioned—or someone like me—the first fear is that he will rock the boat. Make people work six or seven days a week. Call them at midnight with a problem. *Allen is hard to get along with because he demands that everyone earn his pay check*" [italics are in the original].[2]

With his fourth firing by the Rams, Allen became untouchable for NFL owners and he suddenly had a lot of minutes to avoid wasting. Typically, he found something to do. During the 1978 NFL season, Allen worked for CBS as a color commentator during football broadcasts. He was paid $3,000 each for games featuring the Rams against New England, Houston and Atlanta, a game featuring the Redskins against St. Louis and a contest between Minnesota and Seattle. He appeared on WDMV-TV9 in September and wrote a syndicated column for the Times-Mirror Company.

In 1981, Allen became the Chairman of the President's Council on Physical Fitness during the Ronald Reagan administration. He held the post until 1988 and he was not just a figurehead. John C. McCabe accepted Allen's invitation to join the President's Council on Physical Fitness and Sports on April 28, 1986. At the time, McCabe was the Chairman of the Board and CEO of Blue Cross/Blue Shield. An old hand at recruiting, Allen drew attention to the need for continued fitness through life and he attracted important names to the effort.

Allen founded the National Fitness Foundation in 1982 and became the Chairman and CEO of the organization. In that role, Allen joined hands with the nationally prominent to promote fitness and health. For example, the foundation held an awards banquet on June 21, 1989. The National Dinner Chairman was Caspar Weinberger, the Secretary of Defense during the Reagan administration. The guests of honor included Commerce Secretary Robert Mosbacher and RJR Nabisco Chairman/CEO Louis Gerstner. Roger B. Smith, Chairman/CEO of General Motors, accepted the Corporate Achievement Award. Preston Robert Tisch, President/CEO of Loews Corporation, was given an award for public service and University of Tennessee basketball coaching great Pat Summitt was given the Sports Leadership and Achievement Award. That's a heady group of associates for an out-of-work football coach, but, after seven years in Washington, Allen was used to that sort of thing.

Like most coaches, Allen remained available for his former players. He was the featured speaker at a dinner in Los Angeles benefiting the fight against myasthenia gravis, the illness that had struck former Rams defensive end Lamar Lundy. Allen joked with his audience, "It's good to be back as the Rams coach. Excuse me, I have the wrong speech."

For a few months in 1982, Allen was in Canada, trying to revive the fortunes of the Montreal Alouettes. This time he wasn't a coach. George Allen was a minority owner. Montreal Alouettes owner Nelson Skalbania's ballclub was deeply in debt and not winning. The Canadian Football League team compiled a record of three wins and 13 losses in 1981. That was good enough to reach the playoffs but not good enough to make a profit. A *Sports Illustrated* article in the magazine's March 15, 1982, edition estimated the team had lost no less than two and a half million dollars in 1981 and possibly as much as four and half million. Skalbania lived and owned a business in Vancouver, British Columbia, and was away from the ballclub much of the year. The owner and team administrators had differing opinions on who was to blame for the team's financial plight, but the bottom line was the team was in debt, had a poor product on the field and was bleeding season-ticket holders.

Skalbania and his team needed a newsmaker, someone to create interest in a flagging ballclub. A ticket seller. George Allen had built ticket sellers twice but had been out of football since his final tenure with the Rams ended. His reputation for free spending and the sour endings in both Los Angeles and Washington left him unattractive to NFL owners, even those suffering through long stretches of losing seasons. When Skalbania announced in February of 1982 that he had hired Allen, the idea was to change the fortunes of the team that was the biggest one-season loser in the history of the Canadian Football League. But Allen wasn't hired to coach the Als. He was hired to manage the team back to profitability. There was no coach at the time Allen was hired and he *could* have coached. Son Bruce came along to be the team's Vice President of Operations.

"I feel I've proven myself as a coach," Allen told the Associated Press. "One of my goals has been to be an owner. I was once offered 5 percent of a ballclub in the NFL, but the offer was taken back before I could exercise it."[3] Allen put the chances of him coaching the Alouettes at 60–40 that he would not coach.

"We'll simply have to decide whether this thing is salvageable," Allen said. He added, "If I like what I see, I'll exercise my option; it's that simple. But right now you're going to learn just how frugal George Allen can be." When asked about his previously free-spending ways, he said he'd do things differently because "I'm an owner now, you know."[4]

Allen moved to Montreal and lived for a time at the Ritz-Carlton hotel. Etty did not go with him right away. It was the same arrangement the family made when Allen went to Chicago to join the Bears, to Los Angeles to join the Rams in 1966 and to Washington to join the Redskins. Etty was fluent in French and might have helped her husband in Montreal, where the predominant language was and is French.

Money talked in both languages and Allen had to trim expensive contracts from the balance sheet. The same *Sports Illustrated* piece that profiled Allen's foray into Canadian football credited him with trimming $300,000 (Canadian) from front office salaries and more than a million from the player salaries, mostly American players. Vince Ferragamo, a quarterback Allen coached briefly during his final stint with the Rams, had a huge contract by Canadian standards, estimated at $450,000. Most of Ferragamo's deal was a personal services contract with Skalbania. Allen wrote the Rams and gave them permission to renew negotiations with Ferragamo. Other American players with big contracts were either cut or not brought back.

"Ok, this Montreal franchise is at rock bottom now," Allen told *Sports Illustrated*. "I built up two franchises before and I can do it again. The NFL has gotten out of the ticket-selling business. The clubs have grown fat on TV money, but selling season tickets will be one of my jobs here. Six thousand season tickets weren't renewed after last season. O.K., I'm going to sit down and personally sign a letter to each of those people, and we'll send 'em one of these little key chains with the Alouettes' logo on it. I've never signed 6,000 pieces of paper before, but I'm going to do it now."[5]

Bruce Allen told *Sports Illustrated* that the franchise operated without a budget during the 1981 season. He had an accountant from the financial firm Price Waterhouse look at the team's business end and the resulting news, Bruce Allen said, was that everything was a mess. The younger Allen said, "Anytime someone wanted to draw money or write a check, he just wrote it. ... There was no supervision here at all. My little sister would have known better."

George Allen's Montreal contract gave him 20 percent ownership of the club, to be held in escrow with an option for Allen to buy 51 percent by the end of December of that year. Skalbania was to pay off the team's debts. Allen had investors ready to help him purchase the next 31 percent for ownership of the controlling interest by the end of 1982 and then the final 49 percent by the end of 1983 but, according to the Associated Press, the team's unclear financial status blocked the entire purchase from going forward. Shortly after Allen signed on with the club it became obvious that Skalbania could not pay off the Alouettes' outstanding debts. A new deal was struck: Allen investors William Harris, a California real estate businessman, and Chicago financier Tom King would pay off some of the debt if Skalbania could obtain waivers from other creditors. The waivers were never obtained.[6]

Allen told reporters in March, "Well, that's basically it. The team can't stay in limbo the way it's been. ... We've been spinning our wheels and this has to be done for the good of the team."

The Associated Press termed Allen's announcement a last-ditch effort to revive his chances of staying with the club but it didn't work. George Allen was out of football again.

Skalbania never did pay off franchise's debts and he gave the club to the league before the 1982 season. The league technically folded the Montreal franchise and replaced it with the Montreal Concordes, but the

Concordes were awarded with the history and playing records of the Alouettes.[7] In 1986, the Concordes were renamed the Alouettes. A few years later, the franchise went out of business again. A new franchise, also named the Alouettes, was formed years after that.

In September of 1984, at age 66, Allen was concerned enough about certain aspects of his health that he had himself examined by a medical group in Redondo Beach, California. His health, tests showed, was within normal ranges. That was good news. Allen was soon to become a wanted man again.

21

Blitzing and Wrangling with the USFL

As the United States Football League was established as an entity in preparation for playing in 1983, it was announced that the league would not be a challenger for the long-established National Football League. The new circuit would play a spring schedule and avoid the kind of bidding war for top players that the NFL and American Football League conducted in the 1960s. Player salaries would be limited. The games themselves would be the attraction instead of the players but, hopefully, the players would attract a following for the league. The USFL accomplished an important milestone when it attracted and inked a contract with the combination of the ABC and ESPN television networks to carry the games.[1]

George Allen and William Harris, a Southern California businessman, applied for ownership of the Chicago franchise. They eventually came to terms with Arizona doctor Ted Diethrich, who put more money in the pot and became the controlling owner. Allen was made the Chairman of the Board and head coach. Bruce Allen became the General Manager. George Allen immediately got to work, assembling a roster largely made up of NFL veterans with some high-quality draft picks. The best-known players included veteran NFL quarterback Greg Landry, rookie wide receiver Trumaine Johnson and kicker/punter Frank Corral. Allen also acquired running back Kevin Long and drafted another back, Tim Spencer, plus veteran linebacker Stan White. If these were not front-line NFL stars, the full roster was the most expensive in the league in 1983. The Blitz was favored to win the inaugural USFL championship.

Diethrich said of Allen, "He was very friendly, an affable guy. He was a tremendously driven person, driven in the care of his own health, running every day. He was driven in his profession and always thinking about what he was doing in football. He was very intense, particularly at game time and leading up to game time. If it wasn't a good game, you could tell he was very concerned."² But Diethrich added about George Allen, "He was a good football man from the standpoint of X's and O's and calling the plays, but not a good businessman. ... He had no concept about the economics. The person who was responsible for the economics was his son Bruce."

The Blitz played its games at Soldier Field. The league's goal was to provide affordable football in major stadiums, something the Blitz accomplished. But the facility sometimes dwarfed the crowds drawn to see Allen's team. Televised games could not help but display the crowd size within the massive stadium, which hurt the league's image. While it was true that the USFL did not compete with the NFL for television time—due to the USFL's spring schedule—it did compete with baseball. Allen and his Blitz got a bit of a bad break in that regard because the Chicago White Sox won the American League West Division title with a record of 99–63.³ The White Sox had not fielded competitive teams in many years and the fever generated by their division title run hurt the fledgling Blitz at the gate.

Allen headed a coaching staff of himself plus seven assistants. Only two of those assistants had previous experience with Allen, passing coordinator Paul Lanham and offensive coordinator Charlie Waller. Lanham and Waller both worked for Allen in Washington and during the 1978 mess in Los Angeles.

George Allen had been an owner (in theory) during his brief stint in Montreal but had said he probably would not coach the Alouettes. Now he was more than just an owner and more than just a coach. He was building a franchise from scratch, but he was doing more than just that. Allen was the face of the United States Football League. Before the league had players, it had Allen. His love of coaching and his ceaseless energy were not only accepted by the USFL but also were needed, and Allen didn't disappoint. According to Paul Reeths in his detailed history of the league, *The United States Football League 1982–1986*, Allen consulted several times with Oakland Raiders head man Al Davis, who had once been the commissioner of the American Football League.⁴ According to USFL Revisited.webs.com, Allen conducted nine formal tryout camps during the months before the start of training camp. He evaluated as many as 3,200 players and actually signed 268 candidates to one sort of contract or another during that time. It should not come as a surprise that Allen instituted the first trade in USFL history on August 11, 1982, sending the negotiating rights to four players to the Boston Breakers for quarterback Greg Landry, an NFL veteran. Well ahead of the draft, the league assigned member franchises territorial rights to players from specific pro teams from both the NFL and Canadian league, plus players from specific college or universities. Thus, Allen had more than just draft picks to exchange for players he wanted, he also had negotiating rights he could offer.

Allen's energetic efforts to build the Blitz did not always go over well with the other teams in the league. When the Blitz signed Landry, the veteran NFL quarterback, the Boston franchise still owned the negotiating rights to Landry. Thus, the first "trade" in USFL history was really something Allen had to do after inking the deal with Landry. Allen had to put together a package that sent Boston four players from the list of players for which Chicago had negotiating rights. Boston coach Dick Coury joked, "I told George I'd like to be able to talk with my players before he does. [NFL Commissioner Pete] Rozelle couldn't control George for 14 years. If we can somehow do it, we'll already be one step up on the NFL."[5]

Allen was accused of tampering with players he should not have been talking to by other teams, according to USFL Executive Director Steve Ehrhart. Other teams around the league may have been guilty of tampering as well. It was a wild chase for talent and there were good players available to chase. It was, as Anthony Edwards said in the film *Top Gun*, a target-rich environment. Ehrhart said, "Our suspicion was that there was a lot of contact between the Allens and other teams' protected players, where if we'd been in a more established situation, there would have been penalties. But these players were not under contract to anybody. There was no question that there were an awful lot of people blurring the lines, saying, 'I know somebody that knows this guy. We're new, let's just get him in the league,' rather than worrying about if his rights belonged to somebody else. We were in a fast track getting ready for camp that first year, starting from zero, trying to get rosters built. It smoothed out in years two and three."[6]

The first USFL draft was held on January 4, 1983, and Allen was the first to make a draft day trade. He sent the Blitz's first round pick, which was the sixth pick overall, plus the negotiating rights for running back Calvin Murphy, to the Arizona Wranglers for the Wranglers' first rounder, which was the second pick overall. With that second overall choice, Allen selected running back Tim Spencer of Ohio State and later signed him. The Wranglers selected SMU star running back Eric Dickerson with the pick they received from the Blitz. Dickerson became one of the greatest professional runners of all time. He was eventually inducted into the Pro Football Hall of Fame. But he never played in the USFL. Tim Spencer became Allen's top rusher in 1983. Allen wasn't done, of course. He sent his ninth, tenth and eleventh rounders to the Boston Breakers for their first rounder, the 11th choice overall. With his new pick, Allen selected Trumaine Johnson of Grambling. Johnson led the USFL in receiving in 1983. Trader George had maneuvered his way into selecting twice in the first eleven spots, used both picks for offensive players and picked two players who became keys to Allen's offense. It was roughly analogous to using two picks to get Gale Sayers and Dick Butkus for the Bears in the midst of the draft war against the AFL all those years earlier.

The USFL owners had been wary of setting a salary cap out of concerns for a possible anti-trust legal action. The owners *had* set an informal agreement for a cap on player salaries and the Blitz did not stay under that level. That led to some bad blood between the franchise and other league teams. Denver owner Ron Blanding said of Allen: "[We] got along great. I mean, we had our arguments, but once the arguments were over, he was a pleasure to be around. It was just his philosophy of life. It had always been that way even when he was with Washington. He'd pay anybody anything to get whatever he wanted. He didn't care about what the costs were. He didn't care whether there was a profit or a loss. All he wanted to do was win. ... In my mind, he was a nice guy with the wrong philosophy."

The Blitz held training camp at Arizona's Glendale College, near Phoenix, because winter conditions in the Chicago area that time of year were a little too rugged for training camp. League rules limited teams to having 85 players at the start of camp. The USFL rules stated that the franchises had to trim down to a 40-player roster, plus a 10-player Development Squad. During training camp, veteran NFL linebacker White signed a free agent contract with the Blitz.[7]

"This league is for real," Allen told reporters. "The Chicago Blitz is for real. The league is going to go and be successful and expand and there will be expansion after that. Anybody who doesn't think that has ulterior motives. This league is good for America. Football is a sport that is made for television."[8]

Drama is also made for television and the USFL schedule makers knew that, so Allen and the Blitz opened their season on March 6 at RFK Stadium in Washington, D.C., Allen's former stomping grounds. Quarterback Greg Landry and wide out Trumaine Johnson had big days as the Blitz beat Washington 28–7. The game drew 38,007 and gained the USFL plenty of attention.[9]

It was a triumphant return to the nation's capital for Allen, who told reporters after the game, "It was an emotional experience for me because I wasn't just a Redskins coach. I had my heart and soul in the organization and the city. I became emotional a couple of times standing on the sideline during the national anthem. But I'm very proud of my team, the staff and the organization. They played like pros. We didn't make many mistakes and we beat a good football team." Allen admitted that things were different in the new league than they had been during his NFL tenure. "I may have changed because ... in this new league I can't let little things bother me. I used to have this expression that no detail is too small. I still believe that but the other day we went to practice with fifty players and coaches and everything. We didn't have any footballs. That would have bothered me but I thought, 'Every day there is some little thing like that ... and I know that until we get better organized, just roll with the punches.'"

Allen soon had punches to roll with. The Blitz lost a road game to the Arizona Wranglers, 30–29, then lost their home opener, 16–13, when the Denver Gold scored the winning points with 18 seconds remaining. Statistically, Denver did not gain a single yard passing. The Denver game drew 22,600 to Soldier Field. The Blitz, the preseason favorites to win the league championship, were suddenly looking down the barrels of a season on the brink. Typical of an Allen-coached team with its back to the wall, the Blitz rallied. The Blitz drew their record to even on March 27 with a 20–14 victory over the Los Angeles Express in Chicago. In four games, Chicago had scored 90 points and allowed 64, but their record was only 2–2.

Three days after the victory over the Express, Allen traded two picks in the 1984 USFL draft to the Birmingham Stallions for defensive back Carl Allen. Carl Allen was assigned to the Development Squad and then activated on April 6.

Next up were the undefeated Tampa Bay Bandits, coached by Steve Spurrier, at Tampa Stadium. The Bandits got Blitzed, 42–3. Luther Bradley intercepted six Tampa Bay passes and returned one 93 yards for a touchdown to lead the Chicago defense. Greg Landry passed for 277 yards and Trumaine Johnson caught seven passes for 146 yards for the Blitz. The Blitz led 14–3 at the half but scored 21 points in the third quarter to put the game away. Chicago more closely resembled the dominating team Allen was supposed to have and kept rolling with a 22–11 victory over the Birmingham Stallions in Chicago. The Blitz had won four of six and three in a row. They had out-scored opponents 154–81 but their home game against the Stallions drew just 13,859.

Next up was a road game in the Pontiac Silverdome against the 3–4 Michigan Panthers. The Panthers were winless in two home games but the Panthers beat the Blitz 17–12 in front of a sparse crowd of 11,634. The Blitz beat the New Jersey Generals 17–14 in overtime in front of 32,184 in Chicago. The turnout was mostly to see New Jersey runner Herschel Walker, the Heisman Trophy winner from the University of Georgia. Walker's $4.2 million dollar contract was worth more than twice the USFL's recommended *team* salary cap of $1.8 million. Walker was available to play in the USFL because the NFL had a policy that banned drafting and signing players whose college eligibility had not expired and Walker's had not. The Walker signing flew in the face of the idea of affordable, responsible conduct by USFL team owners but, as evidenced by the Chicago attendance count, Walker drew fans to the league.

Allen made a major trade on April 28, after beating the Generals, when he sent eight picks in the 1984 draft and the rights to two other players to the Michigan Panthers for center Tom Piette. Piette was first assigned to the Blitz Development Squad but he was activated on May 5. Pro football history is replete with stories of seemingly one-sided trades. The Rams traded eleven players to acquire linebacker Les Richter in the 1950s, for example, and the New Orleans Saints once traded virtually all of their draft picks one year for Texas running back Ricky Williams. But Richter was an NFL star and Williams was expected to become one. Piette was not.

Mike Keller, the personnel director for the Panthers, said, "They wanted a player we had, a fellow named Tom Piette. Tom was a Michigan State guy. ... He made our team that first year as a backup. We liked him, he was a good team player. ... George and Bruce, a lot of the time they would do it in tandem; they would both be on the line with me. They wanted to trade for Tom Piette. For some reason they thought he was going to be the greatest center who ever played. I talked with them and said, 'Let me think about it. Let me talk to the coach.' ... We didn't think he was as good as George and Bruce thought. They had offered like a third round pick, and I said, 'No, no.'" Eventually the Allens upped the trade ante so high that Keller made the deal. Keller said, "As much as we like Tom Piette ... all these draft choices, we can't turn it down. It was an unbelievable trade. I've never seen anything like it before or since. The more we said, 'No,' the more they wanted him. That was George Allen. George was so paranoid. He figured the reason we wanted this backup guy was because he was so good, he had to have him."[10]

Piette was activated on May 5 and he remained on the active roster through the end of the 1983 season and was active with the Arizona Wranglers for all of the 1984 season.[11]

The victory over the Generals started Chicago on another three-game win streak. Allen returned to the Los Angeles Memorial Olympic Coliseum and the Blitz beat the Los Angeles Express 38–17 in front of 21,123. The team returned to Chicago to beat the Federals again, 31–3, in front of just 11,303. The Blitz was now 7–3. Next up for Allen was a return to another location he knew well, Veterans Stadium in Philadelphia, home of the Stars. Jim Mora, who had been the Redskins' defensive coordinator for the last three years that Allen coached in Washington, coached the Stars. Mora's Stars beat the Blitz 31–24 and were headed for the USFL playoffs.[12]

Next, Chicago ventured to New Jersey to beat the Generals, 19–13, in overtime again, but suffered a major loss when starting quarterback Greg

Landry suffered a broken ankle. Landry went on the Injured Reserve list and Allen traded offensive lineman Kari Yli-Renko and a draft pick to the Generals for quarterback Bobby Scott. Scott was immediately added to the active roster. Another quarterback, Tom Porras, was added to the Development Squad. After Landry was hurt, Tom Rozantz, Bobby Scott and Tim Koegel would all get meaningful playing time under center. In another trade during the same time frame Allen then sent defensive lineman Bob Cobb to the Washington Federals for the Federals' eighth-round pick in the 1984 draft.

The Blitz next came home and avenged their early-season loss to the Wranglers, 36–11. The two wins improved Chicago's record to 9–4, but Chicago lost to the Boston Breakers in Boston the following week, 21–15. On the flight home from Boston, a few players were laughing and joking and the always intense Allen angrily chewed those players out for seemingly taking the loss lightly. They should not have been happy enough to joke around, Allen said. It was a minor incident by itself but it also showed that Allen had not lost his competitive intensity. He had preached all of his coaching life that losing was like dying and the fires still burned within Allen at age 65. Every player interviewed for this book described Allen as a player's coach and no former player described Allen as yelling or shouting at practice. Sometimes, however, as reflected above, 65-year-old Allen would chew them out on airplanes after a loss.[13] Allen hated losing and could not abide players who could laugh after a loss.

A 31–8 victory over the Bandits in Chicago in front of 21,249 and a 29–14 road victory over the Stallions left Allen's club with a record of 11–5 with two games remaining. The Blitz was in danger of missing the playoffs and things looked even worse when the Panthers went to Chicago and beat the Blitz 34–19 in front of 25,041. Allen's Blitz finally secured a berth in the USFL playoffs on the final day of the regular season with a commanding 31–7 victory over the Oakland Invaders in front of 12,346 in Chicago. Allen and his roster of veteran players should have shined in the USFL playoffs. Instead, they blew a double-digit lead and lost to the Stars in Philadelphia, in overtime, 44–38. For the season, including the playoff loss, the Blitz won 12 of 19. They drew an average of 18,163 to their nine home games.

The Blitz led the USFL in scoring in that first year, putting 456 points on the scoreboard, and allowed the second fewest points scored against them, 271. For the first time in the professional ranks a George Allen-coached offense featured two rushers who gained more than a thousand yards: Spencer gained 1,157 yards and scored six touchdowns while Long gained 1,022 yards and scored 12 times. Both men averaged 3.9 yards per carry. Trumaine Johnson led the USFL by catching 81 passes

21. Blitzing and Wrangling with the USFL

and had the best yardage total, 1,322. Johnson caught 10 scoring passes. Kicker Frank Corral finished fifth in scoring. Quarterback Greg Landry was among the league leaders in most passing categories, despite missing part of the season with his leg injury. Most importantly, Landry tossed 16 touchdown passes and only nine interceptions.

Ted Diethrich, the Blitz owner, was based in Arizona and he didn't want to keep traveling back and forth from the southwestern desert to Chicago. A heart surgeon and researcher, Dietrich was constantly on the road with the Blitz and that commitment ate into the time he could spend on his primary career. Diethrich lost millions on the Blitz, which could be expected for a new sports league, but he wanted an operation closer to home. Eventually a complicated deal was worked out whereby Diethrich would become the owner of the Arizona franchise and he would sell the Chicago team. James Hoffman, a Milwaukee-based heart surgeon, was willing to buy the Blitz. Diethrich took over the Wranglers with the understanding that Allen and his players would move from Chicago to Arizona. Hoffman got the woeful Wranglers players, who had gone 4–14 in 1983. The deal amounted to an exchange of franchises and it was a little confusing at first. When Wranglers head coach Doug Shively was replaced by former Allen assistant Marv Levy, Levy thought he'd be coaching Allen's team.

Levy had been offered the general manager's job with the USFL's Express as the league ramped up for its first season, but Levy wanted to coach rather than administrate and he turned the offer down. Instead, he turned broadcaster and helped call USFL games for ABC radio. Levy wrote that when the USFL expanded following the 1983 season, he was contacted by two teams. Before he could accept either of those offers, Levy was contacted by a representative of the Blitz named Ron Potocnik. Levy met with Potocnik in Chicago and, after a discussion, Levy was offered the head coaching position of the Chicago Blitz. Levy thought he would be coaching a strong team in his hometown and he was a happy man.

For a while.

Levy wrote later, "Now, for the first time in my career, I would be taking over a strong team, one that was ready to challenge for the championship right from the outset. On the day I arrived back in the old hometown, I learned that the complicated Chicago/Arizona deal had included an exchange between those two teams of their complete roster of players. I was Chicago's new coach, all right, but Arizona's 4–14 last place team from the year before would be the *new* Chicago Blitz" (italics in the original). Levy continued, tongue in cheek, "After learning about the trade that sent the strong Blitz roster to Arizona in exchange for a much less talented group, I spent several days in intensive care."[14]

Chicago's new owner gave up on the team early in the season, ending his association with the team and the league. The USFL office had to take on the responsibility of running the Blitz. Along with ending his association with the Chicago franchise, Hoffman also quit making payments on his debt to Diethrich for purchasing the Blitz. The stoppage of payments impacted the Allens later.

While his roster of players stayed mostly the same, there were a few changes to Allen's coaching staff and one of the new additions to the Wranglers was an old name in the Allen story. Roman Gabriel joined the team as Allen's quarterbacks coach. Gabriel had served as the offensive coordinator and quarterbacks coach of the USFL's Boston Breakers the year before. From 1980 through 1982, Gabriel had been the head coach at California State Polytechnic University, Pomona, which was better known as Cal Poly Pomona. The Broncos struggled during Gabriel's tenure, going 8–24 over three seasons.[15] The school dropped football after the 1982 season.

After splitting their two preseason games, the Wranglers stumbled their way through the opening weeks of the season, dropping four of their first seven games. They lost close games and won blowouts. After Mora and his Stars beat the Wranglers 22–21 in front of 30,252 in Sun Devil Stadium, the Wranglers beat the Generals in New Jersey, 20–3 and then prepared for a unique challenge: The Houston Gamblers. The Gamblers were coached by Allen's long-time defensive signal caller, Jack Pardee, and Pardee had a hot young quarterback, Jim Kelly, running the volatile run and shoot offense. Houston beat Arizona 37–24, but the teams would meet again. The San Antonio Gunslingers, led by future NFL quarterback Doug Williams, beat Arizona next, 24–23 and Allen's team had a 4–6 record. Allen's record of never recording a losing season in a professional league was in danger and the playoffs seemed out of reach. Arizona split the next four games, then finished the season with a four-game win streak, good enough for a berth in the playoffs.

The first-round game matched Arizona against Pardee's Gamblers and it looked like the Wranglers would lay another playoff egg. Arizona trailed 16–3 with seven minutes remaining in the game, then staged a crazy comeback and won 17–16. The second-round game matched Arizona against the LA Express. The Express was coached by former NFL and AFL passer John Hadl and featured rookie quarterback Steve Young, whose reputed $40 million contract made him the richest professional football player in America. The game should have been played in Los Angeles because the Express had the better record in the regular season. However, the Coliseum was preparing to host the 1984 Olympic Games and the game site eventually switched to Sun Devil Stadium in Phoenix. There are better places to play football than Arizona in the month of July. Kickoff was scheduled for 8:30 p.m. in order to avoid the worst of the heat. The game drew 30,188 and the Wranglers' improbable postseason run continued after a 35–23 victory over the Express. The Wranglers advanced to the USFL championship game against, who else, Jim Mora and the Philadelphia Stars.

The title game was played in Tampa, Florida. The area was soaked by thunderstorms prior to the game but there was no rain during the title match. Philadelphia's offense plowed through the Wrangler defense on its first two possessions to leap out to a 13–0 lead. The Stars' offensive line's domination of those first-quarter drives was so complete that quarterback Chuck Fusina fumbled the ball on an attempted quarterback sneak and scored anyway. The ball rolled into the end zone and Fusina fell on it, scoring Philadelphia's second touchdown. The Stars nearly had another touchdown in the second quarter but that time running back Kelvin Bryant fumbled into the Arizona end zone and the Wranglers recovered for a score-saving touchback. Frank Corral booted a 37-yard field goal to get three points for the Wranglers in the second quarter and the Stars missed a field goal near the end of the half that could have given Mora's team a bigger halftime lead.

The Wranglers had a promising drive going in the third quarter but it terminated when a pass play failed. Philadelphia defensive back Mike Johnson appeared to have committed pass interference on Arizona's Tim Spencer near the sideline. A completion would have given Arizona a first down. No penalty was called and the pass might have been uncatchable anyway. The last chance the Wranglers had to score came late in the third quarter when a Philadelphia pass was tipped at the line of scrimmage and intercepted by Arizona's Ed Smith. Smith returned the play to the Stars' 47 and the Wranglers got the ball to the Philadelphia 23 before the drive stalled on three incomplete passes. Trailing 13–3, Allen chose to try a field goal but Corral's 40-yard attempt failed. The Stars scored twice more and won the game 23–3 in front of 52,662.

During the championship game broadcast, play-by-play man Keith Jackson mentioned the likelihood that the USFL would convert its schedule to play in the fall and compete directly with the NFL. Since he had become the owner of the USFL's New Jersey franchise, Donald Trump had been agitating other USFL franchise owners to switch to playing a fall season. It was an idiotic idea. The USFL was still establishing itself as a business, but its identity was as a high-quality football league fans could watch in the spring. There was a new television contract with ABC on the table that would have included a slightly bigger rights package at $175 million. The money ABC offered each team would not have put every team in the profitable column, but it would have stabilized several and made some difference to the bottom line of all of them. Wranglers principal owner

Diethrich, for example, was never going to see the money he was owed for the Blitz sale and so the ABC money would have made a difference to his franchise. ABC would not agree to follow the USFL to the fall; its desire was to televise spring football.

Trump had tried for years to purchase an NFL team but NFL owners, all of whom understood business and valued stability, refused to consider Trump's repeated attempts to join the club. The USFL was less picky about franchise purchases. As the second season went along, the league discovered some of its owners, particularly its newer owners, could not cover their business losses and several teams were in financial trouble. That was especially true of those who spent the most freely on playing talent. Trump's primary reason for purchasing the New Jersey Generals had nothing to do with the value of the USFL nor any real love for the game of professional football. Trump wanted to force a merger between the NFL and the USFL, thus getting him a new and very valuable toy, a National Football League franchise. Trump eventually convinced enough of the new league's owners to abandon its primary assets, the spring schedule and the network contract, in order to switch to a fall schedule. The USFL had probably expanded too quickly and it might not have lasted much longer anyway but it was the switch to a fall schedule that killed the league.

Diethrich told author Paul Reeths, "I had the prediction this thing was going to go south. He [Trump] was insistent the league should go in the fall. That was in spite of the recommendation we were getting that we were doing pretty well and we should stay where we were. All that made me say that it was time for me to get back to my profession."[16]

Philadelphia Stars owner Myles Taubman said, "I think spring football proved it worked. We had an audience; we had interest; we had the media interested. I think if the owners had been stronger and had they kept the original direction, the theme of how it should work, it would have been successful."[17] Player agent Leigh Steinberg said, "The sadness of the approach they later took was that they in essence committed business suicide. They were growing a following, they had a television contract, they were way ahead in their first year or two of where the AFL had been."[18]

The Wranglers were in financial trouble and plans were made for a merger with the Oklahoma Outlaws, but the merger collapsed. The Wranglers had sold about 17,000 season tickets and already spent the money. The Outlaws ownership did not want that kind of debt. The merger between the teams was not going to happen and the Wranglers ceased to exist. George and Bruce Allen left the USFL to its uncertain future.[19]

22

Long Beach State

In 1989, George Allen edged back towards his college coaching roots when he started the George Allen Classic at Morningside. The Classic was fundraiser for the Morningside football program, bringing along someone from Allen's past each year to serve as an honorary coach.[1] He spent two weeks with the Chiefs during the 1989 training camp and the team ended a 15-game losing streak with a 31–13 victory over Northwest College of Iowa. There were ten Allen Classic games, eight of them after Allen's death, and Morningside went 8-1-1 in those games. Allen had previously funded the George Allen Athletic Scholarship at Morningside, starting in 1974 with a gift of $2,847.[2]

Allen completed his return to the college coaching ranks when he accepted the challenge of taking over the football program at Long Beach State University. He was 71 years old when he took the job and turned 72 a short time later.

"Allen was a huge deal when he got hired here, and though it's silly, probably the most lasting impact was changing the school colors from brown and gold to black and gold, a switch that has stuck since," said Roger Kirk, the Assistant Athletic Director/Athletic Communications at California State University, Long Beach.[3] Allen felt the brown and gold scheme were loser's colors. The black and gold combination was meant to give his new team the same look that the West Point Cadet football team exhibited.[4] It was ironic, given the problems that Allen's NFL teams had beating San Francisco, that Allen would make his return to college football with Long Beach State. Their nickname was and is the 49ers.

While the 49ers' basketball program gained national attention under the direction of coach Jerry Tarkanian in the 1960s, the Long Beach State football program had been less successful and was locally overshadowed. In the 23-year history of the gridiron program, the school enjoyed only a dozen winning seasons and played in only one bowl game, the 1970 Pasadena Bowl.[5] In the three seasons before Allen's arrival, Long Beach State's

Allen working with his Long Beach State players on the sideline. Number 47 is linebacker Ed Lair (courtesy Long Beach State Athletics).

teams went 11–24. Long Beach State's all-time football record was 130 wins, 125 losses and two ties. In addition to competing for wins on the field, the program also had to compete with the nationally prominent programs in Los Angeles, UCLA and USC,[6] for attention. Long Beach State also had to compete with two National Football League teams, the Los Angeles Rams and Raiders, for attention from the sporting public. Despite all the acrimony built up during his four terms of service with the Rams, including the four firings, Allen still harbored dreams of returning to the franchise as its head coach.

Chuck Hayes was among Allen's administrative assistants at Long Beach. Hayes told the author, "The Rams drove Coach Allen. When I say that, his competitive fire was such that he believed that if he turned Long Beach State around that he would get the Rams job again. He believed that. He believed it in his heart of hearts. It motivated him."[7]

Allen's final book, *Strategies for Winning: A Top Coach's Game Plan for Victory in Football and in Life*, was published in 1990. He may have been prescient when he wrote, "Oh, sure, I would be tempted by one more shot at building another team in to a winner and going for a championship. I know I say I'm retired, and I am. But I'm not deceased. Like an old time boxer, start to count 10 over me and I am liable to get up."[8]

Allen's final coaching job might have been his greatest sideline challenge, but his automatic name recognition in Southern California worked in his favor. His stints at Whittier and with the Rams made him a popular memory. His only Super Bowl appearance came with the Redskins in the Los Angeles Memorial Olympic Coliseum and his USFL teams went 4–1 in games against the LA Express, including a 35–23 victory in the 1984 conference championship game. Allen had a winning reputation in the Los Angeles area and he won in Long Beach, forging a 6–5 record.

Shayne Schroeder was part of the sports information staff at Long Beach State when Allen was hired. The announcement, Schroeder recalled, drew sudden attention to the school's athletic department. "The press conference announcing his hiring was *by far* the largest such event in school history. We were informed of his hiring the prior evening at about 11 p.m., just after a men's basketball game we were working on campus. I think word had leaked out because we began to get *a lot* of calls. By noon the next day, *hundreds of people* [fans and media] showed up at the press conference.... How we pulled that off in a span of just 12 hours or so I have no idea. Needless to say, it was all hands on deck to put the press conference together."[9]

"Personally, I think George Allen did bring something special to the campus," Schroeder continued. "He was a legend after all! Even those who weren't football fans knew him. He certainly created excitement on campus and in town and drew national attention to Long Beach State. It was a bold hire and might have worked out had he not passed. We were 6–5 in his first year and though we didn't get large crowds, I believe they were better than previous years and there was a buzz going. ... Since he hadn't coached for five-six years and was 72 years old, I would say his hiring was unexpected and was certainly the talk of the football world."

Shawn Wilburn was a cornerback on the Long Beach State defense and a senior when Allen was hired.

Allen as the new head football coach at Long Beach State (courtesy Long Beach State Athletics).

"I felt we needed a change," Wilburn recalled. "I didn't know what to expect."[10]

Once hired, Allen was busy. He was in demand for interviews. He was still the head of the President's Council on Physical Fitness and had to complete his duties for that office. His position as Long Beach State's football coach, just his being there, lifted the profile of the university and the school took advantage of that fact. He worked his traditionally long hours and Etty frequently called Allen's secretary to be sure her husband didn't skip lunch, which he normally did. Allen's unflagging devotion to physical fitness hadn't faded. Schroeder remembered Allen telling people that, "Anyone can do fifty pushups. Be better, do fifty-one."[11]

Wilburn said, "I was impressed by the way he carried himself. There was an aura about him. Understand, before we met him, we were reading a lot of things about him in the media. He was making statements about what he felt needed to be changed. So, we were reading about that and learning about him before we actually met him. Our expectations were high before we ever met him. Then we met him … the way he spoke and carried himself really excited me to play for the man."

As he had after his initial hiring as head coach of the Rams 24 years earlier, Allen reached out to the Long Beach State campus community, handing out shirts to students to drum up interest in the football team. Among the many notes he wrote to himself and about himself in the third person and left in his desk at home is a sheet headed "LB STATE." Among the points Allen noted in all caps: "ASK ANYBODY WHAT'RE YOU STUDYING? YOU GOING TO THE FOOTBALL GAME? WHAT'S YOUR NAME?" Next to those words, Allen wrote, "CURIOUS IN PEOPLE," and, "EARNEST INTEREST IN YOUTH." Allen recognized that his name drummed up interest in the Long Beach State football program away from campus but most Long Beach State students did not choose to attend Long Beach State football games. So, Allen drummed up interest himself by talking to students he happened upon.

Every one of the high school players Allen signed to attend Long Beach State were Southern California high school products and one of them went on to win two Super Bowl rings. Terrell Davis started his college career at Long Beach State but he did not play for Allen. Davis redshirted as a freshman and then played sparingly as a sophomore after Allen died. When the Long Beach State program was discontinued after the 1991 season, Davis transferred to Georgia. He eventually won two Super Bowls with John Elway and the Denver Broncos.

Somehow, college coaches missed Davis' obvious physical gifts and the story of Davis' arrival at Long Beach is one of those odd tales that somehow make history. Chuck Hayes related to the author that Hayes was in a meeting room during a running backs meeting when a player noticed a list of high school players on a white board. Long Beach coaches were interested in the players on the list and were scouting them. Running back Reggie Webb saw the list and asked about a name he saw.

Hayes recalled, "Reggie says to me, 'Coach, why is my brother's name on the board?' And I'm looking on the board and I said, 'Reggie, I don't see the name. What name are you looking at?' He says, 'Terrell Davis, that's my brother.'"[12]

Hayes told the author that Davis played both nose tackle and fullback at Lincoln High in the San Diego area. Davis also ran hurdles and threw shot put on the track team. There were some coaches who thought Davis was better as a high schooler than future Heisman Trophy winner and Pro Football Hall of Famer Marcus Allen had been. The comparisons came because they played at same high school. "There had been some interest [in Davis] from Utah State but not much," Hayes said. "So, we had Reggie call Terrell; he came up the next weekend."

Davis signed a letter of intent to attend Long Beach State. Davis' talent was obvious but he was still raw and did not have as much experience as some high school running backs coming to the collegiate level. Allen red-shirted Davis. Eventually, the brothers played in the same backfield briefly in 1991.

As he had at Whittier, Allen recruited heavily from junior college programs around Southern California and he signed 16 JC players to the Long Beach State program. Two juco players he snagged for the 49ers had already played Division I football, Chris Stetz and Kelly Schlegel. Both played their junior college football at Mt. San Antonio College in 1989. Stetz was a defensive lineman who had attended Utah State and Schlegel was signed as an offensive lineman who had played at Utah.

California junior college programs have a long history of producing players who excelled at the highest levels of the game. Pro Football Hall of Famer Frank Gifford played at Bakersfield College in California before transferring to USC and then starting for the New York Giants. Another Hall of Fame member, O.J. Simpson, played at City College of San Francisco before winning a Heisman Trophy at USC and then playing for the NFL's Buffalo Bills and San Francisco 49ers. Tom Dempsey, who held the professional football record for longest field goal for many years, played at Southern California's Palomar College. Anthony Calvillo played junior college ball at Mt. San Antonio College, before moving on to Utah State. Calvillo finished his professional career with pro football's all-time record for career passing yards, playing his entire professional career in the Canadian Football League. George Allen knew about the potential for diamonds in the rough among the junior college ranks. More than half the players he brought to Long Beach State for the 1990 season were juco transfers.

Allen's preference for experienced players probably led him to recruit from the two-year college ranks. Max Fields, who played at East Los Angeles City College before joining Allen at Whittier, explained, "It's a bigger jump from high school football to junior college ball than it is from JC ball to Division I." George Allen valued junior college football players.

Despite all the attention Allen brought the Long Beach State program when he assumed the head coaching position, regardless of the headlines he generated by adding former Oakland Raiders star Willie Brown to the coaching staff and even with all the recruiting successes Allen had with the 49ers, one thing could not change: This was Long Beach State, where the dollars did not flow as they had with the Rams and Redskins or even with major college programs of the day. Hayes called the Long Beach State football offices "a PE building," where anyone could walk the hallway freely. Allen felt that was a distraction for both his coaches and players. Hayes said Allen wanted to use some buildings near the Long Beach airport as a suite of offices, ensuring that only team personnel would be allowed to enter. Allen's idea was never activated—it would have been very expensive—but it was reminiscent of his changes to both the Rams and Redskins training facilities.

You could see Allen's point. Hayes recalled that the football offices had a meeting room that housed the valuable video equipment and the meeting room was kept locked for that reason, an obvious security precaution. But the football coach was not issued a key for the use of the meeting room. In order for the football coach and his assistants to use the room, someone had to be sent across campus to retrieve the key from the athletic director's office and then had to hustle back.

"There would be Coach Allen," Hayes said, "with 12 to 14 coaches standing behind him, waiting for the door to be unlocked. He would be standing with his notebook and ... he would be talking under his breath and he goes, 'I'm going to write a book. It'll be called *Chapter 13*. It's going to be the story of my coaching days at Long Beach State. How can we beat Fresno if we can't even open the door to our conference room?' He would just have that disgusted look on his face sometimes like, 'Can you believe this? Can you believe what's going on?' ... That was the AD's decision. He wouldn't even give [Allen's] secretary the key to the conference room. He [Allen] had to come ask for it."

Hayes also said, "Long Beach State was such an underfunded enterprise that the guys that I had worked with [at Long Beach State] in 1987, '88 and '89 and were still on the staff, we knew how to make it happen in a world where there wasn't a lot of resources. That went along with what Coach was trying to do."

Allen's coaches and players had to deal with the 49ers' practice field, which did not have lights. Allen described putting trucks at one end of the field and turning on their lights so the team could finish practice after the annual Daylight Savings time change. Letters in the Allen file at the Pro Football Hall of Fame show the coach was trying to help the school get funding to build a stadium. The stadium, one would assume, would have included lights.[13]

In September of that year, Allen was in discussions with the David Black Literary Agency of New York about producing an autobiography. Allen's *Strategies* had been published earlier that year by McGraw-Hill and Allen's history of producing books made it clear that he could produce a manuscript. His reemergence into the coaching ranks made him a topic of interest again. The agency would have supplied a co-writer for the project.[14]

With the electrifying news of Allen's hiring, recruiting effort and preseason training all behind them, the 49ers opened their 1990 season on the road against Clemson. The game might have given Allen flashbacks of the lamented season opener against Sub-Pac, the service team that drubbed his first Whittier Poets team in 1951. Clemson was loaded, in coaching parlance, and eventually finished the season with a 10-2 record. The Tigers were ranked ninth in two polls when the 1990 campaign ended.

A slightly grainy video shows Allen's pregame talk to his 49ers before the Clemson game. He told them, "You've made a lot of progress. You're prepared. You're together as a team. We have to go out and keep our poise and the most important thing is to stick together, all the way through. Be happy for the other guy's success and be physical and hit, hit, hit, hit. I'm proud to be your coach."[15]

Clemson beat Long Beach State 59–0. Allen told *Los Angeles Times* reporter Dick Wagner, "This is a new experience for Coach Allen to lose 59–0.... I don't want any more games like this. It's not fair to the kids. Anybody who knows football knows you couldn't expect anything much more than this." Reminded by reporters that Long Beach State was scheduled to play the University of Miami the following season, Allen called that "ridiculous."

Smaller Division I college programs then as now frequently play major football powers in games the smaller programs seldom win. The bigger program, Clemson in the case of the 1990 opener for Long Beach State, pays the smaller school a significant fee and the money makes football affordable for a year for the smaller program. Hayes said, "We played ... what would be body bag games to pay the bills to start the season off and then go into our Big West schedule."[16]

The next game was the Big West Conference opener against Utah State, another weekend on the road, but at least the 49ers were competitive. Utah State jumped ahead 17–0 and led 17–3 at the half. Long Beach State scored a touchdown to get the game closer, 17–10 in the third quarter. The final score was 24–13.

San Diego State was next, a short trip down the freeway from Long Beach for a non-conference game. The Aztecs had opened their season against Pac 10 member Oregon and would play Brigham Young University the following week, leaving Allen the chance to spring a trap game effort at the hosts. But San Diego State ran and passed its way to 514 yards of total offense and beat the 49ers 38–20.

Long Beach State was winless in three games and had been outscored 124–33. Still, Allen did not do a lot of yelling at his players and Wilburn said that approach was one of the keys to Allen's success. "Football … is a do it my way or the highway thing," Wilburn said. "You make a mistake and you get yelled at. There is that constant pressure. With coach Allen, though, it was very different. … When you made a mistake, he wasn't in your face screaming at you. It was okay to make a mistake, just play hard. For me, that really worked. That clicked. That took some of the anxiety off. I think that is the key to his success. It was the first time in all my years of football … with Coach Allen … it was have fun, enjoy the game. Don't worry about making mistakes. If you make a mistake, go a hundred percent. He would tell you what you needed to correct but he wasn't screaming at you, he wasn't pulling you off the field. For me, that took the pressure off. It eased anxiety and enabled me to play and not worry about anything other than enjoying the game and having fun. I went on to coach high school and college football. I coach track and field now and I try to coach that way. I want [the athletes] to have fun. You definitely can see the difference when a kid feels anxiety and is under pressure versus when they're able to just let it flow and relax and not worry. … I think there are two keys to what Coach Allen was able to do at Long Beach State. One of them was taking the anxiety out of playing the game. The other thing was basically the organization, the professionalism, the making you feel like you were part of something special. Something as simple as saying, 'Hey, were going to all be wearing the same thing at practice. This is how they do it in the pros, this is how they would do it in big time college football. We're doing it the same.' The upgrades we had in the locker room and the upgrades with our facilities. All of that made us feel important and we felt like, 'Hey, we're making progress,' before we ever stepped onto the field. And I know that with the Rams that rubbed some people the wrong way, spending the money that he spent and the same thing at Long Beach State, the demands he made, changing the uniforms and the money he spent. But it made a world of difference to the players, how we felt. We knew he had our back. It had nothing to do with the Xs and Os, it had everything to do with, basically, how it made the players feel."

It had been a rough beginning but it was only fair to say that the 49ers were in the midst of a major rebuilding program. They had been reasonably competitive against Utah State and San Diego State and they still had not played a home game. Then, from September 22 through November 11, Allen's club played six times at home and twice on the road, winning six of the eight. The 49ers won a couple of nail-biters and, when it was all over, Long Beach State completed a winning season with a record of 6–5. Allen had done it again, produced winners from ashes.

Senator George Allen of Virginia on the occasion of his father's induction into the Professional Football Hall of Fame in Canton, Ohio, August 3, 2002 (Alamy).

As he had done at every other coaching stop, Allen devoted time to building team chemistry at Long Beach State. The reader will remember the barbecue parties at a local park when Allen coached at Whittier. At Long Beach, Allen again used the lure of burgers to bring the team together but in his last season, Allen put a new twist on his camaraderie campaign.

Hayes explained, "Coach had a great relationship with Carl Karcher of Carl's Junior. So, we would have a long practice on a Thursday, a long, long practice. You couldn't see after the season [time] change would happen. We didn't have any lights on the practice field. It's *dusk*, I mean it's dark. The kids would go in and change, all the coaches would come together and the Carl's Junior Honor Crew would roll up in a food truck. In the 1990s, it was very unusual to see a food truck. Today, everyone has a food truck, but back then they didn't. They would set up the tables and everything and we would have burgers and fries and milk and [soft] drinks. [Allen] would play horseshoes with the players. It was really relaxed. ... So here he's playing horseshoes with some kid from wherever and they're playing horseshoes with George Allen and Willie Brown, two guys that are in the Hall of Fame with two kids from Long Beach State. Everyone's eating burgers and bonding as a group. And that's why they'd do anything for him."

Wilburn remembered the food truck arriving after Friday practices prior to home games. But he agreed with Hayes about what their arrival meant to the players. Wilburn told the author that the players felt they were part of a big-time program. "That was something we had not experienced, the players that had been at Long Beach State before that year," Wilburn said.

Finally, they won for him. The September 22 game was Long Beach State's home opener against the University of the Pacific in Veterans Stadium on the campus of Long Beach City College. The *Los Angeles Times* put the attendance at 5,308. It wasn't a sellout, even at the Vet. The 49ers and their famous coach were 0–3. USC and UCLA were on the road, so the attendance was not what the school might have hoped. Long Beach State had lost eight of its last nine games, including the close of the 1989 season, and had narrowly lost to Pacific, 26–25, the season before. But, playing at home for the first time in 1990, Allen's 49ers beat Pacific 28–7.

"This is bigger than an NFL victory because these kids have been down for so long," Allen told the *Times*.[17]

Pacific's run-and-shoot offense had not been successful that season. The Tigers were 1–2 overall and 0–1 in conference play before the game in Long Beach. But Allen's defense played its best game of the season, to date. Allen had installed a new wrinkle for the contest and the change paid off.

He told the *Times*, "Our defense held up the whole game. I used three linemen, two linebackers and six defensive backs. I call it a dime." Defensive formations with five defensive backs were termed "nickel," defenses, so calling the six-back alignment, "a dime," made sense. Regardless of the small change, the defense held Pacific out of the end zone until late in the third quarter, when Long Beach State led 14–0. Long Beach State quarterback Todd Studer, one of those junior college transfers, completed 18 of 29 passes, throwing three scoring passes. Wilbourn intercepted a pass at the goal line to stop one Pacific drive in the third quarter. The players presented Allen with the game ball but the coach gave it to wide receiver Mark Seay. Seay had suffered a gunshot wound two years earlier and lost a kidney. Allen said Seay was inspirational.[18]

The Pacific game was Long Beach State's best defensive result of the season to that point. Wilburn and a linebacker called the defenses for the

49ers. Next to his devotion to special teams play, Allen's coaching legacy was on defense. So, what was it like to play defense for Allen at Long Beach State?

Wilburn said, "I played for some pretty good defensive coaches in the past before Coach Allen, but what Coach Allen did that was special was he basically taught us how to break down every formation, every stance of the opposing player. It was really the first time that we got into the analytics of it. He enabled us to call the defense. I actually called the defense, based off of the down and the distance and the formations, as opposed to taking a signal from the sideline from him. He taught us so well in practice and with our film study ... he put it on us to be in the right defense, based on what the other team was doing. If we made a mistake or if I made a bad call—which at times I would—I would get us into a bad blitz or something—he wouldn't scream. He would tell me why and, basically, you'd learn and you wouldn't do that again. He put so much power in his players that I just think we were so comfortable out there, playing, we weren't thinking."

Long Beach State had to come from behind to win the next week, beating Boise State 21–20. Allen's crew scored first on a 73-yard run by Freddie Leslie, but trailed 10–7 at halftime. In the fourth quarter Boise State scored again to make it 17–7. Studer hit Jeff Exum for 73 yards and a score to close it to 17–14 before Boise State kicked a field goal to lead 20–14. Studer hit Sean Foster on a 33-yard touchdown pass for the game-winning points. Studer finished the game hitting 20 of 38 attempts for 318 yards. He was intercepted twice but he threw those two late-game scoring passes to bring his club back. Exum finished with 188 receiving yards. Boise State finished with 411 yards from scrimmage but the Long Beach State defense forced three fumbles and took two of them away. The *Times* put the attendance at 4,106.[19]

Winning breeds spinning turn styles, usually. Not so at Long Beach State. The *Times* reported 3,926 at the Vet to see the 49ers win their third straight game, a 31–27 victory over New Mexico State. The visitors scored first but Long Beach State led 17–14 at the half. Long Beach led 31–21 in the final period before New Mexico State got a touchdown. A two-point conversion failed and the 49ers won. Studer passed for 212 yards. Freddie Leslie rushed for 74 yards and both Herman Nash and Rickie Clark had scoring runs as Long Beach totaled 428 yards from scrimmage. New Mexico State had 349 yards.

The following game was against San Jose State and was the first of two straight on the road. Long Beach started out well enough, leading 10–3 after one quarter. But the hosts put 22 unanswered points on the board in the second quarter and finally beat the visitors 46–29. The 49ers gained just 36 yards on the ground while giving up 305. Studer hit on 20 of 35 passes and four touchdowns, including a 77-yard bomb to Seay. But Long Beach State fumbled six times, losing the ball twice. Allen's defense forced four San Jose State fumbles. A week later, Fresno State was next and the 49ers started quickly again, leading 10-7 after one quarter and trailing by just 14-10 at halftime. But Fresno State eventually won 28-16.

"Some of the losses that we had, that were close, I felt like we had more talent and I felt that we really mis-aligned a little bit and I think that the other teams were able to take advantage of that," said Wilburn. "Some of the misalignments were a result of us only being with [Allen] one year and not quite understanding some of the adjustments that needed to be made."

The losses left Allen and the 49ers with a record of 3-5 overall and 2-3 in conference play with three home games left to play. To finish with a winning record, the team would have to manufacture a three-game winning streak. That was the bad news. The good news was that none of the remaining opponents—California State University, Fullerton; California State University, Northridge; and the University of Nevada, Las Vegas—were overtly threatening teams. Only one of the three, Northridge, finished the year with a winning record and Northridge played in the NCAA's Division II.

The Fullerton game attracted a crowd of 7,042 and that crowd saw a game that was unlike any a George Allen team ever played. Between them, the teams generated more than a thousand yards of offense. Studer completed 21 of 40 pass attempts for 346 yards and two touchdowns. Fullerton's passer, Paul Schulte, completed 20 of 34 for 343 yards and three scores. The game seemed to turn in Fullerton's favor when Long Beach, trailing 35-34, lost the ball on downs at the Fullerton 42 with just two minutes, 37 seconds remaining in the game. Two plays later, Fullerton's Schulte ran a bootleg play in an attempt to get a first down that would clinch the game for the Titans. But Long Beach defender Pepper Jenkins forced a fumble and Ed Lair recovered to give the 49ers one final chance.

Long Beach did not have a timeout remaining but Studer made do without one. He hit Seay for 19 yards and then completed a third down pass to Jeff Exum to the Fullerton 20-yard line. Fullerton was assessed with a late-hit penalty, which moved the ball to the 10. Jeff Fassett ran for seven more yards before kicker Sean Cheevers booted a game-winning field goal with six seconds left.

Allen said later, "I've never had a bunch of guys who have worked harder than this bunch of kids."[20]

Ironically, Allen did not see Cheevers boot the winning points home and this time he did some yelling. Wilburn recalled, "Their quarterback—who's a good friend of mine—fumbled and we recovered and there were only a few seconds left. We needed to kick a long field goal to win and a couple kids, students from our side, ran out onto the field. I just remember Coach Allen losing his mind, just laying into this drunk kid on the sideline. He didn't even see the ball go through the uprights and know we had won the game because he was too busy laying into this kid at the same time that Sean Cheevers was kicking the field goal."[21]

There was a buy-in to Allen's approach by the Long Beach State players that made the players *want* to play hard. Part of that stemmed from the way Allen allowed them to play the game. It would not have been surprising to discover that Allen retained the play-calling duties at the collegiate level, especially the defensive play calling. But as he did with his professional teams, Allen coached a defensive framework and allowed his players to make most of the calls on the field.

"He believed that the players on the field on defense should be accountable and they should run the game," said Chuck Hayes. "So, Chris Tsangaris was a transfer linebacker from Ventura College. He'd call all the defenses on the field, based upon the defenses we were in. [Allen] gave him a lot of responsibility right away. So, he [Allen] was trusting kids. Sometimes it would work and sometimes it wouldn't work. But, with that said … he didn't have a playbook on defense. He had defenses that he liked." Hayes said Allen brought in a package of film of defenses for the coaches to review. "There might be 4–3 coverages with blitzes that he liked and there might be 35 different variations of the 4–3 that he wanted to put in."

Wilburn said, "We would go over it in the meeting room, myself and the middle linebacker. We spent the most time, one-on-one with [Allen] in the meeting rooms, watching the films. You'd have the defensive meeting and position meeting and then myself and Chris Tsangaris would sit down with him. He would give us these formation sheets and he would have options, what defenses we should be in for the particular formation or personnel that was coming out onto the field. We were very well rehearsed during the week as to what we should be calling. We had some parameters but we still felt like we were allowed to [call the defenses]. It could be third down and long or something and I could walk back to the huddle and we would know we had a couple of different options for a defense and I could say to Chris Tsangaris, 'Chris, call this blitz. I really feel like if we call this blitz that we can get there [to the quarterback].' So, we kind of had the confidence from the film study and if we sensed something or saw something, me and Chris could talk in the huddle and we would make the call."

A game against Cal State Northridge was next. The Matadors played in the NCAA's Division II in those days and had a chance to earn a berth in the playoffs. The Matadors were ranked 13th in Division II going into the game with Long Beach. Northridge had an excellent running back named Albert Fann and Fann was the lynchpin for the Northridge offense. When he finished his collegiate career, Fann was the all-time leading rusher for the Northridge program. The week before Long Beach was due to play Northridge, the Matadors had a rare Friday game and the 49ers coaches were planning to scout the game in person. They were in the meeting room—someone had retrieved the key—and readying for the short trip north to the Northridge campus when Allen somehow discovered that Fann had an injured ankle and would not play for two weeks. Fann would miss the game with Long Beach State. Another player, a juco transfer named Victor DeVaughn, would start in Fann's sted. Hayes related that Allen wanted to know everything about the replacement player immediately. One of the assistants recalled the 49ers had recruited DeVaughn, so Allen asked to see film of the player, game film of DeVaughn sent by Grossmont College in San Diego for the Long Beach staff to study. But Long Beach had not kept the film of the player or copied it—that would have been expensive—before sending it back to Grossmont. Allen was perplexed at *that* news and then asked about the player's high school career. All this while everyone was supposed to be leaving to drive to Northridge. Eventually Allen and the staff decided they would drop the matter for the time being because they were about to scout the entire Northridge team in person.

"The next week we play Northridge," said Hayes. "[Allen's] got this guy to be built up to be the second coming of Jimmy Brown. This kid was the greatest thing since sliced bread. Seriously, that's all [Allen] talked about. We start the game off. A different kid breaks one, right up the middle for forty-plus yards and a touchdown. On the sideline, you've seen scattering? The coaches just moved ten yards that way, ten yards that way. He [Allen] was standing by himself as the defense jogged off the field." Hayes added that the coaches scattering was like a biblical parting of the sea.

The contest drew 3,090 to the Vet and they were treated to another seesaw struggle. Led by "Sliced Bread" DeVaughn's 121 yards on just 13 carries, Northridge rushed 46 times against Long Beach State, gaining 229 yards. The 49ers scored two touchdowns in the third quarter to take a 17–10 lead. Northridge scored a pair of touchdowns to go back in front 24–17 with 10:39 to go in the game. Long Beach scored a touchdown with a minute, 17 seconds remaining to get within a point at 24–23. Allen sent in a two-point conversion play, which appeared to fail when Northridge safety Clayton Bamberg tipped Studer's pass attempt. But the tipped ball floated to Long Beach's Seay, who caught it for the game-winning points.

"We didn't play well in that game," said Wilburn. "I don't remember

22. Long Beach State

why. I think, as a team, we had started to win some games and they were a Division II team and I do think we over-looked them. We were kids and I think we felt, 'Ah, we've arrived, we're playing good and now we're playing this Division II team and we hardly had any fans in the stadium for that game and we didn't play well."

Hayes said, "We won a lot of games down the stretch and that was all belief and will."[22]

The last football game George Allen coached was on November 17, 1990, at the Vet as Long Beach State faced UNLV. It was the last chance the 49ers would get to complete the season with a winning record. Allen had coached two franchises each in the NFL and USFL in playoff games, including a Super Bowl with the Redskins and the USFL title game with the Wranglers. Allen had turned both the Rams and Redskins from losers to winners in a season and his first USFL team was brand-spanking new, as was the rest of the league. Allen had won under all those circumstances. He had coached winners at Morningside and Whittier. He had been an assistant with two NFL teams and seen both winning and losing from that perspective. His Long Beach State team was badly over-matched in its opener and started the season with three straight losses before fighting back to even, five wins and five losses. When you look back on Allen's career you see winners throughout but he had not coached since the failure of the USFL. Allen must have felt there was something to prove on that day. Months later, Jennifer Allen was going through her father's desk and found a note he had written to himself after receiving the news that the Pro Football Hall of Fame had not voted him in again. The note Allen wrote himself said, in part, "George Allen, he never had a losing season." That consistent winning meant something to Allen.[23]

And achieving that record, winning more than losing, meant a great deal to the Long Beach State players, too. Wilburn said, "We treated that as our bowl game. That's how George Allen built it up. [He said,] 'Look, this is your bowl game.' We said that all week going into that game and after we won, it was an incredible feeling. That year was the most fun I had in a lot of years of playing football."

Long Beach State led 16–14 at the half, the difference being a safety recorded by the Long Beach defense in the first quarter. Second half field goals of 30 and 39 yards by Cheevers and a scoring pass from Studer to Exum gave the 49ers what they needed to win 29–20 in front of 4,649 attendees. In his final coaching effort, Allen's defense recorded a safety and his kicking game contributed two conversions and two field goals. The safety, conversions and field goals were worth 10 points in a nine-point victory.

The 49ers had earned a winning record and they had won the Allen way.

The question that must be answered is how did it happen? What did George Allen do that was different from Long Beach State coaches before him? The program's funding was the same, the facilities had not changed, most of the players on the roster had been there the year before and Allen had not been allowed to dismiss the assistant coaches he inherited. How did things change for the 49ers? Why did a program that was 11–24 for the previous three seasons win six of 11 under Allen?

Chuck Hayes worked with Allen for just one season but had been a coach before that and has been around sports his entire professional career. He summed up the answer as well as anyone when he said of Allen, "He had attention to detail and he could get everybody pulling on the rope in the same direction. He had a way about him and the players loved him. He was a players' coach. ... He had a sense of humor that was real subtle. He could turn a phrase. He had a way to do things."

Allen was doused with ice water when the final game ended. Not Gatorade. The traditional victory bath for the head coach was done with ice water because, as Allen said, Long Beach State couldn't afford Gatorade. Allen reportedly stayed on the field after the game in his wet clothing, talking to reporters and fans. He was reportedly still wet when the team returned to campus. There has been a persistent story that the ice water shower, the resulting wet clothing, cooling ambient temperatures as the evening came on and the delayed changing into dry clothes somehow brought on Allen's death 44 days later. In its January 1, 1991, edition, the *New York Times* ran an obituary which quoted Allen as saying that he had not felt "completely healthy" since the ice water bath following the final game of the 1990 season.[24] That final game was played on November 17, which can be a cool time of year, even in Southern California. According to multiple weather reports found online, the low temperature in Long Beach that day was 55 degrees, with a high of 73. Off-shore breezes at the Vet can cool things off in a hurry and the ice water would have felt, well, icy. Allen was a 72-year-old football coach by then, albeit a man with an exercise regimen that might put younger men to shame. He jogged daily, drank his milk and remained physically fit. Still, the septuagenarian spent a long time in cold, wet clothes that evening.

Wilburn said he saw Allen on either December 29 or 30 of that year, in Allen's office on campus at Long Beach State. Allen was planning on coaching in an all-star game in a few weeks and he told Wilburn that Wilburn had been added to the list of alternate players for the game. If a player expected to participate could not play in the game for some reason, Wilburn might get called to fill the spot on the roster. Nothing seemed amiss, Wilburn said. Then, while Wilburn was home visiting his parents on New Year's Day, the family phone rang. An Associated Press reporter was calling to get a reaction to Allen's passing. It was the first Shawn Wilburn had heard of it.

"I felt like I had lost a family member," said Wilburn. "I mean, it floored me."

Allen had lived twice the life expectancy for men born in his birth year, 1918. Men born that year lived an average of less than 40 years.[25] The double-whammy of the Great Depression and the Second World War ended a lot of lives early for men who turned 22 years of age in 1940. Allen lived through both of those world-wide calamities and then maintained a devotion to fitness through his adulthood and into his senior years. His death, even at 72, came as a surprise.

Jack Pardee, Allen's on-field defensive general, said shortly after Allen's passing, "I talked to Coach Allen a few weeks ago and he was just so excited about the winning season he had at Long Beach State. Coach Allen always thrived on building something out of very little. And he was very excited about the continuing challenge that he had at Long Beach."[26]

Jennifer Allen told an interviewer that attending her father's funeral seemed like going to a Redskins game. "It was that same sense of purpose and urgency, that what you were about to do is life and death," she said. "And that's when I really realized that, really, we believed everything that he said and we lived a life as he said it, which was that winning is living and losing is dying. ... A funeral can feel as intense as a football game. It's pretty incredible. It's a lot of emotion."[27]

Epilogue

This book was written with an eye toward finding the elusive answer to a question: What made George Allen a winner? How did he manage to turn losing franchises into winners? The Los Angeles Rams flopped around like a hooked fish on a dry dock from 1958 through 1965, but Allen had them winning in 1966. The Washington Redskins suffered through losing Vince Lombardi after the 1969 season and had a losing record in 1970, but Allen had them winning in 1971 and playing in the Super Bowl a season later. He became the first NFL head coach to go 10 consecutive seasons without posting a single losing season. Allen's USFL teams won immediately, too. He was a winner at three different college stops as well. How did he manage to turn Long Beach State into a winner in his only season there? The 49ers' 6–5 record in 1990 doesn't sound like much until you take into account where they'd been in the recent past.

Everyone interviewed for this book mentioned Allen's attention to detail and his long, grinding hours of game preparation. Dick Vermeil's comment that Allen understood and valued each position on the field went along with Allen's unrelenting search for an advantage against an opponent. All NFL coaches work that same time pattern now, but that was not so when Allen got his first head coaching assignment at the professional level in 1966. As we've seen, Allen spent so much time preparing for games that his wife frequently called the local police to find her husband and be sure he was okay. He was ahead of his time when it came to breaking down the habits of opposing players. Allen was a tremendous judge of talent as well. Whether he was preparing for the draft, bringing veterans to his pro teams through trades or recruiting for his college teams, Allen appreciated talent when he saw it.

Allen was the first NFL or AFL coach to put serious emphasis on coaching the kicking game. The two best-known plays for Allen-coached teams at any level were the punt blocked by Allen's Rams against the Packers in 1967 and the blocked field goal against the Dolphins in the Super

Bowl at the end of the 1972 season. It has to be said, too, that Allen knew how to coach defensive football. Starting with Allen's time under George Halas in Chicago, Allen's defensive teams made scoring difficult for the opposition. His ability to break down the opposing team's offensive tendencies, then find a way to put his players in position to take advantage of his discoveries, was masterful. It didn't hurt that he inherited a Rams defensive team that included Deacon Jones, Merlin Olsen, Jack Pardee and Eddie Meador. But the Rams had those players before Allen got there and they weren't winning. Otherwise, they would not have needed a new head coach.

Billy Kilmer, the Redskins passer, credited something else. Kilmer said that when he started with Allen in Washington, "I saw the organization and I saw things around me that I'd never seen before. You get caught up in that enthusiasm, you get caught up in the whole atmosphere and it breeds winning."

John Wilbur, the offensive guard who began his career with Tom Landry and the Cowboys in the late 1960s before Allen brought him to Washington in 1971, called Allen "[o]ne of the greatest motivators of all time and I got a Doctorate in motivation from George Allen." Wilbur also said of Allen, "He taught us you had to find ways inside of yourself to commit yourself to the group effort."

Allen usually was not a yeller. He seldom raised his voice at practice. He coached the players, yes, and he sometimes put them through grueling workouts. He challenged them constantly. But his motivational techniques did not come at the top of his lungs and a lot of players appreciated that, especially his veteran players. Allen said virtually every week that the next game would be the most important one of the season. It always *was* the most important game to Allen. Sometimes those comments wore thin with his coaches and players but there is no denying that those players responded to Allen's pushing.

"It was the relationships that he built with his players," Shawn Wilburn said. "[I see it] especially now that I coach men and women in college track and field and the better the relationship that I have with my athletes, the more enjoyable it is for me as a coach and I believe it is enjoyable for the athlete as well. If you can build a strong relationship with your athletes, they'll run through a wall for you. At the time [with Allen] I didn't realize that but it was the first head coach that I had a real close relationship with. Because of that relationship, I would have done anything that he asked me to do. I think that is the biggest thing as a coach, wherever I've been, I've tried to build strong relationships with my athletes." Wilburn added, "I believe it really evolves around anxiety. If you can take an athlete and alleviate their anxiety to where they're comfortable because they trust you, they trust that you believe in them and that you're not going to scream and yell and degrade them, I think that's the biggest piece. ... If your athlete knows that you're in it for them instead of just you, that's what it's all about when it comes to coaching and getting your athletes to perform at a high level."

And Allen worked very hard to develop team chemistry. When Allen acquired Bears linebacker Bill George for the Rams in 1966, he did so because he knew that George would show Rams players how a winner prepared for a season or for games. Allen developed chemistry with his assistant coaches, too, giving his kicking teams assistant input on which players to keep when the final cutdown day loomed at the end of preseason training camp. Allen sometimes put chemistry at risk, like when he vacillated between quarterbacks Kilmer and Sonny Jurgensen, but generally Allen did everything he could to promote that most elusive thing, team togetherness. Whether it was barbecued burgers in the park at Whittier or a Carl's Junior food truck at Long Beach State, the coach found ways to bring his charges together. His players and coaches never forgot those moments.

The answer to the big question then is multi-faceted. Allen's work ethic meant that his teams were prepared and had the best equipment and facilities Allen could acquire for them; his game preparation left nothing unobserved or underestimated. Allen understood and valued each position and did whatever was needed to put the best player available in each spot. Then he developed a strong sense of togetherness amongst the players and his coaching staff. Allen never stopped trying to learn new ways to motivate. More than a passion for the game, Allen had an overpowering desire to win and that led to him being creative about finding ways to attack an opponent.

No coach is perfect. Allen never won a professional championship as a head coach, although he reached the championship game in two different leagues. While he was regarded as a players' coach, he was a free-spender and that meant that he was not an owners' coach. That fact got him fired in both Los Angeles and Washington. It should be pointed out that coaching at the professional level is not a ticket to job security in any scenario.

After his final stint with the Rams, Allen never coached an NFL team again and he attracted no interest. In a league where coaches move from team to team frequently, Allen was never hired again. He had changed the fortunes of two moribund franchises and never coached a professional team to a losing season. Still, he couldn't get hired. Jennifer Allen wrote about her father getting a call from an owner and traveling to meet with the owner, only to wait in vain. The owner never showed for the meeting.

Allen's methods—literally trading the future for the now—were questioned, certainly. He was an expensive hire and he wanted his players paid well, too. He wanted top-notch facilities. He was seen as an eccentric winner. His final, aborted fling with the Rams probably damaged Allen's standing with league teams. The word was out that Allen could not function unless he was hired as both general manager and coach—and it was expensive to make him the GM.

Joe Theismann wrote in his book that a change in NFL rules regarding free agency might have also made teams leery of hiring Allen. If Allen's Redskins, for example, signed a free agent from the Rams, the Rams would have to be compensated with draft choices from the Redskins. "It wasn't that George Allen could no longer coach, but that his philosophy—'Give me older players who don't make mistakes and I can beat anybody'—became outdated," Theismann wrote.[1]

The NFL's rules regarding free agent players have since been modified.

It is only fair to point out that Allen had a contract offer from the Redskins which sat unsigned for nearly a year before the team ended its relationship with him. The contract Allen never signed would have made him the best-paid coach in the NFL.

With the story ended, you are left to wonder what it all meant. What did George Allen's lifetime of devotion mean to the game of football?

We know what football meant to George Allen. He loved the game and he loved coaching it. He was driven to succeed to the point where he took slower trains instead of the express so that he'd have more time to study his game plan notes on his way home from Chicago Bears practices. He brought home films of practices to study his Rams and Redskins players, watching in an office he had in his home. He preferred to eat food that didn't require much chewing because he felt chewing his food was too time-consuming, taking him away from his game-planning. He frequently avoided eating altogether, drinking milk instead. When he was rejected by every NFL owner after his final, brief tenure with the Rams ended, Allen was haunted by the lack of interest in his services.

That brings us to what George Allen meant to the game of football. How did he change it? How did his devotion to winning impact the National Football League? How did Allen impact his players and his assistant coaches? How did his mere presence impact the California State University at Long Beach? Those are the questions that more accurately reflect Allen's decades of activity within the football world.

Allen changed the way teams prepared for games through his study of each player at each position. His ability to use film study to break down the opposition was revolutionary. So was his willingness to work through the small hours of the morning. Allen changed the way franchises operated when he convinced the Redskins to build Redskins Park. No team has approached Allen's propensity for building teams through trades for veteran players, but his success through that method has influenced the way teams are constructed. It is a good guess that George Allen would have reveled in the modern-day free agency rules. And Allen's willingness to put players on the rosters of his professional teams primarily because of their special teams skills was ahead of his time. Now, with expanded roster sizes, every professional team does that.

One method Allen used did not influence future coaches at the collegiate or professional levels: Allowing his players to call their own signals. He felt he could prepare his players properly so that he did not need to call signals for them or have his assistants do so.

George Allen's life was heavily impacted by growing up during the Great Depression. As a boy, he contributed to his family's income and he helped grow food in the basement. Many families of the era were similarly uncertain about finances from the time of the stock market crash in 1929 through the end of the Second World War. The need to produce earnings "right now" was a fact of life for many American families. Building strong teams for the future, Allen felt later in life, meant building strong rosters for the next coach. A nice legacy perhaps, but the next coach would be the one employed, not the guy who built the legacy.

Obviously then Allen was not afraid to spend the money of his team owners in pursuit of winning. Allen's expensive ideas frequently turned out to be just the beginning of trends in the NFL. He pushed the Rams to improve the conditions of their preseason training camp and then got the Redskins to build the first team facility of its kind. Every team has a facility like it now. Allen tended to side with the players in contract negotiations, which is as rare now as it was then. Allen was a trailblazer in terms of the importance he placed on special teams play and his teams won games because of that—remember the blocked punt and the blocked field goal. His ability to analyze the opposition's offensive schemes was unique for the time and, because of that, his defenses were tough to score upon.

His offenses were less conservative than his memory indicates even though he preferred quarterbacks who avoided interceptions, like Gabriel, to gunslingers like Jurgensen. Joe Theismann played very little for Allen and Theismann later won a Super Bowl with a different Redskins coach but while Allen coached the Redskins, Theismann did not play as well as he did later. Even the offensive formation shifts that Allen's Morningside and Whittier teams employed to switch from the modern T-Formation into the Single Wing was less about conservatism and more about inducing opponents' penalties. Allen was far from the only coach—regardless of the level—who made his quarterbacking decisions based upon avoiding turnovers. Criticism of Allen for his offensive style isn't fair because he wasn't more conservative than others.

No franchise since George Allen coached in the NFL has been as willing as Allen was to trade away draft picks for veteran players. But you could argue that very few coaches or general managers have had Allen's eye for talent either, and nobody turned losing teams around faster than George Allen. Allen's ability to see how another NFL team's player would fit into a position of need on his own team was unique but it made an impression on Dick Vermeil when Vermeil was a young Rams assistant coach in 1969. The draft picks Allen did make, starting during his time in Chicago, prove that he was a tremendous judge of college talent. It is easy to look back now and say that Gale Sayers and Dick Butkus were easy selections for the Bears to make, but two running backs were selected by other teams before Allen's Bears picked Sayers and no team in the American Football League selected Butkus on the first round of that league's draft. Allen's mantra about the immediate future (the future is now) was born of a man who grew up during the Great Depression and had that generation's concern for job security. George Allen always figured he had to win immediately and he set out to do that.

The bottom line about George Herbert Allen is that his methods won games everyplace where he coached. He was determined to do things his way and that determination made life difficult for him. His teams did not fare well in postseason play but to lose playoff games those teams had to reach the playoffs first. Allen's teams won enough to make regular appearances in the postseason. In Allen's era, it was more difficult to reach the playoffs than it became later because there were fewer playoff slots available.

Ron McDole said he enjoyed playing for Allen's Redskins teams and told the author about the freedom he and other defensive players had to operate within the confines of the defensive call on a given play. Allen trusted veteran players like McDole or punt blocker Bill Malinchak to make the assigned play and gave them the freedom to react when they saw an opportunity for a minor adjustment that could result in a big play. Thus, the complaints from veteran players like Sonny Jurgensen and Isiah Robertson ring hollow. Allen's system allowed for a veteran's insight to lead to an adjustment at the line of scrimmage that frequently resulted in a big play by Allen's squad. He gave the same freedoms to his college players.

And Allen trusted his veteran players to create and maintain the team chemistry that was so vital to his success. Veteran players, Allen believed, made fewer mistakes and all coaches believe that the team which makes the fewest mistakes will win most games. Winning is also a very fine thing for team chemistry. During his two seasons in the USFL, Allen had the opportunity to build an entire roster himself. He stocked it with NFL veterans, which made for one of the most expensive payrolls in the young league. But that roster won. Allen's two-season USFL record was 22–14 in regular season games and 24–16 including the playoffs. He coached his teams to the playoffs both years and into the league title game in the second year.

Allen's least appreciated work might well have been his best, when he coached at Morningside, Whittier and Long Beach State. He could recruit at the college level, but he could not trade a draft pick for a veteran. As Dick Vermeil told the author, Allen had to teach the game more at that level. He did so. The articles Allen wrote for the coaching magazines while he was at both Morningside and Whittier bespoke of his detailed approach to coaching individual positions and specific plays. Fields, Allen's running back at Whittier, talked decades later about Allen's crisp, well organized practices. By the time he coached at Long Beach State, Allen was a coaching legend and the players were attracted to him as a proven winner. But when he coached at Morningside and Whittier in the 1940s and 1950s, Allen was an unknown. He found ways to build team chemistry, like the picnics he had with his players and young family at Whittier, that did not cost much but meant a lot to the players. Very few college football players have ever turned down a free hamburger.

The answer to the question about what Allen meant to football is pretty simple, then: George Allen innovated as a coach and he won everywhere he went. He won by building team chemistry—which was expensive at times—and by being a players' coach. He was driven to succeed at least partially due to growing up during the Great Depression. No detail was unimportant to Allen, up to and including checking the angle of the sun in a stadium where he had previously coached for five seasons. Assistant coaches like Dick Vermeil and Marv Levy took Allen's examples to heart and won championships.

Pro football head coaches are judged by how many championships they win. Allen was 0–2 in professional championship games and his teams had a losing record in playoff games. Other Hall of Fame coaches have suffered the same fate. Bud Grant tormented some of Allen's teams while Grant coached the Minnesota Vikings. Grant never won a Super Bowl but he has been enshrined in the Hall.[2] Levy, Allen's assistant in both Los Angeles and Washington, lost four straight Super Bowls as head coach of the Buffalo Bills and never won the NFL title as a head coach, but he is also in the Hall of Fame.[3] Marty Schottenheimer won 200 regular season games as head coach of the Browns, Chiefs, Redskins and Chargers, but he never won a Super Bowl.[4] Grant and Levy are enshrined with Allen in the Pro Football Hall of Fame. Schottenheimer probably should be.

What did Allen mean to his players? Like all coaches who have long careers, Allen made an impact. An undated letter from the son of John Audikian, one of Allen's players at Whittier, said in part, "You had quite a bit to do with the development of my father, not only as a football player but as a man." The letter described the senior Audikian's successful business career and mentioned that the elder Audikian's wife had recently passed away. Allen called his former player after receiving the letter.[5]

Fields, who also played for Allen at Whittier, described the last time he saw Allen. The two men were attending a funeral more than 30 years after Allen left the school to join the ranks of assistant coaches in the NFL. Fields described approaching Allen. "He smiled and said, 'I recruited you,'" Fields said.

Of all the great questions about George Allen's coaching career, the one that seems most intriguing is what might have happened to the Chicago Bears had George Halas stepped down as head coach after the 1963 championship season or after the 1964 season and named his smart, driven young assistant, George Allen, head coach of the Bears. In Allen, Halas had a man who saw the Halas way as the right way. With Halas there to guide Allen's instincts, what might the Bears have accomplished? We'll never know the answer to that question, but we can surmise that Halas might have appreciated Allen's approach to the game better than Dan Reeves did in Los Angeles. We can comfortably assume that Allen would have had a harder time spending Halas' money than he did spending Edward Bennett Williams' funds in Washington because Halas was famously conservative when it came to expenses. But it could also be said that Allen's exuberance for the job might have energized the Chicago franchise. Allen's willingness to side with players during contract negotiations, as he did with draftee Dick Butkus, might have helped the Bears with employee relations. So, it is fair to assume that as much as working for Halas might have helped Allen in some ways, Allen's work ethic and team-chemistry skills probably would have helped the team as much as his great coaching talent. We'll never know, obviously, but it is a great what-if question.

You also wonder what might have happened had Allen lived long enough to coach a few more seasons at Long Beach State. The winning season in 1990 created a positive atmosphere and would have made recruiting easier. Allen's system had been implemented already, so all that was needed was the annual refinement that all college programs undergo. The 49ers had a stud running back with four years of playing eligibility remaining in Terrell Davis, who was waiting to become a star. In the end, the football program at Long Beach State survived Allen by just one season. It is impossible to tell what might have been, but it would have been interesting to watch.

Appendix 1
Trades

Los Angeles Rams (1966–1970): 59 trades
Washington Redskins (1971–1977): 87 trades[1]

The total number of trades for Allen's NFL years is 146. The table on the following pages includes the records of transactions where Allen acquired a free agent and then had to give compensation to the player's previous team as a trade. In some cases, the exact draft choice involved in a transaction was not clear at the time of the transaction. Free agent signings where there was no compensation required are not included, although one of those incidents was interesting.

In 1970, Allen and the Rams claimed running back Elijah Pitts off the waiver list. Pitts played two games for the Rams before Allen traded Pitts to the New Orleans Saints for an undisclosed draft pick. Basically, Allen got a player any team could have claimed for virtually nothing and then traded him away for what was probably a late-round draft pick.[2]

Allen's reputation as a coach who squandered his franchise's future by trading draft picks for veteran players has been over-stated through the years. As head coach, Allen oversaw 146 NFL trades. In 34 of those instances (or 16.4 percent of the trades), his only compensation was one or more draft choices. On 18 other occasions (12.3 percent), Allen's team reaped at least one draft pick along with one or more players. That brings the total to 52 trades in which Allen's team scored at least one draft choice (35.6 percent). On the flip side, Allen completed 66 trades in which he gave away draft choices but no players (45.2 percent) and 18 in which he sent off both players and draft picks (12.3 percent).

It is difficult to determine exactly how many draft choices changed hands in trades where Allen's teams were participants. In some cases, the number of draft choices traded depended upon player performance. In other cases, the trades were voided because players failed their physical examinations or they retired. The trades that were voided are included here because a deal was struck, even if it was later cancelled. However, the draft picks included in trades that were later cancelled are not counted among those that were exchanged. It appears Allen's teams received 65 draft choices through trades. His teams sent away 137, slightly more than a two-to-one ratio.

Los Angeles Rams

Date	Acquired	Other Team Involved	Value Surrendered
3/15/66	David Ray	Browns	Undisclosed draft choice
4/1/66	Maxie Baughan	Eagles	Frank Molden; Fred Brown; 1967 draft choice
4/26/66	Tom Moore	Packers	Ron Smith; Rights to Dick Arndt; 2nd round, 1967 draft
6/8/66	Irv Cross	Eagles	Aaron Martin; Willie Brown
7/1/66	Mike Dennis	Falcons	6th 1967
7/8/66	Myron Pottios	Steelers	Draft choice, 1967
7/26/66	Gerald Circo	Eagles	Draft choice, 1967
8/1/66	Bob Nichols	Steelers	Roger Pillath
8/10/66	Earl Leggett	Bears	4th, 8th 1967
3/14/67	Hal Bedsole; Tommy Mason; 2nd round, 1967	Vikings	Marlin McKeever; 1st 1967
6/9/67	Willie Daniel	Steelers	Undisclosed draft choice
7/1/67	Dave Cahill	Saints	Mike Capshaw
7/1/67	2nd 1967	Saints	Agreement, Rams joined scouting combine
7/7/67	2nd 1968	Packers	Ben Wilson
7/10/67	Bernie Casey	Falcons	Tom Moore
7/17/67	Bob Whitlow	Falcons	Undisclosed draft choice
8/28/67	3rd 1968	Browns	George Youngblood
9/7/67	Roger Brown	Lions	1st, 3rd 1968; 2nd 1969
9/11/67	4th 1968	Falcons	Tommy McDonald
9/11/67	Undisclosed draft choice	Giants	Bruce Anderson
1/8/68	Ron Smith	Falcons	Undisclosed draft pick

Appendix 1: Trades

Date	Acquired	Other Team Involved	Value Surrendered
5/1/68	Pat Studstill; Tommy Watkins; Milt Plum; 1st 1969	Lions	Bill Munson; 3rd 1969
5/30/68	James Wilson; Bob Sanders	Falcons	Bucky Pope
6/14/68	1st 1969	Redskins	Gary Beban
7/29/68	Jim Garcia	Saints	Undisclosed draft choice
7/31/68	Coy Bacon	Cowboys	5th 1969
8/13/68	Jay Bachman	Packers	Undisclosed 1969 draft choice
8/22/68	Kent Kramer	Saints	5th 1970
9/19/68	Frank Marchlewski	Falcons	Undisclosed draft choice
1/28/69	Dick Absher; 6th 1969	Falcons	4th 1969
5/12/69	Bob Brown; Jim Nettles	Eagles	Joe Carollo; Don Chuy; Irv Cross
5/14/69	4th 1970	Vikings	Kent Kramer
5/17/69	Richie Petitbon	Bears	Lee Calland; 4th 1970; 3rd 1971
6/20/69	Karl Sweetan	Saints	4th 1970; 3rd 1971
7/7/69	Claudis James	Packers	Undisclosed draft choice
7/7/69	Izzy Lang	Eagles	Harold Jackson; John Zook
7/11/69	Jim Purnell; 2 undisclosed draft choices	Eagles	Tony Guillory; 2nd 1970
7/14/69	Undisclosed draft choice	Giants	Henry Dyer
7/20/69	Undisclosed draft choice	Giants	Milt Plum
7/20/69	Jon Kilgore	Giants	$1
7/20/69	Undisclosed draft choice	Packers	Claudis James (earlier trade voided due to James failing physical exam)
7/22/69	Undisclosed draft choice	Redskins	Vilnis Ezerins
8/4/69	Undisclosed draft choice	Vikings	Don Martin
8/5/69	Alvin Haymond	Eagles	Billy Guy Anderson; Jimmy Rae; 3rd 1970
8/12/69	Dave McDaniels	Bears	7th 1971
9/12/69	Rick Cash	Falcons	Undisclosed draft choice
9/9/69	Mitch Johnson	Redskins	2 undisclosed draft choices

Date	Acquired	Other Team Involved	Value Surrendered
9/10/69	Dave Cahill	Falcons	Undisclosed 1970 draft choice
1/1/70	7th 1970	Falcons	To be determined
1/20/70	Undisclosed 1971 draft choice	Saints	Frank Marchlewski
1/27/70	Kermit Alexander; 2nd 1970	49ers	Bruce Gossett
4/21/70	Draft choice not exercised	Chargers	Lamar Lundy[3]
5/2/70	Frank Richter	Browns	Izzy Lang
5/30/70	Tommy Joe Crutcher	Giants	2 undisclosed draft choices
7/1/70	Bob Long	Redskins	Undisclosed draft choice
8/25/70	John Wilbur	Cardinals	Mike LaHood
9/1/70	Dick Evey; 4th 1971	Bears	Jim Seymour, Ron Smith
9/9/70	5th 1972	Vikings	Ted Provost
10/10/70	Undisclosed draft choice	Saints	Elijah Pitts

Washington Redskins

Date	Acquired	Other Team Involved	Value Surrendered
1/23/71	Billy Kilmer	Saints	Tom Roussel; 4th and 8th 1971
1/28/71	Maxie Baughan; Myron Pottios; Jeff Jordan; John Wilbur; Diron Talbert; 5th 1971	Rams	1st, 3rd 1971; 3rd, 4th, 5th, 6th, 7th 1972
1/28/71	Boyd Dowler	Packers	5th 1971
1/29/71	Mike Taylor	Saints	Leo Carroll; 17th 1971
3/31/71	Tommy Mason	Rams	Undisclosed draft choice
5/6/71	Jimmy Jones	Jets	6th 1973
5/7/71	Sam Wyche	Bengals	Henry Dyer; Undisclosed draft choice
5/11/71	Ron McDole	Bills	3rd, 4th, 7th, 1973
5/26/71	Speedy Duncan (free agent)	Chargers	3rd, 4th, 5th 1973— compensation
6/5/71	1973 draft choice	Broncos	Walt Roberts

Appendix 1: Trades 223

Date	Acquired	Other Team Involved	Value Surrendered
6/10/71	1972 draft choice (included with acquisition of Verlon Biggs)	Jets	1st, 1972; 2nd 1973
6/29/71	1973 draft choice	Saints	Jim Ward
7/8/71	Bob Grant	Colts	2nd, 7th 1972
7/10/71	George Burman	Rams	2 choices, later returned when Burman retired
7/24/71	Undisclosed draft choice	Chiefs	George Starke
7/31/71	Roy Jefferson; 9th, 1973; 9th, 1974	Colts	Cotton Speyrer; 1st, 1973
8/4/71	Richie Petitbon; 2 undisclosed choices, 1972; 1 undisclosed choice, 1973	Rams	6th, 1973; 1st, 1974
8/4/71	Tom Barrington; Undisclosed draft choice	Saints	Bruce Anderson; Undisclosed draft choice
8/31/71	Mike Hull	Bears	Steve Wright; Danny Pierce
10/26/71	Clifton McNeil	Giants	5th, 7th 1972[4]; Richmond Flowers
1/19/72	George Nock	Jets	3rd, 1974; Undisclosed draft choice
3/13/72	Ocie Austin; John Lanier	Steelers	Conditional 1973 draft choice if Austin or Lanier made the team[5]
5/12/72	Rosey Taylor; 2 undisclosed draft choices	49ers	Undisclosed choices 1974, 1975
5/21/72	Undisclosed draft choice	Raiders	Michael Taylor
6/15/72	Mike Wilson	Bills	Conditional draft choice if Wilson made the team[6]
6/16/72	Undisclosed draft choice	Saints	Bob Grant, 3 undisclosed draft choices
7/15/72	Ike Lassiter	Patriots	9th, 1973
7/9/72	Alvin Haymond	Rams	Undisclosed 1973 draft choice
7/31/72	Mitch Johnson; 8th, 1974	Browns	3rd, 1973

Appendix 1: Trades

Date	Acquired	Other Team Involved	Value Surrendered
8/31/72	5th, 1973	Falcons	Willie Germany
9/5/72	5th, 1975	Lions	John Hilton
1/30/73	Dave Robinson	Packers	2nd 1975
1/31/73	Clancy Williams	Rams	15th 1973
1/31/73	John Pergine	Rams	11th 1973
2/8/73	Fred Miller	Colts	10th 1974
4/17/73	5th, 1974	Oilers	Alvin Haymond
5/15/73	Ken Houston; 6th, 1974	Oilers	Jim Snowden, Mack Alston, Clifton McNeil, Mike Fanucci, Jeff Severson
5/28/73	Alvin Reed	Oilers	5th, 6th 1974
6/7/73	Paul Staroba	Browns	6th 1975
7/1/73	Undisclosed draft choice	Bills	Mike Taliaferro
7/19/73	Duane Thomas	Chargers	1st 1975; 2nd 1976
7/26/73	5th 1974	Patriots	Mel Lunsford
8/6/73	Undisclosed draft choice	Chiefs	Lincoln Minor
8/7/73	Undisclosed draft choice	Rams	Steve Boekholder
8/27/73	Bill Malinchak	Chargers	15th 1974; 8th 1975
8/29/73	9th 1974	Patriots	Charlie Richards
9/6/73	Brad Dusek	Patriots	Donnell Smith; 7th 1974
10/23/73	Willie Holman; 5th 1975	Bears	3rd 1974
1/25/74	Joe Theismann	Dolphins	1st 1976
1/29/74	Walt Sweeney	Chargers	5th 1974; 6th 1975; 4th 1976
1/30/74	Cornelius Johnson; 17th 1975	Colts	George Nock; 17th 1974
1/30/74	Ed Mooney	Colts	12th 1974
1/30/74	Joe Sweet	Rams	9th 1974
2/18/74	6th, 11th 1975	Browns	Rights to Jon Keyworth
3/8/74	Fred Sturt	Cardinals	Jimmie Jones; 7th 1975; 5th 1976
4/10/74	Bryant Salter; 8th 1975	Chargers	3rd 1976; 2nd 1977
5/14/74	Larry Smith	Rams	5th 1977
8/10/74	Deacon Jones; Undisclosed draft choice	Chargers	Undisclosed draft choice
8/17/74	Bill Cappleman	Lions	Sam Wyche
8/21/74	Howard Kindig	Dolphins	10th 1975

Appendix 1: Trades

Date	Acquired	Other Team Involved	Value Surrendered
8/28/74	Jim Tyrer	Chiefs	8th 1975; 6th 1976; 4th 1977
9/5/74	Carlester Crumpler	Bills	Undisclosed[7]
1/28/75	Rights to Ray Parson	Cardinals	15th 1976
1/29/75	Cotton Speyrer; Glenn Ressler	Colts	12th 1975; 16th 1976
1/29/75	Eddie Foster	Patriots	12th 1975
1/29/75	Rights to Karl Lorch	Dolphins	10th 1976
3/11/75	Rights to Glenn Hyde	Falcons	8th 1978
6/2/75	4th 1977	Colts	Herb Mul-key
6/23/75	Marv Fleming	Dolphins	Rights to Charlie Harraway; 4th 1977
8/12/75	Undisclosed draft choice	Dolphins	Cotton Speyrer
8/23/75	Dennis Nelson	Colts	12th 1976; 4th 1977; 2nd, 3rd, 5th 1978[8]
9/4/75	10th 1976	Bears	Ted Vactor
9/4/75	Tim Stokes; 6th, 8th 1976	Rams	2nd, 3rd, 4th 1978; 5th 1979
9/4/75	5th, 15th 1976; 6th 1977	Cardinals	1st 1977, 1st 1978, 2nd 1979[9]
4/2/76	Rights to Steve Hanstedt[10]	Oilers	Rights to Duane Thomas
8/4/76	Undisclosed 1977 draft choice	Oilers	Felix Lobdell
8/4/76	Joe Lavender	Eagles	Manny Sistrunk; 6th 1977; 5th 1978 4th 1979
8/17/76	Ron Saul	Oilers	7th 1977; 6th 1978; 3rd 1979
8/24/76	Jake Scott; 4th, 1977	Dolphins	Bryant Salter
8/24/76	John Matuszak	Chiefs	8th 1977; Undisclosed draft choice
8/29/76	Dave Thompson	Buccaneers	Undisclosed draft choice
9/6/76	Dan Nugent	Rams	2nd, 3rd 1980
9/6/76	Ted Fritsch	Falcons	6th, 9th 1977
5/3/77	7th, 9th 1977	Rams	3rd 1981
8/22/77	Harold Hart	Patriots	Conditional draft choice

Appendix 2
Draft Selections

Los Angeles Rams

1966 Key Draftees: The NFL 1966 draft was conducted before George Allen joined the Rams.

1967 Key Draftees: (Round 2) Willie Ellison, running back, Texas Southern; (5) Nate Shaw, defensive back, Southern Cal; (9) Tommie Smith, receiver, San Jose State.

1968 Key Draftees: (Round 2) Mike LaHood, guard, Wyoming; (11) John Pergine, linebacker, Notre Dame; (12) Harold Jackson, receiver, Jackson State; (13) Dean Halverson, linebacker, Washington; (16) Jimmy Raye, defensive backs, Michigan State. Note: Gary Beban, the Heisman Trophy-winning quarterback from UCLA, was also a second-round pick by the Rams.

1969 Key Draftees: (Round 1) Larry Smith, running back, Florida; (1) Jim Seymour, receiver, Notre Dame; (1) Bob Klein, tight end, USC; (6) Pat Curran, tight end, Lakeland; (8) Richard Harvey, defensive back, Jackson State; (13) Roger Williams, defensive back, Grambling.

1970 Key Draftees: (Round 1) Jack Reynolds, linebacker, Tennessee; (2) Donnie Williams, receiver, Prairie View A&M; (7) Ted Provost, defensive back, Ohio State; (7) Bill Nelson, defensive tackle, Oregon State; (8) Rich Saul, center, Michigan State; (14) Bob Geddes, linebacker, UCLA.

Washington Redskins

1971 Key Draftees: (Round 9) Mike Fanucci, defensive end, Arizona State; (11) George Stark, tackle, Columbia; (12) Jeff

Severson, defensive back, Long Beach State; (13) Dan Ryczek, center, Virginia. Note: The Redskins did not have selections in the first, third, fourth or eighth rounds. Second-round pick Cotton Speyer had a four-year NFL career but did not play for the Redskins, sixth-round pick Conway Hayman did not play for Washington but played six seasons in the league, seventh-round pick Willie Germany played four NFL seasons, none with the Redskins.[1]

1972 Key Draftees: (Round 8) Moses Denson, running back, Maryland-Eastern Shore. (13) Frank Grant, receiver, Colorado State–Pueblo. NOTE: The Redskins did not have selections in the first seven rounds. Denson did not play for the Redskins until 1974 and Grant did not appear in a game until 1973. Washington's first-round draft pick for the 1972 draft went to the New York Jets in the 1971 trade for defensive end Verlon Biggs. Biggs started 55 of a possible 56 regular-season games for Washington, recovered eight fumbles and scored two touchdowns. The Jets drafted Michigan linebacker Mike Taylor with the pick they got for Biggs. Taylor played two seasons for the Jets, starting eight games. Taylor had one interception during his career and he scored one touchdown.

1973 Key Draftees: (Round 8) Mike Hancock, tight end, Idaho State. (10) Ken Stone, defensive back, Vanderbilt. (13) Dennis Johnson, defensive end, Delaware. NOTE: The Redskins did not have a choice until the fifth round.

1974 Key Draftees: (Round 6) Jon Keyworth, running back, Colorado. (7) Mike Varty, linebacker, Northwestern. (9) Jimmie Kennedy, tight end, Colorado State. (13) Stu O'Dell, linebacker, Indiana. NOTES: The Redskins did not have a selection until the sixth round. Keyworth played in seven NFL seasons, all with the Denver Broncos. Kennedy played in three NFL seasons, starting in 1975 and all were with the Baltimore Colts.

Also acquired: QB Joe Theismann, DE David "Deacon" Jones, K. Mark Moseley.

1975 Key Draftees: (Round 5) Mike Thomas, running back, UNLV. (9) Dallas Hickman, defensive end, California. (15) Art Kuehn, center, UCLA. NOTE: Hickman did not play in 1975. Kuehn played eight seasons with the Seahawks and Patriots.

1976 Key Draftees: (Round 6) Tommy Marvaso, defensive back, Cincinnati. (8) Brian Fryer, wide receiver, University of Alberta. (12) Walter Tullis, wide receiver, Delaware State. NOTES: The Redskins did not have a pick until the fifth round. Marvaso played two seasons with the Jets, Tullis played 1978–79 with the Packers.

1977 Key Draftees: (Round 7) Reggie Haynes, tight end, UNLV. (11) Don Harris, defensive back, Rutgers. NOTE: The Redskins did not have a pick until the fourth round. The draft was shortened to twelve rounds.

Appendix 3
The Offensive Truth

In the years since George Allen coached the Rams and Redskins, his defenses for both teams have enjoyed rave reviews. Allen inherited the Fearsome Foursome in Los Angeles, sprinkled a few veterans into the defensive mix and developed one of the fiercest units in the game. Then he brought a bunch of those Rams with him to Washington and built another stout group of defenders, acquiring a few more veteran tough guys along the way. Allen's groundbreaking genius for coaching the defensive game, which was chiefly his ability to break down the opposing offense and determine how best to attack it, served his teams very well during his dozen NFL seasons. Nobody would argue against the defensive accomplishments of Allen's teams.

Allen's offenses were a different story, right? Ultra-conservative, ground-based and low scoring. Allen's offenses depended upon his defenses to generate turnovers and keep the opposition's score low. Sonny Jurgensen said after he retired from the game that Allen was more interested in field goals than touchdowns. Allen was too controlling, the story went, and the offense paid the price for that conservatism. An NFL Films interview with Jurgensen supports that view. As we have seen, Jurgensen related a story during an interview with Steve Sabol of NFL Films about throwing a scoring pass when Allen wanted a running play to set up a field goal and, during the interview, a film clip of a practice drill was shown where Allen told Jurgensen a field goal was the objective. Just playing Billy Kilmer instead of Jurgensen was proof of Allen's inflexibility when it came to his conservatism, the school of thought goes. In Los Angeles, where there was no quarterback controversy, the offense was still conservative. Everybody knows that.

And so, the question is begged: Were Allen's offenses really so conservative that the team was damaged? Did Allen's preference for veteran players keep younger, more capable players off the field or get them traded to other teams and thus limit the Rams' and Redskins' scoring potential?

Surprisingly, the statistics say no. The offenses of the Rams and the Redskins were less conservative than Allen's critics might have you believe. While it is true that liars can figure and numbers can be bent to reflect a prismed view of life, data is still data. Facts are facts. The truth is that Allen's offenses produced. They scored points, gained yards and won games. Allen's record as a head coach in the National Football League was 116-47-5 in the regular season and 118-54-5 including the playoffs. If you include the meaningless Playoff Bowl (his Rams won two of those games), his overall mark improves to 120-54-5. Allen's teams reached double-digits in wins seven times in twelve 14-game seasons. He never coached a losing season in the professional ranks and got to the NFL postseason seven times. He took losing franchises and reached the playoffs within two years in LA and in his first season in Washington.

And the statistics show that Allen's teams passed the football.

As a team, Allen's 1966 Rams ranked third in passing attempts and quarterback Roman Gabriel was seventh among quarterbacks in passing yards among the 15-team NFL. Notably, Gabriel was among the league leaders with a low interception average of just 4.0 percent. Tom Moore set a league record for running backs by leading the team in receptions with 60 and veteran flanker Tommy McDonald, whom Allen acquired by trade and who played without a facemask, caught 55. The Rams were seventh in the league in rushing yards as Dick Bass set a franchise record by gaining 1,090 yards. Bass played in the Pro Bowl at the end of the season. The 1966 Rams ranked 10th in scoring, which wasn't much to brag about, but they were seventh in total yards gained.

The Rams led the league in scoring in 1967 with 398 points. A George Allen-coached team once led the NFL in scoring. Gabriel rated sixth in passing attempts, third in the percentage of his passes that went for scores, 6.7 percent, and had the second-lowest interception percentage, just 3.5 percent. It is interesting to note that Gabriel was sixth in the NFL with 371 pass attempts while Jurgensen led the league with 508. Jurgensen enjoyed one of his finest seasons as an individual that year, throwing 6.3 percent of his passes for touchdowns and surrendering just 3.1 percent for interceptions. Jurgensen led the NFL with 31 scoring passes in a 14-game season while Gabriel threw 25 (good for fourth place). The Rams went 11-1-2 that year, won the Coastal Division and reached the playoffs. One of those ties was against Jurgensen and the Redskins. Washington finished third in the Capitol Division with a record of 5-6-3. In what was arguably Jurgensen's most heroically-successful season, his Redskins did not win half their games.

Appendix 3: The Offensive Truth

The Rams' Dick Bass finished sixth in carries in '67 and 13th in yards gained. Bernie Casey, the flanker Allen acquired by trade and who caught the pass to beat the Packers to save the season, was 10th in the NFL with 53 receptions, eighth in the league with yards gained, 871, and tied for eighth with eight scoring receptions. Casey tied with four others at the eight TD plateau and one of the four was Rams split end Jack Snow. Roman Gabriel spread the ball around and so none of his receivers had huge numbers as individuals.

The 1968 campaign, which ended with such a loud thud in the 13th week, had less offensive sparkle but it still refutes the conservative image Allen's teams had. The Rams finished fifth in points scored and seventh in passing attempts. Gabriel completed the season sixth in the league with 19 scoring passes and running back Willie Ellison gained 616 yards, good for 12th in the rushing standings. Tight end Billy Truax led the club with 35 receptions, just 28th in the league. Los Angeles did manage to score more points than the playoff-bound Minnesota Vikings.

The 1969 Rams were probably Allen's best team on the West Coast and it had a pass-based offense. The Rams led the NFL in scoring passes with 25 (all by Gabriel). Los Angeles ran the ball 382 times that season, an average of 27.28 runs per game, the second-lowest number in the league that year. Larry Smith was the team's leading rusher with 599 yards, twelfth among all runners in the NFL. The Rams scored 320 points, fourth-best, and Gabriel spread the ball around when he threw it. No Rams receiver finished in the top 10 for touchdown receptions but flanker Wendell Tucker was fourteenth with seven, split end Jack Snow was fifteenth with six and tight end Billy Truax was nineteenth with five. Snow led the team with 49 receptions and running back Larry Smith was next with 46. Gabriel had the league's lowest interception average; a skinny 1.8 percent of his passes were caught by opposing defenses.

Allen's 1970 Rams did not enjoy the same success as the 1967 and 1969 clubs, failing to reach the playoffs, despite nine wins in a 14-game season. But the 1970 Rams were second in the league with 426 passing attempts and fourth in points scored with 325. As an individual, Gabriel led the league in passing attempts with 407 and, while he threw only 16 scoring passes that year, his interception percentage was 2.9, bettered only by San Francisco's John Brodie. Snow was fourth in the league with 51 catches and Josephson was 18th with 44. The Rams ran the ball 430 times, which was 18th in the league, averaging the 9th-best total of 4.1 yards per attempt.

When you put the package together as a whole, Allen's Rams were a passing team. Gabriel seldom threw interceptions—he didn't get hurt often, either, which was distinctly different from Sonny Jurgensen. Gabriel and Bill Munson were both on the roster by the time Allen became the

Rams coach but neither had convinced previous Rams coaches who was the better man under center. Allen was convinced *when he got there* and made his decision quickly. The Rams reaped the benefits.

In Allen's five seasons with the Rams, they consistently finished among the league leaders in some very telling categories. Those categories were points scored (an average of 4.8 among NFL teams), pass attempts (6.0), the percentage of touchdowns among the attempts (9.0), the percentage of interceptions among attempts (2.8) and passing yards (8.6). Subtracting Allen's first season, 1966, when the Rams finished 10th in scoring, they finished an average of 3.5 among the league's teams. In the four years from 1967 through 1970, the Rams were never lower than fifth in scoring and, as noted above, led the league in 1967. In Allen's five seasons they were never lower than 10th in pass attempts and were eighth or better four times. They were never lower than fourth in interception percentage.

These are not the traditional hallmarks of a conservative offense. As evidenced by the 60 passes caught in 1966 by Moore, a running back, Gabriel had great passing discipline. He did not ignore the fundamentals of Allen's game plan, as Jurgensen and Theismann later admitted they did. Gabriel did what he was coached to do instead of what he probably wanted to do (most quarterbacks want to throw the ball down the field instead of throwing shorter, safer passes). That cut the Rams' odds of making mistakes and helped moved the football. George Allen's passing game will never be confused with that of the Oakland Raiders, from whom Allen wooed Gabriel away. Al Davis' aggressive Raiders teams threw the ball deep often and scored a lot of points. But Allen's Rams teams did throw the football often. Gabriel ran Allen's offense successfully enough that the Rams ranked eighth or better in passing yardage in three of Allen's five seasons in LA.

Once Allen moved to Washington, the team passing statistics were more indicative of his offense than numbers for individual quarterbacks because three different passers had significant playing time. In 1971, the "Skins" finished 12th among NFL teams with 276 points (for comparison, Dallas led with 406). Washington passers threw 13 scoring passes and 15 interceptions. The stats mostly belong to Kilmer, as he started 13 games, but Jurgensen played in five and started one and the team scored on 3.9 percent of its passes and got intercepted 4.5 percent of the time.

The season in which Allen and the Redskins advanced to the Super Bowl, Washington, was 23rd in passing attempts but had the best touchdown percentage in the league. The Redskins passers were 13th in the league in interception percentage and 12th in passing yardage, but they were seventh in points scored. Some of those points came from the defense and special teams.

Washington threw fewer passes than most teams around the league in 1972 but threw more scoring passes, 21, than the league average of 15.5. The New York Jets quarterback, Joe Namath, gained more passing yards than the two Washington passers added together but Kilmer went to the Pro Bowl after throwing 19 touchdown passes against 11 interceptions. Kilmer's touchdown pass-to-attempt ratio was the best in the league. It is important to note that Washington's running attack in 1972 was probably the best any team Allen had with the Rams or Redskins.

The 1973 Redskins were ninth in attempted passes and sixth in touchdown percentage, interception percentage and yards gained. Receiver Charley Taylor finished second in the league with 59 catches and second in touchdown receptions with seven. Roy Jefferson caught 41 passes and Larry Brown caught 40 coming out of the backfield. Brown finished second to Buffalo's O.J. Simpson in rushing and Brown scored more touchdowns than Simpson, but Brown also fumbled nine times. The team's running game overall did not produce, finishing 25th out of 26 teams with only 1,439 yards and nine touchdowns on the ground. The Redskins were a pass-oriented team that year.

In 1974, the orientation of the offense grew still more pronounced toward the passing game. Allen's passers gained the most yardage in the league, compiled the third-highest total of pass attempts, finished seventh in touchdown percentage and had the second lowest interception percentage.[1] The Redskins' run game averaged just 3.1 yards per attempt gaining 1,443 yards and scoring 11 touchdowns. Washington finished fourth in scoring but those points included two interceptions returned for scores, plus a punt return, kickoff return and fumble recovery that resulted in scores.

In 1975, Allen's passers ranked third in attempts and scoring passes and finished second in passing yards, but they also threw the third-most interceptions. Mike Thomas, a rookie running back who played his collegiate ball at both Oklahoma and Nevada–Las Vegas, caught 40 passes coming out of the backfield in the same manner as Brown and Tom Moore had done for past Allen teams, gaining 483 yards. Thomas started 10 games and averaged 3.9 yards a carry. Still, the best the Redskins could do on the ground was finish 20th in rushing yards and the team had to put the ball in the air to move it.

The statistic that is by far the most important of the 1976 Redskins' season is the 90 punts Mike Bragg kicked. At that time, it was the most by a George Allen-led pro team. The Redskins ranked 11th in points scored but Kilmer and Theismann combined to toss 20 scoring passes, sixth-best in the league. They also threw 20 pass interceptions, ninth-worst in the league. Despite the efforts of Thomas and John Riggins, the Redskins ranked just 14th in rushing yards with 2,111.

Bragg punted 91 times in 1977, sixth in the league. The five teams who punted more—Atlanta, the New York Giants, Tampa Bay, Philadelphia and Detroit—had a combined record of 25 wins and 45 losses. Only Atlanta won as many as half of its games. The Redskins went 9–5, despite all those punts, and did not reach the playoffs. Three other teams with 9–5 records—Minnesota, Chicago and Pittsburgh—reached the playoffs. Washington was 21st in points scored and 20th in yards gained. The "Skins" finished 13th in scoring passes. There was a growing sentiment within the Redskins organization that Theismann should be the quarterback and, in his six starts, Theismann helped produce four wins. But Theismann's touchdown pass percentage was 3.8, while interceptions ended 4.9 percent of his attempts. Kilmer, who was 5–3 as a starter, was slightly better with 4.0 percent touchdowns and 3.5 percent interceptions. Worse, the Redskins were just 23rd in rushing yardage.

Allen's teams never had a breakaway back in the style of Gale Sayers. He had John Riggins in Washington and Riggins became a star after Joe Gibbs became the Washington coach, but that did not happen while Allen was coaching the Redskins. Larry Brown was a top-flight runner and he was very adept as a receiver, but he was not a breakaway threat. With all of that said, Allen's teams depended upon the passing game to move the football. In Los Angeles, Gabriel did that without turning the ball over. That was not the case in Washington.

Jurgensen, by his own admission, did not always follow Allen's game plan. He took chances and threw interceptions. One of the best passers in the history of the game, Jurgensen never-the-less lacked the discipline he needed to reduce his interception totals.

Theismann probably should have played more and sooner. But he also lacked the discipline he needed to prove to Allen that he was ready to be a leader. In his book, the former Notre Dame star described ignoring the game plan in practice, ignoring the needs of the team when he led the scout team offense as the defense prepared for the next game. He jumped out on the practice field to run pass patterns, he wrote. Theismann did not please Allen in practice, making it difficult for Allen or any other coach to trust him in a game. Theismann later became a Super Bowl quarterback for the Redskins and was rightfully very popular with fans, but he threw more interceptions than touchdowns the first five years he was in the league (1974 through 1978) and twice more later in his career. It should be noted that he completed his career with more scoring passes (160) than he did interceptions (138). He was a first-team All Pro selection once and went to the Pro Bowl once.

In Kilmer, Allen had a passer who accepted the game plan and distributed the ball well. He threw fewer interceptions than Jurgensen or Theismann did during the time they were teammates. Kilmer's toughness appealed to his teammates and his head coach. The Redskins went 49–22–1 in games Kilmer started under Allen. In 1978, after Allen was gone, Kilmer started two more times and went 1–1. Kilmer went 2–5 as a starter in playoff games and his playoff wins were the only playoff games George Allen ever won as a head coach in the NFL.

Both Allen's Rams and Redskins teams depended upon the passing game to move the ball. Some have called Allen's scheme a controlled passing game, but whatever it was, it worked. What Allen did not have in Washington was a Roman Gabriel–type passer, a guy who could make any throw but had the discipline to avoid interceptions. A guy who moved well in the pocket and could run when he had to. Gabriel seldom missed a start until later in his career, when he was sacked 97 times as an Eagle. It should be pointed out that Gabriel's only postseason victories as a starting quarterback were in Playoff Bowl games.

Allen's USFL teams finished first and third in points scored. Quarterback Greg Landry was among the league's leading passers both seasons. His totals for 1983 and 1984: He completed 471 of 783 passes for 42 scores and 24 interceptions. In '83, despite missing games due to injury, Landry was fifth in scoring passes and sixth in attempts, completions and yards. Trumaine Johnson led the league in receptions and receiving yards in 1983 and he was fourth in scoring receptions that year. Johnson was among the leaders in 1984 and his totals in Allen's offense were 23 scoring receptions, 2,590 yards all in 171 receptions. Both the Blitz and Wranglers had effective rushing attacks. Spencer finished fourth and fifth in yards gained and Long finished third in the league in rushing touchdowns in 1983.

How conservative were Allen's offenses? While it is true that no Allen passer was ever nicknamed "The Mad Bomber," as Oakland Raiders quarterback Daryle Lamonica was, it is also true that Allen's quarterbacks threw the ball frequently and generally called their own plays. Allen's NFL teams were consistently in the top half of the league in pass attempts, usually among the leaders in that department. Like football coaches of all eras, Allen looked for versatile players. His running backs had to be good receivers and men like Tom Moore and Larry Brown were very effective in that role. Yet, it is also true that wide receivers like Snow, Tucker, Jefferson and Taylor enjoyed productive careers in Allen's offense. The single year when Allen's Washington offense was by far his most productive as a running team, 1972, the Redskins advanced to the Super Bowl. In his five years as the Rams coach, Allen's offense produced only one rusher who gained 1,000 yards in a single season and that was Dick Bass in 1966.

The conservative offense brand is unfairly burned into Allen's hide. His NFL offenses might have produced more with more consistent running attacks, as his USFL teams proved.

Appendix 4
Coaching Comparison

George Allen's overall coaching record in professional leagues, viewed in the abstract, is impressive. His regular-season record in the NFL and USFL, combined, was 138–61–5. But viewed against the teams he coached and left, his record is instructive. The only head coach in the National Football League who had the same job from 1960 through 1977 was Dallas Cowboys head man Tom Landry. The graph below compares the Bears, Cowboys, Rams and Redskins during Allen's primary coaching stints in the NFL. The periods of comparison include Allen's time as an

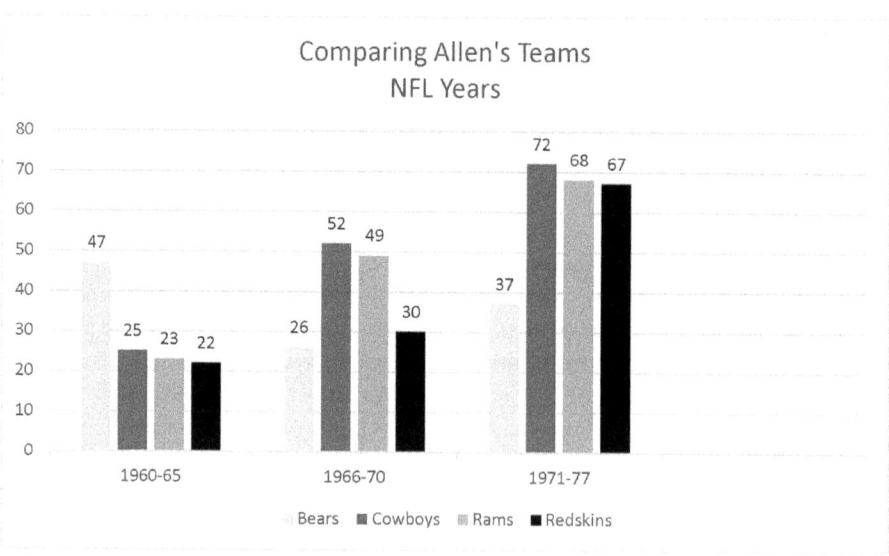

Comparing Allen's teams (author's illustration).

Appendix 4: Coaching Comparison 237

assistant in Chicago (1960–65), and his time with the Rams (1966–70) and in Washington (1971–77). The reader is reminded that the Bears won an NFL title and the Cowboys won two Super Bowls during the same period.

Allen's regular-season record for his two USFL seasons was 22–14. He is compared here with five coaches who coached teams for two seasons during the same period and had won-loss records equal to or better than Allen's. The coaches were Jim Mora (Stars), Spurrier (Bandits), Pardee (Gamblers), Dotsch (Stallions) and Stanley (Panthers). The Stars and Panthers won titles.

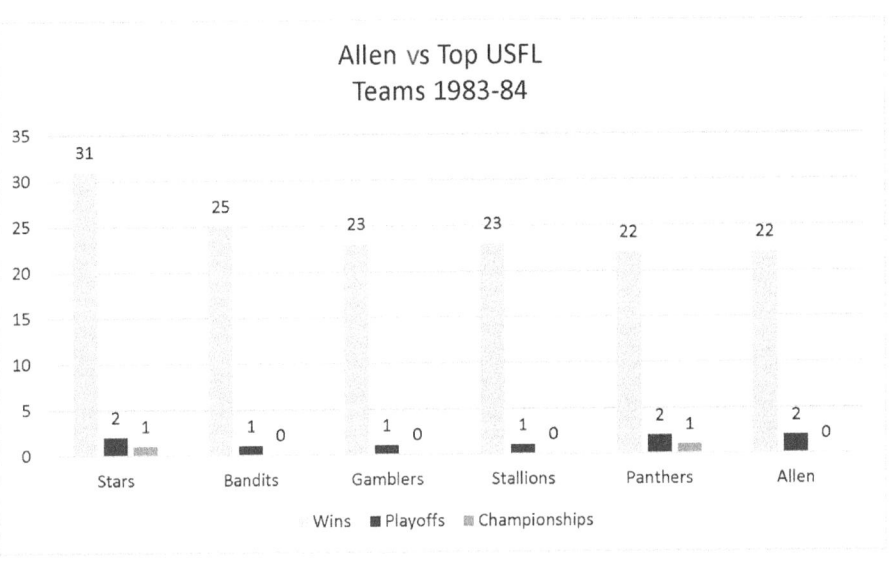

Allen vs. top USFL teams, 1983–84 (author's illustration).

Chapter Notes

Preface

1. Allen's 1948 Morningside team finished at 3–6 and his 1951 Whittier team went 2–7.

Chapter 1

1. The author carefully reviewed game film to determine how the Rams lined up to rush the punter.

Chapter 2

1. 1920 United States Census, viewed online September 7, 2020.
2. 1930 United States Census, viewed online September 7, 2020.
3. George Allen's draft card, seen online September 7, 2020.
4. 1940 United States Census, viewed online September 7, 2020. The Census worker who filled out the form with the information on the Allens put a mark next to Loretta's name, indicative that she was the family member who gave the information.

Chapter 3

1. Allen, Jennifer. *Fifth Quarter: The Scrimmage of a Football Coach's Daughter*, page 57. From here on, *Fifth Quarter*.
2. Ibid., page 55.
3. Ibid., page 55.
4. *New York Times*, *Henriette "Etty" Allen, Wife of NFL Coach and Mother of Senator, Dies* by Marc Fisher, January 7, 2013.
5. Allen's version of his hiring at Morningside is in *Strategies*, p.32.
6. *The Sioux City Journal*, *For the Record* column by Terry Hersom, December 14, 1989.
7. New Head Football Coach at Morningside, *The Morningsider*, May 1948.
8. *The Morningsider*, November 1948.
9. The author's interview with Morningside Sports Information Director Dave Rebstock, 2017. Callahan was drafted by the Detroit Lions in 1950 but did not make the team.
10. Allen Collection at Professional Football Hall of Fame, Box 22C.
11. Ibid.

Chapter 4

1. Allen, George. *Strategies for Winning: A Top Coach's Plan for Victory in Football and in Life*, p. 124.
2. Quotes from McNichols came from the author's interview with him August 22, 2017.
3. All quotes from Fields come from a 2017 interview with the author.
4. The 1952 Whittier preseason notebook shows four assistants, Dan Tebbs, Bill Payne, Jerry Burns and Beach Leighton. Burns played on Allen's junior varsity team at Michigan.
5. Author's interview with Vermeil.
6. Allen, George. *How to Scout Football*, 1953, School-Aid Company, Danville, Ill. The edition the author owns was published by Martino Publishing, Mansfield Centre, Connecticut. From here on, *Scout*.
7. *Scout*, pages 57–61.

8. *Scout*, page 93.
9. *Scout*, page 94.
10. The George Allen Collection, Pro Football Hall of Fame.
11. Whittier College Football 1955 letter, Allen collection, Pro Football Hall of Fame. From here on, PFHoF.
12. Allen, George H. and Joseph C. Pacelli, *George Allen's Guide to Special Teams*, page xi (see Acknowledgments). Whittier's 28-7 victory over Chico State was Chico State's third game of the 1955 season. The Wildcats finished with a 7-2 record.
13. *Motivation in Athletics*, Allen collection, PFHoF.
14. *The Law of Effect* was published in 1905.
15. The letter is in the George Allen Collection's box 21B at the PFHoF.
16. The game was played at Whittier on November 10, 1956.
17. Allen Collection, Pro Football Hall of Fame. Box 25C.
18. The author interviewed multiple former Whittier players from the Allen era. Trueblood's name came up every time and always with respect and appreciation.
19. Allen collection, Pro Football Hall of Fame.
20. Wilkinson to Allen, Allen Collection Box 25C.
21. George and Etty eventually raised four children: George, Bruce, Gregory and Jennifer.

Chapter 5

1. The Rams also won the 1945 NFL title game and lost the 1949 championship contest.
2. Katzowitz, Josh. *Sid Gillman: Father of the Passing Game*, pages 132-135. Katzowitz quotes Gillman as telling a reporter, "It seems that the one important thing in the city of Los Angeles, even of more importance than the elections, is who is going to call the Rams signals."
3. Gildea and Turan. *The Future Is Now: GEORGE ALLEN, Pro Football's Most Controversial Coach*, 1972, page 200.
4. Pro-football-reference.com, 1957 Los Angeles Rams, accessed August 6, 2019.
5. Treat, Roger. *The Encyclopedia of Football* (Sixteenth Revised Edition), page 137.
6. Charles Genuit, Magic Million: Rams Re-wrote Attendance Figures in 1957 Season, *Pro Football*, pps. 42-43.
7. Josh Katzowitz, *Sid Gillman: Father of the Passing Game*, Clerisy Press, Covington, Kentucky, 2012, 138-141.
8. *Fifth Quarter*, pages 38-39.
9. George Allen Collection, Pro Football Hall of Fame, Box 21B.
10. *Fifth Quarter*, pages 38-39. As we will see, George Allen was not done with the car wash and his first stay in Chicago was short-lived.
11. The game statistics for the Colts game came from Pro-football-reference.com, the 1958 Chicago Bears page, viewed August 7, 2019. The information on the Bears, Mather and Korch all came from Davis, *Papa Bear: The Life and Legacy of George Halas*, pages 333-336. From here on, *Papa Bear*.
12. *Papa Bear*, page 335.
13. *Papa Bear*, page 332.
14. *Papa Bear*, page 335.
15. George Allen Collection, Pro Football Hall of Fame, Box 8C.
16. *Fifth Quarter*, page 39.
17. Pro-football-reference.com, 1959 Chicago Bears page, viewed August 7, 2019.
18. *Papa Bear*, pages 356-357.
19. Pro-football-reference.com, 1959 Chicago Bears page, viewed August 7, 2019.
20. *Papa Bear*, page 336.
21. Pro-football-reference.com, 1959 Chicago Bears page, viewed August 7, 2019. See also Ed Brown's page.
22. Pro-football-reference.com, 1958 Los Angeles Rams page, viewed August 7, 2019. See also Del Shofner's page.
23. *Papa Bear*, page 357.
24. *Papa Bear*, pages 368-370.
25. *Papa Bear*, page 370.
26. *Papa Bear*, page 386.
27. *Papa Bear*, page 386.
28. The statistics for the 1963 Bears came from Pro-football-reference.com, the 1963 Bears page.
29. The statistics for the 1963 Giants and for the league leaders came from Pro-football-reference.com. See the 1963 New York Giants page and the ProFootballReference.com 1963 statistical leaders page.
30. See Pro-football-reference.com, the page for the 1963 championship game. See

also Roger Treat, *The Encyclopedia of Football*, 16th Edition, Dolphin Books, Garden City, New York, 1979, page 168.

31. Davis, Ben. *Papa Bear: The Life and Legacy of George Halas*, page 398.

32. *Papa Bear*, page 399.

33. NFL Films: George Allen—*Winning Is Living, Losing Is Dying*. Viewed online by the author 5/31/2020.

34. *Fifth Quarter*, page 231. Allen wrote that her father was serenaded by the Bears in the locker room with the ditty: "Hooray for George! Hooray at last! Hooray for George, he's a horse's ass!"

35. Pro-football-reference.com, see the 1963 Chicago Bears page and the pages for Galimore and Farrington for the statistics. Viewed by the author August 11, 2019. The story on the fatal accident is available via any number of sources. See *Papa Bear*, pages 411–412. George Halas was famously tight with money but Davis wrote that Halas paid for the college educations of Galimore's children. One of Galimore's sons became an Olympic gymnast.

36. ProFootballReference.com, see the 1964 Chicago Bears page.

37. The Bears players did receive $5,899.77 each as their winners' share of the championship game purse. The game drew 45,801. Roger Treat, *The Encyclopedia of Football*, page 168.

38. The spelling is reproduced here as it was written in Allen's book. See *Strategies*, page 127.

39. The italics are in the original. *Strategies*, page 127.

40. Spelling is correct.

41. *Strategies*, pages 101–113.

42. Allen and Olan, *Pro Football's 100 Greatest Players, Rating the Stars of the Past and Present*, page 165.

43. *Pro Football's 100*, pages 66–67.

44. In the seventh round, the Los Angeles Rams selected a little-known linebacker from Lamar named Tony Guillory. Guillory eventually played three seasons with the Rams and another with the Philadelphia Eagles. It was the same Tony Guillory who, a few years later, made what was arguably the biggest play a George Allen-coached team ever produced. See the 1965 NFL draft page on Pro-football-reference.com. Viewed by the author August 12, 2019. The AFL selected a gimpy quarterback out of Alabama with the first overall selection for that league in 1965. The kid had been in and out of Alabama coach Paul "Bear" Bryant's dog house during his college career. But Joe Namath, who was drafted by the NFL's St. Louis Cardinals as their first-round pick, also has a bust in the Pro Football Hall of Fame. See the 1965 AFL draft page, ProFootballReference.com.

45. Brian Piccolo's story is well-known. See Pro-football-reference.com for his NFL career statistics.

46. *Pro Football's 100*, page 165.

47. See Pro-football-reference.com for the Bears 1965 statistics. The author added the points scored for and against Chicago in the first three games and subtracted those totals from the seasonal totals with help from his trusty, hand-held calculator before performing the division function with the same calculator to get the stats for the final 11 games.

48. *Pro Football's 100*, page 66.

Chapter 6

1. The author found many references for Allen's birthdate, all online. See his draft card, Registration Card D.S.S. Form 1, Serial number 3701, Order No. 1379 for George Herbert Allen, Local Board No. 2, Washtenaw County, Michigan. See also Social Security Applications and Claims Index 1936–2007 for George Herbert Allen. See also California Death Index 1940–1997 for George Herbert Allen. All viewed online, 11/10/2020.

2. In 1965 the Rams averaged 40,333 per game, while the league as a whole averaged 43,489. In 1966 the Rams averaged 49,776 per game, compared to the NFL's 45,732. In 1967 the Rams averaged 60,000 to the league's 48,606. Most stadiums of the day had less seating capacity than did the LAMOC.

3. *Fifth Quarter*, page 39.

4. Professional Football Hall of Fame, George Allen collection.

5. *Fifth Quarter*, page 38.

6. January 13, 1966, *Chicago Sun-Times*, The George Allen Collection, Pro Football Hall of Fame.

7. *The Evening Sun*, January 12, 1966, The George Allen collection, Professional Football Hall of Fame.

8. Sid Ziff column, *Los Angeles Times*,

The George Allen Collection, Professional Football Hall of Fame.

Chapter 7

1. The statistics for the 1966 Rams are available in many places. The author accessed pro-football-reference.com on March 4, 2019. From here on, pro-football-reference.com.
2. The Rams quarterback saga is responsible for the joke about who the most popular man in town was at any given time. In Los Angeles it was the Rams' back-up quarterback.
3. *Headslap*, pages 320–321.
4. The information about Pardee's surgery is available from a number of sources. See the April 1, 2013, *Houston Chronicle*, among others. See also Dent, Jim *The Junction Boys: How Ten Days in Hell with Bear Bryant Forged a Championship Football Team*, 1999, Thomas Dunn Books for the remarkable story of the college career that produced Pardee.
5. Author's interview with Vermeil.
6. *Strategies for Winning: A Top Coach's Game Plan for Victory in Football and in Life*, page 44.
7. Ibid., page 46. The book was written after Allen's tenure with the Redskins.
8. NFL Films: *George Allen—Winning Is Living, Losing Is Dying*. Viewed online by the author 5/31/2020.
9. Ibid.
10. Ibid.
11. This was the mid-1960s and the proposed trade was with a team in the deep south.
12. The George Allen files at the Pro Football Hall of Fame, box 21A.
13. Author's interview with Chuck Hayes, August 19, 2020. Schnellenberger told Hayes the story while the two were traveling to Japan.
14. *Allen Denies "Stool Pigeon" Helped Rams*, The Washington Post, Times Herald, September 2, 1966. See also a roundup story about a luncheon meeting of the Southern California Football Writers Association in the *Los Angeles Times*, *Nine Troy Gridders Hit with Food Poisoning*, September 13, 1966.
15. The Rams-Bears game was played on a Friday night, September 16, 1966. The author attended the game with his father and clearly recalls a fan racing onto the field. The fan drew a little too close to the Bears' offensive huddle and was clotheslined by Mike Ditka. The man's decision to race onto the field during a game may have been aided by alcohol and he got what he deserved.
16. George Allen Papers, Pro Football Hall of Fame, box 26A.

Chapter 8

1. George Allen Papers, Pro Football Hall of Fame, box 23A.
2. *Headslap*, pages 325–326.
3. *Fifth Quarter*, page 67.
4. The author found the *Sports Illustrated* piece at the Pro Football Hall of Fame, folder STL 1966–1969.
5. The teams are linked through a history of unique notes. It was the Rams who, in a week eleven game of the 1960 season, ended John Unitas' 47 consecutive game streak in which Unitas completed a touchdown pass. The Rams did not allow Unitas to throw a scoring pass that day in 1960 but the Colts won anyway, 10–3. The odd relationship was rekindled in 1972, when Rams owner Robert Irsay and Colts owner Carroll Rosenbloom exchanged franchises.
6. Redskins quarterback Sonny Jurgensen completed only 18 of his 41 passes in that tie game, but he threw four touchdown passes and gained 334 yards through the air. The Rams did not intercept him.
7. The Packers-Chiefs game was played in the Coliseum.
8. *Instant Replay*, page 221.
9. Bisheff, Steve. *Great Teams, Great Years: Los Angeles Rams*, page 96–97.
10. Ibid.
11. *Instant Replay*, page 223.
12. Ibid.
13. *Special Teams*, page 74.
14. *Washington Post*, December 11, 1967, On Today's Scene.
15. *Washington Post*, December 11, 1967, On Today's Scene.
16. Author's interview with Joe Doherty, December 12, 2021. The Rams-Packers game was the only football game Doherty ever attended.
17. The author was among those who avoided the news all day in order to see the game without knowing the final score.

18. *Pro Football's 100*, page 13.
19. Kramer, *Instant Replay*, page 240.
20. Pro-football-reference.com, accessed March 3, 2019.
21. *Headslap*, page 377.

Chapter 9

1. Bob Golic, who played 14 seasons with the Patriots, Browns and Raiders, told the author in 1991 that high school and college defensive linemen who played in front of the offensive center might be termed nose *guards* but, in the NFL, such a defensive player was a nose *tackle*. Golic was an affable player and a great interview but he also stood six feet, two inches tall and played at 260 pounds. The author elected to agree with Golic's terminology.
2. The author found the clipping at the Pro Football Hall of Fame, folder STL 1966–1969.
3. *Headslap*, page 409
4. *Headslap*, pages 413–414
5. *Headslap*, page 424.
6. *100 Greatest*, pages 26–27.
7. *Headslap*, pages 414–415.
8. There are several versions of Allen's words to Reeves but the versions the author has read are all very close to what is written here.
9. *Headslap*, pages 425–425.
10. Melvin Durslag's column. Date uncertain, Pro Football Hall of Fame.
11. Sid Gillman had 28 wins as head coach of the Rams and Hamp Pool was next with 23.
12. *Special Teams*, page 4. Ezerins' first name is properly spelled Vilnis, according to numerous sources. The Rams drafted Ezerins in 1966 but he did not make the roster in '66 or 1967. According to Allen in *Special Teams* Rams assistant Ray Prohaska recommended the Rams keep Ezerins in 1968 because he was fast for his size at 6-feet-2 and about 220 pounds and would thus be a good player for special teams coverage. Ezerins was a running back and had two carries for a yard each during the season. It was his only season in pro ball. The play was viewed by the author on YouTube in a highlights package from the game on April 30, 2020. The highlight package can be viewed at https://www.youtube.com/watch?v=jPtTHlZyQzo.
13. The Bears game was historically important for another reason: Piccolo was the leading rusher with 62 yards and a touchdown on 22 carries. He also caught three passes for 20 more yards.
14. *Fifth Quarter*, page 3.
15. Ibid.
16. Melvin Durslag's column. Date uncertain, Pro Football Hall of Fame.
17. *St. Louis Globe-Democrat*, January 3, 1969. The author found it in folder STL 1966–1969 at the Pro Football Hall of Fame.
18. Allen Fired: What's New? Morton Moss, *Los Angeles Herald Examiner*, December 27, 1968, viewed at the Pro Football Hall of Fame.
19. *Fifth Quarter*, page 6.
20. *Fifth Quarter*, page 13.
21. *Headslap*, page 424.
22. NFL Films: *George Allen—Winning Is Living, Losing Is Dying*. Viewed online by the author 5/30/2020.
23. *Fifth Quarter*, page 9.
24. NFL Films: *George Allen—Winning Is Living, Losing Is Dying*. Viewed online by the author 5/30/2020.
25. The AP story was viewed at the Pro Football Hall of Fame.
26. *Fifth Quarter*, page 12.
27. *Fifth Quarter*, page 60.
28. *Special Teams*, pages 4–5.

Chapter 10

1. Schnellenberger, Vermeil told the author in 2019, belongs in the college football Hall of Fame. "He isn't because they have a rule that a coach has to have won 60 percent of his games, which is a stupid rule. He should be in the Hall of Fame because of all the teams he coached and he turned them all into winners." Author's interview with Vermeil.
2. Allen, *Special Teams*, pages v–vi.
3. Pro-football-reference.com, accessed April 21, 2019.
4. *Headslap*, pages 454–455.
5. *Fifth Quarter*, page 78.

Chapter 11

1. *You Win! You're Fired!*, *Sports Illustrated*, September 7, 1970.
2. *Headslap*, pages 464–465.

3. Levy, Marv. *Where Else Would You Rather Be?* Pages 128–129.

4. *Where Would You Rather Be?*, page 130.

5. *Where Would You Rather Be?*, page 131.

6. Jerry Kramer was interviewed for the NFL Films feature on Olsen, *#27: Merlin Olsen | NFL's Greatest Players (2010)* | NFL Films. Accessed on YouTube April 21, 2019. "He had a great headslap," Kramer said of Olsen. "He'd put that right hand up against your earhole on your helmet, so it was kind of half boxing match and half football."

7. Morton, who played for Levy when Levy was the head coach at the University of California at Berkeley, played 19 NFL seasons. Morton was traded to the New York Giants during his 10th season with Dallas in 1973, played parts of three seasons there and finished with six seasons in Denver.

8. *Where Else Would You Rather Be?*, pages 134–135.

9. *Where Else Would You Rather Be?*, page 145.

10. *Fifth Quarter*, page 80.

11. Allen eventually made good on Beban, trading the former *second* round selection to the Redskins for a *first* round pick.

12. *Where Else Would You Rather Be?*, page 137.

Chapter 12

1. *Fifth Quarter*, page 143.

2. William Gildea, Kenneth Turan, *The Future Is Now: GEORGE ALLEN, Pro Football's Most Controversial Coach*, page 201.

3. *The Future Is Now*, page 199–200.

4. *Los Angeles Herald-Examiner*, January 29, 1971, *Allen Tomahawks 'Skins* by Melvin Durslag. The author saw a copy of the article at the Pro Football Hall of Fame in box Was 1970–1971.

5. *Green Bay Press-Gazette*, *'Double-0 Skin Secret Serviceman,'* January 12, 1973. Viewed at the Pro Football Hall of Fame, Box Was 1972–1973.

6. If Talbert was Washington's first round choice that year, the Rams used the first-round choice Allen sent to Los Angeles to select linebacker Isiah Robertson, who played eight seasons for the Rams and four more with the Buffalo Bills. Robertson played in six Pro Bowls, was a first-team All Pro selection twice, was voted the 1971 Defensive Rookie of the Year by the Associated Press and would later be named a Pro-football-reference.com First Team All 70s selection. Talbert played ten seasons for the Redskins and started 130 of a possible 142 games. Talbert played in one Pro Bowl and was a selectee to Pro Football Reference's second team, All-70s squad. Both teams were happy with the results of that deal.

7. See Appendix 2 for the full trade details.

8. *Sport Special: A Most Revealing Look at the George Allen Formula for Winning, Behind the Redskin Turnaround*, found by the author at the Pro Football Hall of Fame in folder Was 1970–1971.

9. *Where Else Would You Rather Be?* Pages 141–142.

10. Petibon was the only player Allen coached on the Bears, Rams and Redskins.

11. If the 1971 draft days trades that brought so many veteran players from Los Angeles was Allen's "Brink's job," then another trade between the Rams and Redskins was, without question, his Golden Fleece. But this trade happened in 1968 when Allen was still coaching the Rams. The Rams had drafted UCLA quarterback and Heisman Trophy winner Gary Beban in the second round and discovered quickly that Beban would never be a starter in the NFL. In fact, the Rams did not sign Beban to a contract. Instead, Allen traded Beban to the Redskins for a *first* rounder in the 1969 draft. The Redskins eventually tried Beban at running back and defensive back, to no avail. Allen had turned a second-rounder into a first rounder while giving up a player whose best playing days were at the collegiate level.

12. Author's interview with Ron McDole.

13. *Ibid.*

14. George Allen, *Pro Football's 100 Greatest*, page 185.

15. *Washington Redskins 1972*, NFL Films, viewed online by the author August 23, 2020.

16. *Pro Football's 100*, pages 184–185.

17. Mike Hull, *A Player's Tribute to George Allen*, George Allen Collection, Pro Football Hall of Fame, box 22C. From here on, Hull letter.
18. NFL Films production about the 1972 Redskins. Viewed online by the author May 24, 2020.
19. Interview with Steve Sabol of NFL Films in NFL Films Present: *Sonny Jurgensen—Did You Ever See Him Play?* Viewed online April 7, 2020.
20. Hull letter.
21. *Where Else Would You Rather Be?*, page 161.
22. NFL Films, *Did You Ever See Him Play?*
23. Pro-football-reference.com. See the Redskins team pages for 1971–1974.
24. Clipping found at the Pro Football Hall of Fame, folder Was 1970–1971, *Skin Hopes Ride on Dramatic LA Trip*.
25. Bob Oates, *Allen Views Ram-Redskin Confrontation as "Another Civil War,"* Los Angeles Times, December 11, 1971.
26. Ibid.
27. *Wary Gabriel Prepares for Allen Reunion*, Washington Post, December 8, 1971. See also *Emotional Factor Makes Game One of High Points of Season*, Los Angeles Times, December 7, 1971, for Gabriel on possible trade to Redskins.
28. *Fifth Quarter*, pages 136–137.
29. *Fifth Quarter*, page 137.
30. *Pro Football's 100*, page 21.
31. The author saw the video of Allen's address in the locker room online on May 5, 2020, but the name of the film was obscured. It was part of an NFL Films presentation.
32. *The Sporting News*, February 18, 1978. Seen by the author in folder Was 1976–1980 at the Pro Football Hall of Fame.

Chapter 13

1. *Sports' Forgotten Heroes* podcast, accessed March 10, 2019.
2. George Allen Collection, Pro Football Hall of Fame, Box 25B.
3. George Allen Collection, Pro Football Hall of Fame, Box 25B.
4. *Pro Football's 100*, page 179.
5. The author viewed the clipping at the Pro Football Hall of Fame, folder WAS 1972-73.
6. Allen Issues His Manifesto, *The Evening Star and Washington News*, October 11, 1972. The author viewed the clipping at the Pro Football Hall of Fame.
7. *Pro Football's 100*, pages 206–207.
8. Pro Football Hall of Fame, Folder WAS 1972–1973. It was an ironic twist of fate for the Redskins to settle their quarterback conundrum through an injury. Two weeks earlier, in a game against the San Diego Chargers, Miami Dolphins quarterback Bob Griese suffered a broken ankle. Veteran quarterback Earl Morrall, who had once replaced Johnny Unitas for a season when the Colts' Hall of Famer injured his elbow, stepped in and the Dolphins did not miss a beat. The Dolphins completed the regular season undefeated and advanced to the Super Bowl, where they played the Redskins.
9. George Allen Collection, Pro Football Hall of Fame, Box 25B.
10. *Washington Redskins 1972*, NFL Films Production; Viewed by the author online August 23, 2020.
11. *100 Greatest Players*, p. 16.
12. *Fifth Quarter*, p. 148–149.
13. Author's interview with McDole, 3/13/2019.
14. Shula was criticized after his Colts lost Super Bowl III for not replacing Morrall earlier than he did, in favor of Johnny Unitas. It was not a fair criticism. Unitas' right elbow was not healthy enough to throw well that year and that was why Morrall played the entire regular season instead of Unitas in the first place. But in the 1972 AFC title game, Shula had a healthy Bob Griese on the bench. Solid as Morrall had been in the regular season, the Dolphins needed a spark against the Steelers and Griese provided it.
15. Author's interview with McDole, 3/13/2019.
16. *Where Else Would You Rather Be?*, page 174.
17. NFL Films Presents *Sonny Jurgensen*.
18. WASHINGTON QUOTES PAG1 [sic], Pro Football Hall of Fame, box Was 1972–1973.
19. REDSKIN PLAYER QUOTES PAGE III, Pro Football Hall of Fame, box Was 1972–1973.

20. Author's interview with McDole.
21. https://www.dailymotion.com/video/x3ywera, accessed by the author August 1, 2019.
22. *Garo's Goof: Cypriot Kicker Is No Passer*, January 15, 1973, *Los Angeles Times*, by Jeff Prugh. Reviewed by the author at the Pro Football Hall of Fame, box Wash 1972–1973.
23. *It Was Super Bore VII*, January 15, 1973, *Los Angeles Times*, by Jim Murray. Reviewed by the author at the Pro Football Hall of Fame, box Wash 1972–1973.
24. WASHINGTON QUOTES PAG1 [sic], Pro Football Hall of Fame, box Was 1972–1973.
25. *Fifth Quarter*, page 158.
26. *Where Else Would You Rather Be?*, pages 178–179.

Chapter 14

1. Allen file, Pro Football Hall of Fame, Box Was 1972–73. See *George Allen Must Appease Three Backs*, *The Repository*, August 12, 1973.
2. The Grey Cup Game is the championship game of the CFL. Levy's Montreal teams won in 1974 and 1977, losing in 1975. Levy coached the Kansas City Chiefs from 1978 to 1982 without significant success, then coached the Buffalo Bills for a dozen seasons. Levy's Bills played in four Super Bowls, losing each time, but had an 11–8 record in the playoffs.

Chapter 15

1. *Headslap*, page 544.
2. The full title is a paragraph by itself: *Theismann: On Theismann, Bad Breaks, L.T., Riggo and the Hogs, Cowboys, Cathy Lee, Madden, Gamblers, CBS, McMahon, President Reagan, Redskins, Stabler, the Golden Dome, Five O'Clock Club, Midnight Meetings, Etc.* From here on, *Theismann*.
3. *Theismann*, page 53.
4. Theismann's CFL statistics at statscrew.com, viewed 4/7/2020.
5. *Theismann*, page 57.
6. CFL rules allow each side to play with 12 players on the field.
7. *Theismann*, pages 61–62.
8. *Theismann*, pages 64–65.

9. NFL Films *Sonny Jurgensen: Did You Ever See Him Play?*
10. *Strategies*, page 127.
11. *Headslap*, page 544.
12. *Headslap*, page 545.
13. *Theismann*, page 73.
14. *Redskins Hard Put to Put Loss Out of Mind*, *The Washington Post*, November 30, 1974.
15. *Headslap*, page 546.
16. Moseley told the story at the Shenandoah Apple Blossom Festival Valley Health Fast Forward Luncheon. Accessed by the author online May 5, 2020.
17. George H. Allen and Joseph G. Pacelli, *George Allen's Guide to Special Teams*, page 170. Petitbon also played for Allen in Los Angeles but was not the holder for Allen's Rams teams, that was done by Eddie Meador. Meador and Petitbon started next to each other as defensive safeties in Los Angeles. Redskins defensive lineman Ron McDole was one of Allen's all-time best kick blockers, along with Alan Page of the Vikings.
18. *Special Teams*, pages 19–20.
19. *Special Teams*, page 20.

Chapter 16

1. *Theismann*, page 72.

Chapter 17

1. *Theismann*, pages 67–68.
2. *Theismann*, page 68. Tillman played for the Redskins from 1970 through 1977 and had three starts. He did not play for another NFL team.
3. *Theismann*, page 69.
4. *Theismann*, page 70.
5. *Theismann*, page 68.
6. In the Jets game, Malincheck caught a 12-yard pass, his only reception ever as a Redskin.
7. *Burgundy and Gold Flashback* podcast, September 4, 2014. Watched by the author online 5/31/2020.
8. Ibid.

Chapter 18

1. Allen files at the Pro Football Hall of Fame, Box Was 1976–1980. See Leonard

Shapiro's *Washington Post* article dated November 14, 1977.
  2. *Theismann*, page 784.
  3. Leonard Shapiro, "Theismann, Defense Scramble Eagles," *Washington Post*, Oct. 31, 1977, pages D1, D4.
  4. Pro-football-reference.com, accessed March 31, 2020.

Chapter 19

  1. See Allen files at the Pro Football Hall of Fame, Box Was 1976–1980. See the Associated Press story headlines, *Redskins Fire Allen* dated 1/9/78.
  2. See Allen files at the Pro Football Hall of Fame, Box Was 1976–1980. See Dave Brady's story, *Allen's Redskin Reign Ends in War of Words*.
  3. It should be noted that the Redskins, coached by Ray Flaherty, won NFL championships in 1937 and 1942, a span of less than seven years.
  4. See Allen files at the Pro Football Hall of Fame, Box Was 1976–1980. See Dave Brady's story, *Allen's Redskin Reign Ends in War of Words*.
  5. The Associated Press quoted a letter from NFL Commissioner Pete Rozelle. The *Los Angeles Times* broke the story on July 18; the AP story was found in the Allen papers at the Pro Football Hall of Fame, box WAS 1976–1980. See *Allen Gets $3,000 Fine for Remarks on 'Skins*. The same AP report has Rozelle cautioning Allen for remarks which, Rozelle said, bordered on player tampering. Allen had reportedly commented on Redskins quarterback Billy Kilmer who had not agreed to a contract with Washington for the 1978 season at that time.
  6. Malavasi coached the Rams to their first Super Bowl appearance at the end of the 1979 season. They lost Super Bowl XIV to the Pittsburgh Steelers in the Rose Bowl in Pasadena, California, 31–19. Malavasi coached the Rams for five seasons.
  7. Associated Press, August 8, 1978, from the *Eugene Register-Guard*, viewed online August 30, 2020.
  8. Associated Press, August 8, 1978, from the *Eugene Register-Guard*, viewed online August 30, 2020. The quotes from Allen, Mack, Haden, France and Youngblood came from the same source. The Rams lost five of their six preseason games under Knox in 1977.
  9. Carroll Rosenbloom drowned while swimming off a Southern California beach.
  10. Dominic Frontiere was later convicted of scalping Super Bowl tickets for the Rams-Steelers Super Bowl and then not reporting the earnings on his taxes. He served nine months of incarceration after the conviction and the Frontieres were divorced after his release.

Chapter 20

  1. *Strategies*, page 22.
  2. *Strategies*, pages 128–129.
  3. *The Star-News*, February 20, 1882. Viewed online March 15, 2020.
  4. "We'll simply … can be," *For Allen, This Is Alien Territory, Sports Illustrated*, March 15, 1982. "I'm an owner now, you know," Associated Press April 23, 1982, viewed in *The Times-News* online March 15, 2020.
  5. *Sports Illustrated, For Allen, This Is Alien Territory*. March 15, 1982. Viewed online April 15, 2020.
  6. *The Times-News*, April 23, 1982. Viewed online March 15, 2020. Information on Harris and King came from the March 15, 1982, editions of *Sports Illustrated: For Allen, This Is Uncharted Territory*.
  7. Years later, the National Football League would do the same thing when Cleveland Browns owner Art Modell moved his team to Baltimore and renamed the team the Ravens. When a new franchise started in Cleveland, named the Browns, that franchise was given the records and history of the old Browns.

Chapter 21

  1. ABC and ESPN had the same corporate owner then and still do.
  2. Reeths, Paul. *The United States Football League 1982–1986*, page 35.
  3. The Cubs were more cooperative, finishing fifth in the National League East at 71–91.
  4. *The United States Football League 1982–1986*, page 35.
  5. *The United States Football League 1982–1986*, page 45. Allen was a head coach for 12 full seasons in the NFL, not 14.
  6. *The United States Football League 1982–1986*, page 46.
  7. White deserves special mention. As

a high school player for Roosevelt High in Kent, Ohio, White scored in every possible way in a game during his senior year. He scored a touchdown and on a two-point conversion play, kicked both a conversion and a field goal, and tackled the opposing quarterback in the end zone for a safety. See Stan White page on Wikipedia.

8. *USFL The Big Plays*, Week 1 highlights, viewed online February 18, 2020.

9. The crowd counts cited for the 1983 USFL season come from team pages on Wikipedia, viewed September 10, 2020.

10. *The United States Football League, 1982-1986*, page 47.

11. Piette's participation chart is available at USFLrevisited.com for both the 1983 Blitz and the 1984 Wranglers. Viewed by the author September 13, 2020.

12. Mora later became famous for a postgame rant after his NFL team, the Indianapolis Colts, surrendered five turnovers, all on pass interceptions, in a single game and lost to the San Francisco 49ers. He was asked whether his team could still make the playoffs and Mora famously reacted with the incredulous words, "Playoffs? Don't talk about—playoffs? You kidding me? Playoffs?" Jim Mora finished with 184 wins as a head coach, counting his college and professional tenures, but he remains best-known for that 10-second sound bite. The irony of the incident was that the defensive coach of the 49ers that day was Mora's son.

13. The story of the plane trip chew-out was related to Paul Reeths by Blitz administrator Don Kojich. *The United States Football League, 1982-1986*, page 107.

14. Levy, *Where Else Would You Rather Be?*, page 266.

15. The author served as color commentator on the radio broadcasts of the Cal Poly games on Corona, California, radio station KWRM. Veteran broadcaster John Rebensdorf did the play-by-play. The sports world lost a great broadcaster and an even better man when Rebensdorf passed away suddenly in 1992.

16. *The United States Football League, 1982-1986*, page 263.

17. *The United States Football League, 1982-1986*, page 377.

18. *The United States Football League, 1982-1986*, page 378.

19. The USFL filed an anti-trust suit against the NFL on October 17, 1984.

Eventually the court found in favor of the USFL owners and fined the NFL just a dollar because the court found the USFL had caused many of its own problems. Anti-trust settlements are tripled by law and so the USFL owners won three dollars for their troubles. The USFL played one more spring season but by the end of its 1985 campaign, many teams were unable to pay their bills. The switch to playing in the fall never materialized and the USFL was out of business.

Chapter 22

1. The guest coaches included men Allen had coached in the NFL: Pat Fischer, Dick Bass, Deacon Jones, Roy Jefferson and also Leon Shortenhaus who had played for Allen at Morningside. Willie Brown, who coached with Allen at Long Beach State, was a guest coach and so were Etty and Jennifer Allen (1991), Bruce Allen (1992) and Greg Allen (1995). Author's interview with Dave Rebstock, sports information director at Morningside College.

2. George Allen papers, Pro Football Hall of Fame. Note from James Walker, the Director of Development at the school 6-7-1974.

3. Email from Kirk to the author, March 30, 2020.

4. Author's interview with Chuck Hayes August 20, 2020.

5. Long Beach State tied Louisville 24-24 in that bowl game.

6. The University of California at Los Angeles and the University of Southern California.

7. Author's interview with Chuck Hayes August 20, 2020.

8. Allen, *Strategies*, page 23.

9. Email from Schroeder to the author March 31, 2020. Emphasis is in the original.

10. Author's interview with Shawn Wilburn, August 29, 2020.

11. Email from Schroeder.

12. The story of Terrell Davis' recruitment to the Long Beach State program was related to the author by Chuck Hayes during the author's interview with Chuck Hayes, August 20, 2020.

13. Letters in the George Allen papers, Box 22C, Pro Football Hall of Fame.

14. *Ibid.*
15. Clip of ESPN's news coverage of the game, viewed online April 1, 2020.
16. Author's interview with Chuck Hayes, August 20, 2020.
17. *Allen Enjoys a Day at the Beach with 49ers, 28–8*, Dick Wagner, *Los Angeles Times*, September 23, 1990. Viewed on line March 17, 2020.
18. *Ibid.*
19. Box score, *Los Angeles Times*, September 30, 2020. Viewed online March 17, 2020.
20. *Long Beach Triumphs on Cheevers' Field Goal*, Dick Wagner, *Los Angeles Times*, October 28, 1990. Viewed online March 17, 2020. The game information and attendance all came from the same source.
21. Wilburn interview.
22. Author's interview with Chuck Hayes, August 20, 2020.
23. *Fifth Quarter*, page 234. Of course, it wasn't fully accurate. Allen's first team at Whittier, the 1951 bunch which was beaten so badly by the submarine team, finished with a record of 2–7. It was fully accurate to say Allen's *professional* teams never suffered through a losing season.
24. *George Allen, Coach, Dead at 72; Led Redskins in Super Bowl VII, New York Times*, January 1, 1991. Viewed online September 7, 2020.
25. The author found two sources for lifespan averages online. The first, found at u.demog.berkeley.edu/~andrew/1918/figure2.html, reported that the average age for a man born in the U.S. in 1918 was 36.6 years. The second, found at simplyinsurance.com/average-us-life-expectancy-statistics, listed life expectancy for men born that year to be 39.4 years. The simplyinsurance report showed life expectancy for men born in 1915 was much better, 54.7 years. Both were viewed on August 29, 2020.
26. *George Allen, Coach, Dead at 72; Led Redskins in Super Bowl VII, New York Times*, January 1, 1991. Viewed online September 7, 2020.
27. NFL Films, *George Allen—Winning Is Living, Losing Is Dying.*

Epilogue

1. *Theismann*, page 75.
2. Grant did win four Canadian Football League championships as a head coach.
3. Levy coached two Canadian Football League champions.
4. Schottenheimer coached the Virginia Destroyers to the championship of the United Football League in 2011.
5. George Allen Papers, Box 22C, Pro Football Hall of Fame.

Appendix 1

1. The information for Allen's trades as a head coach in the National Football League comes from the website prosportstransactions.com. Accessed February 20, 2021.
2. Pitts played six games for the Saints in 1970, then completed his career with the Packers in 1971.
3. Lundy retired.
4. Originally, the Redskins sent their fifth- and sixth-round choices in the 1972 draft to the Giants. The Redskins did not have a sixth-round choice left for that year, having traded it away. They sent Flowers to the Giants in compensation.
5. Neither Austin or Lanier made the Redskins roster.
6. Wilson did not make the Redskins roster.
7. Crumpler failed his physical exam, voiding the trade. The teams attempted the same deal five days later but Crumpler failed another physical exam, voiding the deal again.
8. The trade was voided when Nelson retired four days later.
9. This complicated package was the compensation for the Redskins signing of free agent Dave Butz of the Cardinals a month earlier.
10. When Hanstedt signed with the Redskins, they sent an undisclosed draft pick to the Oilers.

Appendix 2

1. No rookie played for the Redskins in 1971. Fanucci, Stark, Severson and Ryczek played for Allen in 1972 or later. Ryczek played three seasons for the Redskins, two more for Tampa Bay and then two for the Rams, where Allen brought him

during Allen's brief final tenure in Los Angeles. Ryczek's final professional football game was in Super Bowl 14, where he and the Rams lost to the Pittsburgh Steelers. Severson played his college ball at Long Beach State, Allen's final coaching stop.

Appendix 3

1. For comparison, Joe Namath was named the NFL's Comeback Player of the Year that season with fewer yards and touchdown passes, plus more than twice the interceptions.

Bibliography

Books

Allen, George. *How to Scout Football*. Mansfield Centre, CT: Martino, 2009.
Allen, George. *Strategies for Winning: A Top Coach's Game Plan for Victory in Football and in Life*. New York: McGraw-Hill, 1990.
Allen, George, and Ben Olan. *Pro Football's 100 Greatest Players*. Indianapolis: Bobbs-Merrill, 1982.
Allen, George H., and Joseph G. Pacelli. *George Allen's Guide to Special Teams*. Champaign, IL: Leisure Press, 1990.
Allen, Jennifer. *Fifth Quarter: The Scrimmage of a Football Coach's Daughter*. New York: Random House, 2000.
Bisheff, Steve. *Great Teams, Great Years: Los Angeles Rams*. New York: Macmillan, 1973.
Carroll, Bob, Michael Gershman, David Neft, John Thorn, and the Elias Sports Bureau. *Total Football II: The Official Encyclopedia of the National Football League*. New York: HarperCollins, 1999.
Davis, Jeff. *Papa Bear: The Life and Legacy of George Halas*. New York: McGraw-Hill, 2005.
Gildea, William, and Kenneth Turan. *The Future Is Now: George Allen, Pro Football's Most Controversial Coach*. Boston: Houghton Mifflin, 1972.
Katzowitz, Josh. *Sid Gillman: Father of the Passing Game*. Covington, KY: Clerisy, 2012.
Klawitter, John, and Deacon Jones. *HEADSLAP: The Life and Times of Deacon Jones*. Amherst, NY: Prometheus, 1996.
Kramer, Jerry. *Instant Replay: The Green Bay Diary of Jerry Kramer*. Cleveland: New American Library, 1968.
Levy, Marv. *Where Else Would You Rather Be?* Champaign, IL: Sports Publishing, 2004.
Reeths, Paul. *The United States Football League, 1982–1986*. Jefferson, NC: McFarland, 2017.
Theismann, Joe, and Dave Kindred. *Theismann: On Theismann, Bad Breaks, L.T., Riggo and the Hogs, Cowboys, Cathy Lee, Madden, Gamblers, CBS, McMahon, President Reagan, Redskins, Stabler, the Golden Dome, Five O'Clock Club, Midnight Meetings, Etc.* Chicago: Contemporary, 1987.
Treat, Roger. *The Encyclopedia of Football*, 16th Revised Edition. Garden City, NY: Doubleday, 1979.

Interviews

Fields, Max. Telephone interview, August 20, 2017.
Hayes, Chuck. Telephone interview, August 19, 2020.
Kirk, Roger. Telephone interview, March 30, 2020.
McDole, Ron. Telephone interview, March 13, 2019.
McDole, Ron. Interview with Warren Rogan. *Sports' Forgotten Heroes*. Podcast audio.

Bibliography

March 5, 2019. https://sportshistorynetwork.com/captivate-podcast/51-ron-mcdole-nfl/?utm_source=rss&utm_medium=rss&utm_campaign=51-ron-mcdole-nfl.
McNichols, John. Telephone interview, August 22, 2017.
Milburn, Shawn. Telephone interview, August 29, 2020.
Rebstock, Dave. Telephone interview, 2017.
Schroeder, Shane. Emails exchanged, March 31, 2020.
Vermeil, Dick. Telephone interview, 2017.

Websites

Ancestry.com.
Dailymotion.com/video/x3ywera.
Profootballarchives.com.
Pro-football-reference.com.
Simplyinsurance.com/average-us-life-expectancy-statistics.
Statscrew.com.

Collections

George Allen Collection, Pro Football Hall of Fame.

Index

Alexander, Kermit 121
Allen, Bruce 66, 153, 180, 182, 192, 248*ch22n*1
Allen, Etty 9–10, 20, 32, 34, 46, 50, 86, 88, 121, 150, 165, faith of 10, father of 10
Allen, George Herbert: birthdate 19; claims about age 8, 34, 47; George Allen Athletic Scholarship (Morningside College) 193; George Allen Classic 193; as a motivator 23; scouting 19–20; volunteer coach for Rams 27
Allen, Greg 248*ch22n*1
Allen, Jennifer 9, 10, 31, 33, 38, 49, 50, 66–67, 84, 85, 86, 88, 89, 97, 103, 107, 111, 120, 121–122, 132, 139, 165, 207, 209, 213
Alma College 7
American Football League (AFL) 28, 34, 43, 44, 45, 56, 63, 70, 72, 88, 94, 113, 128, 182, 183, 185, 190, 192, 211, 216, 241*ch5n*44
Anderson, Donny 3
Arnett, Jon 39, 42
Atkins, Doug 34, 36, 66
Austin, Bill 107

Baker, Terry 54
Bakersfield College 197
Bamberg, Clayton 206
Barney, Lem 91
Bass, Dick 53, 88, 94, 230, 231, 235, 248*ch22n*1
Bass, Mike 127, 138, 158
Baugh, Sammy 123, 137
Beban, Gary 65, 104, 169, 244*ch12n*11
Bednarik, Chuck 43, 57
Belichick, Bill 107
Bengtson, Phil 78, 108
Berry, Bob 101
Big 10 Conference 20
Bigler, Dave 14
Blanda, George 159

Boise State University 203
Bowman, Ken 70–71
Boyd, Bob 29
Boynton, Ed 110
Brady, Dave 172
Bratkowski, Zeke 35, 37, 54, 78
Brian's Song 44, 82
Brodie, John 68, 79, 95, 102, 122, 231
Brown, Bill 34
Brown, Ed 35
Brown, Jim 30, 33, 133
Brown, Larry 108, 112, 125, 128, 130, 131, 137, 145, 233, 234, 235
Brown, Roger 66, 77, 102
Brown, Willie 198, 202, 248*ch22n*1
Brundige, Bill 114, 138
Bryant, Kelvin 191
Bryant, Paul (Bear) 60, 92, 108, 155
Bukich, Rudy 45
Bull, Ronnie 36
Buoniconti, Nick 135, 136, 137
Butkus, Dick 5, 42, 43, 45, 51, 58, 82, 116, 185, 216, 218

Caan, James 44
Cahill, Dave 70
Caldwell, Charles W., Jr. 26
California Institute of Technology (Cal Tech) 18
California State University, Chico (Chico State) 21
California State University, Fullerton (Cal State Fullerton) 204
California State University, Northridge (Cal State Northridge) 204, 205, 206
Callahan, Connie 13–14, 239*ch3n*9
Calvillo, Anthony 197
Campbell, Gary 24
Carollo, Joe 53
Casey, Bernie 59, 60, 69, 72, 75, 80, 138, 231
Chandler, Don 70

253

Cheevers, Sean 204, 205, 207
Childs, Clarence 82, 91
Chuy, Don 53
City College of San Francisco 197
Clark, Don 33
Clark, Rickie 203
Clarke, Leon 29
Claxton, Myron 17
Clayton, Frank D. 26–27
Clemson University 199
Clift, Bob 16
Coffee, Junior 60
Concannon, Jack 82
Cooke, Jack Kent 64, 139
Cornish, Frank 44
Coryell, Don 15, 17, 168, 169
Cosell, Howard 121
Cowan, Charlie 53, 88
Crabb, Claude 3, 4, 70, 71, 72, 73
Crisler, Fritz 7–8, 25
Crutcher, Tommy Joe 71
Csonka, Larry 133, 135
Curran, Pat 105
Curtis, Mike 43

Dale, Carroll 70
Daniels, Willie 83
Daugherty, Duffy 26
David Black Literary Agency 199
Davis, Les 11
Davis, Terrell 196, 197, 218
Defensing the Running Pass 25
DeLong, Steve 43
Dempsey, Tom 197
DeVaughn, Victor 206
Devine, Dan 130
Ditka, Mike 33–34, 35, 242*ch7n*15
Doherty, Joe 73, 242*ch8n*16
Dooley, Jim 36, 37, 38, 51, 82
Dowler, Boyd 109, 112, 134, 142
Dowling, Tom 127
Droullard, Clayton 11–12
Duncan, Leslie (Speedy) 121, 128, 129
Dunn, Perry Lee 60
Durslag, Melvin 81, 85, 89
Dyer, Henry 56

Earhart, Amelia 101
East Los Angeles College 17, 18,
Eller, Carl 96
Ellison, Willie 67, 82, 90, 94, 102, 104, 105, 121, 231
Enberg, Dick 73
Evey, Dick 103
Exum, Jeff 203, 204, 207
Ezerins, Vilnis: correct spelling 91; misspelled 82

Facenda, John 114, 116
Farrington, Bo 39, 40
Fassett, Jeff 204
Faulkner, Jack 30
Fears, Tom 4, 28,
Fearsome Foursome 30, 53, 70, 77, 101, 227, 229
Fields, Max 17, 18, 20, 21, 23–24, 75, 198, 217, 218
Fischer, Pat 127, 128
Fleming, George 34
Fleming, Marv 75
Foster, Sean 203
Frederickson, Tucker 43
Fugett, Jean 169
Furillo, Bud 73, 81, 89
Fusina, Chuck 191

Gabriel, Roman 53, 54, 57, 58, 59, 63, 67, 68, 69, 70, 72, 74, 75, 78, 79, 80, 82, 83, 84, 87, 88, 90, 94, 95, 96, 102–103, 105, 117, 119, 120, 121, 124, 138, 143, 157, 190, 215, 230, 231, 232, 234, 235
Galimore, Willie 39, 40, 42, 44
Garrett, Mike 56, 63, 115
Garrison, Walt 129
Geddes, Ken 121
George, Bill 38, 43, 57, 213
Gibron, Abe 51
Gibson, Claude 34
Gifford, Frank 37, 121, 197
Gildea, William 72, 73
Gilliam, John 67
Gillman, Sid 3, 4, 27–28, 29, 30, 32, 33, 48, 53, 84, 85, 105, 134, 240*ch5n*2, 243*ch9n*11
Godfrey, E.R. 26
Gordon, Dick 44
Gowdy, Curt 138
Grange, Red 32, 45
Grant, Bud 95, 217
Grant, Frank 169
Graytek Associates 23
Great Depression 6, 22, 39, 177, 209, 215, 216, 217
Gregg, Forrest 75
Grier, Roosevelt (Rosie) 53, 66, 77, 78, 102
Griese, Bob 133, 147
Griffith, Coleman R. 22
Grossmont College 206
Guillory, Tony 3, 4, 5, 70, 71, 72, 73, 82, 241*ch6n*44
Guzik, Jon 35

Hadl, John 101, 190
Halas, George 3, 31, 32, 33, 34, 36, 38, 39, 40, 42, 44, 45, 46, 47, 48–49, 50, 51, 61, 65, 74, 105, 116, 132, 212, 218, 241*ch5n*35

Index

Hanburger, Chris 110, 123, 125, 126, 130, 166, 172, 173
Haraway, Charley 112
Harget, Ed 101
Harrington, Judge Cornelius J. 48, 49, 50, 51
Harris, Cliff 158–159
Harris, James 154
Hart, Doug 4, 71
Hawkins, Alex 69
Hawkins, Ralph 109
Hayes, Chuck 162, 194, 196–197, 198, 199, 201, 202, 205, 206, 207, 208
Haymond, Alvin 103, 129
Hecker, Norb 61
Heisman Trophy 7, 15, 43, 54, 56, 65, 104, 115, 186, 197
Hill, Calvin 129, 144
Hill, Jess 27
Hirsch, Elroy 7, 28, 29, 48, 65, 66, 90
Hock, John 29
Hoskins, Bob 122
Hula Bowl 34
Hull, Mike 115, 116, 117
Humphrey, Buddy 54
Hunter, Scott 130

I Formation 15
Iman, Ken 53

Jackson, Harold 104, 105
Jackson, Keith 191
Jefferson, Roy 121, 141, 150, 170, 233, 235
Jencks, Robert (Bob) 61
Jenkins, Pepper 204
Jenner, Albert E. 49
Johnson, Al 26
Johnson, Clyde 17, 18
Johnson, Dennis 157
Johnson, Mike 191
Johnson, Randy 101, 157, 159
Johnson, Trumaine 182, 184, 185, 186, 188, 189, 235
Johnsos, Luke 41
Jones, David (Deacon) 53, 57, 58, 63, 66, 67, 70, 75, 77, 78, 79, 80, 81, 83, 86, 87, 88, 92, 93, 96, 98, 100, 101, 102, 114, 120, 121, 136, 146, 150, 151, 152, 153, 212, "Follow me to the Super Bowl" 152; place kicking 66, 153
Jones, Howard 20
Josephson, Lester 69, 94, 95, 102, 231
Jurgensen, Sonny 35, 54, 110, 112, 116, 117, 118, 119, 124, 125, 126, 127, 128, 129, 135, 139, 142, 143, 144, 148, 149, 150, 154, 157, 160, 172, 215, 216, 229, 230, 231, 232, 234, 242ch8n6

Karcher, Carl 201
Kemp, Jack 15
Kezar Stadium 79, 80, 81, 84, 95, 102
Kiick, Jim 133, 136
Kilgore, Jon 156
Killroy, Bucko 68
Kilmer, Billy 54, 101, 112, 117, 118, 119, 121, 122, 124, 125, 126, 129, 130, 131, 134, 135, 136, 137, 139, 142, 144, 146, 147, 148, 149, 150, 154, 157, 158, 159, 160, 161, 162, 163, 164, 166, 167, 168, 169, 172, 212, 213, 229, 232, 233, 234, 235
Kindig, Howard 136
Kirk, Roger 193
Klawitter, John 54, 79, 150–151
Klein, Bob 105, 121, 154
Knight, Curt 121, 130, 131, 137, 155
Knox, Chuck 154, 173, 174
Korch, Frank 31
Kramer, Jerry 70, 71, 74, 244ch11n6
Kreitling, Rich 39
Kristofferson, Kris 15

Ladd, Ernie 34
LaHood, Mike 104
Lair, Ed 204
Lake Shore High School 6
Lamonica, Daryle 235
Lamson, Chuck 63
Landry, Greg 101, 182, 183, 185, 186, 189, 235
Landry, Tom 23, 67, 68, 75, 101, 128, 129, 131, 132, 134, 150, 151, 177, 212, 236–237
Langer, Jim 135
Lavender, Joe 40, 169
Leslie, Freddie 203
Levy, Marv 99, 100, 101, 102, 103, 104, 106, 109, 112, 116, 118, 119, 125, 128, 130, 132, 134, 136, 137, 139, 140, 142, 155, 156, 189, 217, 244ch11n7
Lincoln, Keith 34
Little, Larry 135
Lombardi, Vince 3, 33, 40, 45, 58, 69, 72, 74, 78, 85, 88, 89, 103, 107, 108, 109, 114, 122, 123, 172, 211
Longley, Clint 152
Los Angeles Memorial Olympic Coliseum 3, 4, 5, 30, 62, 64, 67, 69, 73, 82, 90, 101, 102, 104, 120, 121, 134, 152, 187, 190, 195, 242
Los Angeles Rams: attendance 30, 47; players threaten strike 88, 89–90
Luckman, Sid 35, 44
Lundy, Lamar 30, 53, 63, 66, 77, 78, 88, 102, 178
Lynch, Dick 37

Mack, Tom 56, 57, 72, 111, 174
Madden, John 88, 89
Madro, Joe 30
Malavasi, Ray 174, 247*ch*19*n*6
Malinchak, Bill 125, 126, 216
Marchibroda, Ted 109, 124, 125
Marconi, Joe 36
Marquette University 7
Mason, Tommy 95, 112
Mather, Chuck 31, 32
McCormack, Mike 109, 142, 143
McCray, Bennie 36
McDole, Ron 112, 113, 114, 115, 118, 124, 125, 130, 133, 134, 137, 146, 216, 246*ch*15*n*17
McDonald, Tommy 230
McElhenny, Hugh 18
McKeever, Marlin 61, 110, 112
McLinton, Harold (Hal) 136
McNichols, John 17, 18, 20–21, 23, 24
Meador, Eddie 53, 63, 88, 95, 212, 246*ch*15*n*17
Mercein, Chuck 70, 71
Meredith, Don 33, 121
Michaels, Lou 69
Michigan State Normal College 7
Miller, Ron 54
Montreal Alouettes 139, 142, 178, 179, 180, 181
Moore, Lenny 17, 69
Moore, Tom 58, 59, 60, 230, 232, 233, 235
Mora, Jim 15, 187, 190, 191, 237, 248*ch*21*n*12
Morrall, Earl 78, 133, 134
Morris, Arthur 45
Morris, Larry 37, 38
Morris, Mercury 133
Morton, Craig 101, 128, 129, 143
Motivation in Athletics 22–23
Mt. San Antonio College 197
Mullen, James C. 50
Munson, Bill 53, 54, 55, 124, 231

Namath, Joe 102, 103, 129, 233
Nance, Jim 44
Nash, Herman 203
National Football Foundation 17
Nelson, Bill 105
Nettles, Jim 102
New Mexico State University 203
Nixon, Richard M. 15, 127, 134
Noll, Chuck 88

Oates, Bob 77, 78, 96, 120, 123, 171, 172, 173
O'Bradovich, Ed 36, 37, 38–39
Occidental College 15; Shoes Game 17
Oklahoma Outlaws 192

Olsen, Merlin 53, 57, 70, 77, 78, 79, 100, 102, 114, 212, 244*ch*11*n*6
Oosterbaan, Bennie 8, 25
Orr, Jimmy 94
Over-the-Hill Gang 1, 24, 114, 149
Owens, Brig 143

Pardee, Jack 5, 51, 55, 68, 78, 84, 96, 103, 112, 113, 114, 120, 121, 173, 190, 209, 212, 237; cancer surgery 55
Pasadena Bowl 193
Pastorini, Dan 158
Patton, Jimmy 37
Payton, Walter 44
Pearson, Drew 152
Peoples, Woody 56
Percival, Mac 82
Pergine, John 104, 158
Perkins, Forrest 27
Perkins, Ray 108
Perry, Joe 18
Petitbon, Richie 33, 36, 38, 120, 155, 246*ch*15*n*17
Piccolo, Brian 44, 82
Pivec, Dave 44, 82
Plum, Milt 82
Plunkett, Jim 126
Pollom, Norm 68
Pool, Hamp 29, 32
Povich, Shirley 141
President's Council on Physical Fitness 85, 178, 196
Pro Bowl 51, 90, 128, 134, 230, 233, 234
Professional Football Hall of Fame 1, 3, 5, 18, 28, 29, 31, 33, 34, 35, 36, 37, 38, 42, 48, 53, 64, 69, 70, 74, 80, 88, 90, 100, 115, 133, 135, 140, 146, 152, 159, 184, 197, 199, 208, 217
Prothro, Tommy 97, 99, 104, 119, 120, 154, 173, 174
Putnam, Duane 29
Pyle, Mike 34

Rams Car Wash 31
Rams-Cowboys spy allegations 67–68
Rasinski, Dr. Jules 89
Rauch, John 88–89, 113
Ray, David 57, 154, 155
Rebstock, Dave ix
Reeves, Dan 5, 48, 49, 55, 65–66, 76, 77, 80, 81, 83–84, 85, 86, 87, 88, 89–90, 91, 93, 98, 99, 103–104, 105, 121–122, 218
Reynolds, Jack 105
Rhee, Jhoon 150, 151
Richardson, Jerry 88
Richardson, Willie 69
Roach, John 37

Index

Robbie, Joe 146
Robertson, Isiah 154, 216
Robinson, David 143
Rogan, Warren 124
Rose Bowl 20, 55
Rosenbloom, Carroll 173, 174, 242*ch*8*n*5
Rozelle, Pete 49, 50, 184
Rush, Clive 88
Ryan, Frank 54

Saint Francis of Assisi 155
San Diego State University 18, 21, 200, 201
San Jose State University 203, 204
Sanders, John 49, 65, 68
Saul, Rich 105
Sayers, Gale 5, 43–44, 45, 61, 82, 115, 116, 185, 216, 234
Schlegel, Kelly 197
Schnellenberger, Howard 60, 61, 92
Schottenheimer, Marty 43, 217
Schroeder, Shayne 195, 196
Schulte, Paul 204
Schweda, Brian 44
Scibelli, Joe 53
Scott, Jake 135, 137, 166
Seay, Mark 202, 204, 206
Shapiro, Len 166–167
Shaughnessy, Clark 35, 84
Sherlag, Bob 61
Sherman, Gene 14
Shofner, Del 35, 37
Short, Charles F. 48–49
Shula, Don 73, 85, 134, 135, 138, 149, 177, 245*ch*13*n*15
Simpson, O.J. 65, 115, 197, 233
Sipe, Brian 158
Sistrunk, Manny 40
Skalbania, Nelson 178–180
Smith, Ed 191
Smith, Jerry 110, 121, 125, 126, 137, 159, 161
Smith, Larry 94, 102, 104–105, 150, 231
Smith, Ron 59, 60
Snow, Jack 53, 69, 70, 80, 231, 235
South Dakota State University 13
South Dakota University 11, 12, 13, 14
Southern California Intercollegiate Athletic Conference (SCIAC) 15, 17, 24
Starr, Bart 35, 36, 37, 70, 74, 78, 95, 114
Staubach, Roger 101, 131, 143, 144, 152, 158, 159, 162, 164, 167
Steinberg, Leigh 192
Stetz, Chris 197
Storm, Lowell 30
Studer, Todd 202, 203, 204, 206, 207
Studstill, Pat 156
Stydahar, Joe 29, 84, 90
Sub Pac military team 16, 199

Sullivan, Joe 109, 142
Svare, Harland 4, 47, 48, 53, 57, 84
Swiacki, Bill 30
Szezecko, Joe 61

T-Formation 17, 35, 215
Talbert, Diron 56, 70, 102, 110, 112, 120, 170
Tarkenton, Fran 80, 125, 131, 144
Taubman, Myles 192
Taylor, Charley 125, 130–131, 143, 166, 233, 234
Taylor, Rosey 36, 125
Teague, Eddie 26
Teele, Jack 65
Theismann, Joe 54, 118, 146, 147, 148, 151, 154, 158, 159, 160, 161–162, 165, 166–167, 168, 169, 170, 172, 214, 215, 232, 233, 234
Thomas, Duane 141, 142, 170
Thomas, Mike 158, 167, 233
Thorndike's Law of Effect 22
Thorpe, Jim 32
Tittle, Y.A. 37, 38
Torgeson, LaVern 109
Toronto Argonauts 146–147, 165
Trinity College 11
Truax, Billy 53, 94, 231
Trueblood, Rufus 24–25, 240*ch*4*n*18
Trump, Donald 191, 192
Tsangaris, Chris 205
Tucker, Wendell 82, 83, 94, 95, 231, 235
Twilley, Howard 136

Unitas, John 31, 35, 69, 70, 73, 74, 78, 94, 95
United States Air Force Academy 24
United States Navy V12 Program 7, 16
University of California at Los Angeles (aka UCLA) 55, 64, 65, 97, 99, 104, 108, 194, 202
University of Michigan 7, 14, 29, 34, 56
University of Nevada, Las Vegas (UNLV) 207
University of Northern Iowa 13
University of Oklahoma 26
University of Redlands 27, 28
University of Southern California 20, 27, 65, 104, 105, 115, 194, 197, 202
University of the Pacific 202
Utah State 197, 200, 201

Vactor, Ted 121, 129, 138, 143
Vadini, Joseph 14
Van Brocklin, Norm 4, 28, 29, 54
Vanderhaven, Ed 16
Ventura College 205
Vermeil, Dick 18, 55, 56, 57, 92, 93, 96, 97, 99, 106, 156, 175, 211, 216, 217
Voit 31

Wade, Billy 35, 36, 37, 38, 42, 45, 54
Wagner, Dick 199
Waller, Charlie 109, 183
Warfield, Paul 133, 135, 136
Washington, Gene 102, 122
Waterfield, Bob 4, 30, 53, 54, 57, 84, 88
Webb, Reggie 197
Webster, Alex 88
Wenatchee Valley College 15
Whitlow, Bob 60
Whitsell, Dave 36
Wilbur, John 112, 212
Wilburn, Shawn 195–196, 200, 202, 203, 204, 205, 206, 207, 208, 209 209, 212
Wilkinson, Bud 26
Willard, Ken 43

Williams, Billy Dee 44
Williams, Clarence (Clancy) 53, 63
Williams, Edward Bennett 109, 111, 142, 165, 171, 172, 218
Williams, Roger 105
Williams, Travis 70
Wilson, Ralph 89, 113
Winner, Charley 109, 142
Woodall, Al 102
Wooden, John 64, 108
Wrigley Field 37
Wyche, Sam 124

Yepremian, Garo 137–138
Young, Steve 190
Younger, Tank 29

www.ingramcontent.com/pod-product-compliance
Ingram Content Group UK Ltd.
Pitfield, Milton Keynes, MK11 3LW, UK
UKHW021844140426
5217IPUK00022B/1584